THE STUDENT'S MANGA COOKBOOK

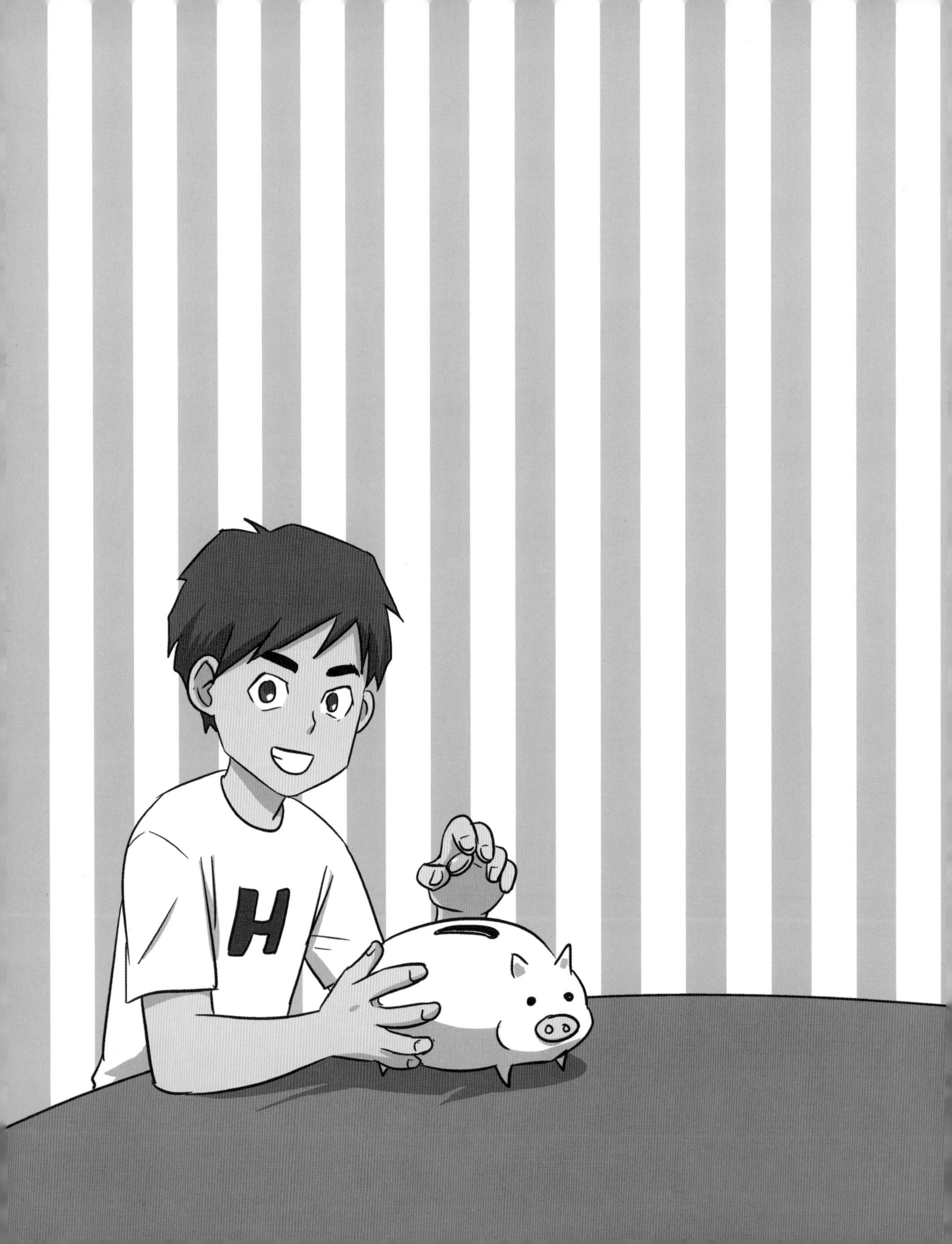
H

THE STUDENT'S MANGA COOKBOOK

YOUR FAVORITE RECIPES MADE EASIER THAN EVER...

...WITH STEP-BY-STEP MANGA INSTRUCTIONS!

YISHAN LI &
CARA FROST-SHARRATT

ilex

An Hachette UK Company
www.hachette.co.uk

First published in the UK in 2016 by ILEX,
a division of Octopus Publishing Group Ltd
Carmelite House, 50 Victoria Embankment,
London, EC4Y 0DZ
www.octopusbooks.co.uk

Design, layout, and text copyright
© Octopus Publishing Group 2016

Distributed in the US by
Hachette Book Group
1290 Avenue of the Americas, 4th
and 5th Floors, New York, NY 10020

Distributed in Canada by
Canadian Manda Group
664 Annete St., Toronto, Ontario, Canada
M6S 2C8

Publisher: Roly Allen
Commissioning Editor: Zara Larcombe
Managing Specialist Editor: Frank Gallaugher
Senior Project Editor: Natalia Price-Cabrera
Editor: Rachel Silverlight
Art Director: Julie Weir
Designer: Ginny Zeal
Assistant Production Manager: Marina Maher

ISBN 978-1-78157-335-8

A CIP catalogue record for this book
is available from the British Library

Printed in China

Introduction   6

SURF & TURF

Tray Bake Herb Chicken   10

Grilled Chicken Salsa   14

Fast Chicken Curry   18

Spicy Mexican Burgers   22

Beef Fajitas   26

Meatball Tagine   30

Classic Bolognese   34

Shepherd's Pie   38

Sweet & Sour Pork   42

Pork & Red Bell Pepper Chili   46

Spicy Pea & Ham Risotto   50

Potato & Bacon Patties   54

Macaroni Cheese with Ham   58

Quick Sausage & Bean Casserole   62

Fish Pie   66

Spicy Fish Skewers   70

Creamy Garlic Mussels   74

CONTENTS

VEGETARIAN

Black-eyed Bean
& Red Bell Pepper Stew   80

Hearty Minestrone   84

Chunky Pasta Sauce   88

Quick One-pot Ratatouille   92

Greek-style Omelet   96

Spinach & Mushroom Lasagne   100

Quick Cauliflower Cheese   104

Potato Gratin   108

Mixed Bean Kedgeree   112

Onion & Mushroom Quesadillas   116

SWEET STUFF

Pineapple with Lime
& Chili Syrup   122

Banoffee Chocolate Muffins   126

Raspberry Muffins   130

Chocolate Chip Cookies   134

Victoria Sponge Mug Cake   138

Index   142

Acknowledgments   144

INTRODUCTION

As you get ready to leave home and begin a new adventure as a student, chances are you're not worrying about which kitchen appliances to pack, or where your closest farmers' market will be. With more pressing concerns like parties, dating, social clubs ... oh, and studying ... to worry about, food often gets pushed way down the list of priorities.

But in order to enjoy any of the other activities on offer at college, you need to eat—preferably well and regularly. While you can resort to canteen staples, takeout, and endless rounds of toast and butter, you'll pretty soon be bored, bloated, and broke. If you want to make mealtimes more exciting, you need to have a few go-to recipes under your belt—easy meals that are cheap, quick, and easy to prepare.

If you have a phobia of cookbooks and have difficulty following instructions for opening a package of pasta, fear not. There's been a revolution on the kitchen bookshelf, as we ditch the traditional recipe formula and prepare meals manga-style.

Meet Hungry Hiro, Sue Shi, and their culinary cohorts Cat, Squid, Shrimp, and Chile. Together they'll take you step-by-step through each recipe, offering tips, advice, and a bit of banter along the way. They've chosen a wide selection of foolproof recipes that should see you through every conceivable college situation—from date nights and mate nights, to post-party kitchen raids, and that unexpected visit from your parents.

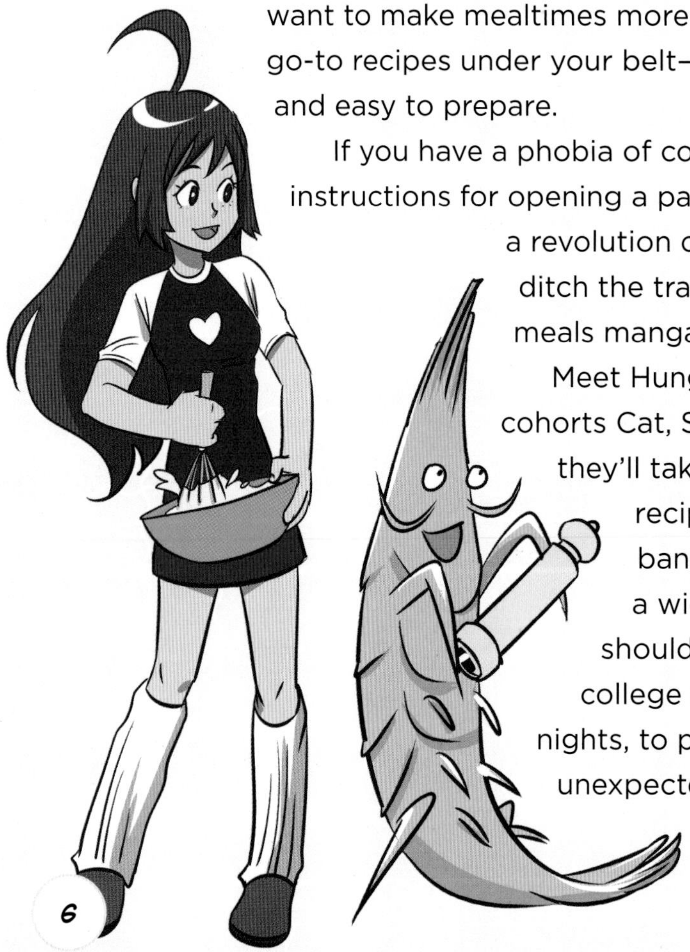

So, even if you're not on first-name terms with the contents of your fridge, and the only time you use a knife is to pierce the lid of a ready-meal, you'll soon be making masterpieces in your kitchen. Your comic-inspired creations will gain you an instant circle of friends, potential partners, and your choice of housemates.

KITCHEN KIT

It goes without saying that you'll need some basic equipment for slicing, dicing, cooking, and serving your dishes. But don't worry—nothing in the book requires specialist utensils, and you should be able to make every recipe with just the essential kitchen equipment.

You'll obviously need a couple of sharp knives and chopping boards for chopping vegetables and cutting meat. Then a couple of saucepans, a skillet, sieve or colander, vegetable peeler, spatula, wooden spoons, and a decent-sized ovenproof dish should see you through most mealtimes. An immersion blender would be really useful and these aren't expensive, but you can manage without if you don't want to sacrifice beer or bill money to kitchen utensils.

The manga way of cooking proves that anyone can rustle up a decent meal with a bunch of everyday ingredients and equipment.

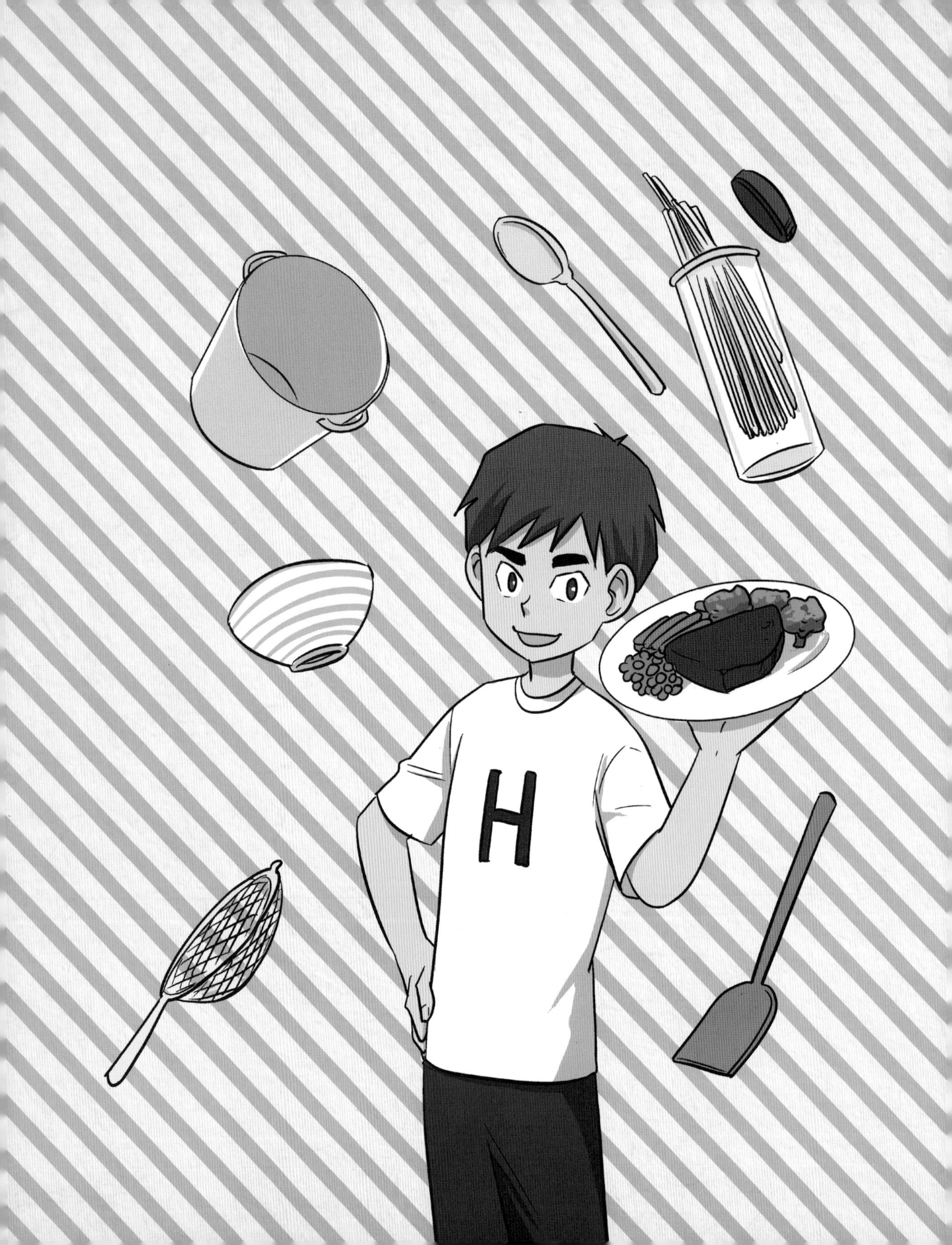

SURF & TURF

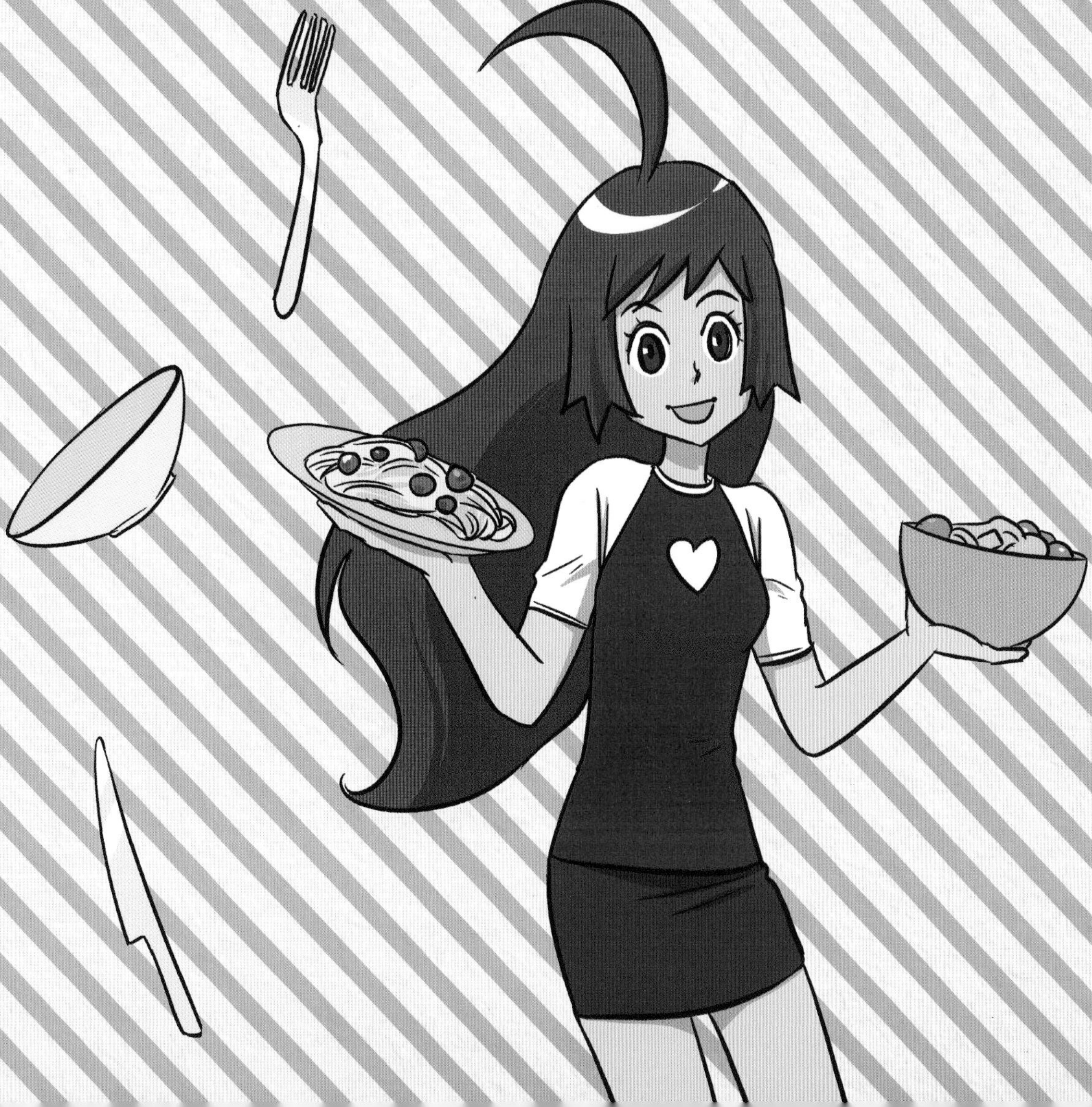

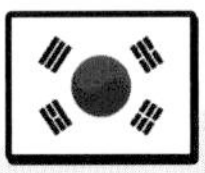

TRAY BAKE HERB CHICKEN

A WEEKNIGHT STAPLE THAT USES THE MINIMUM AMOUNT OF EQUIPMENT.

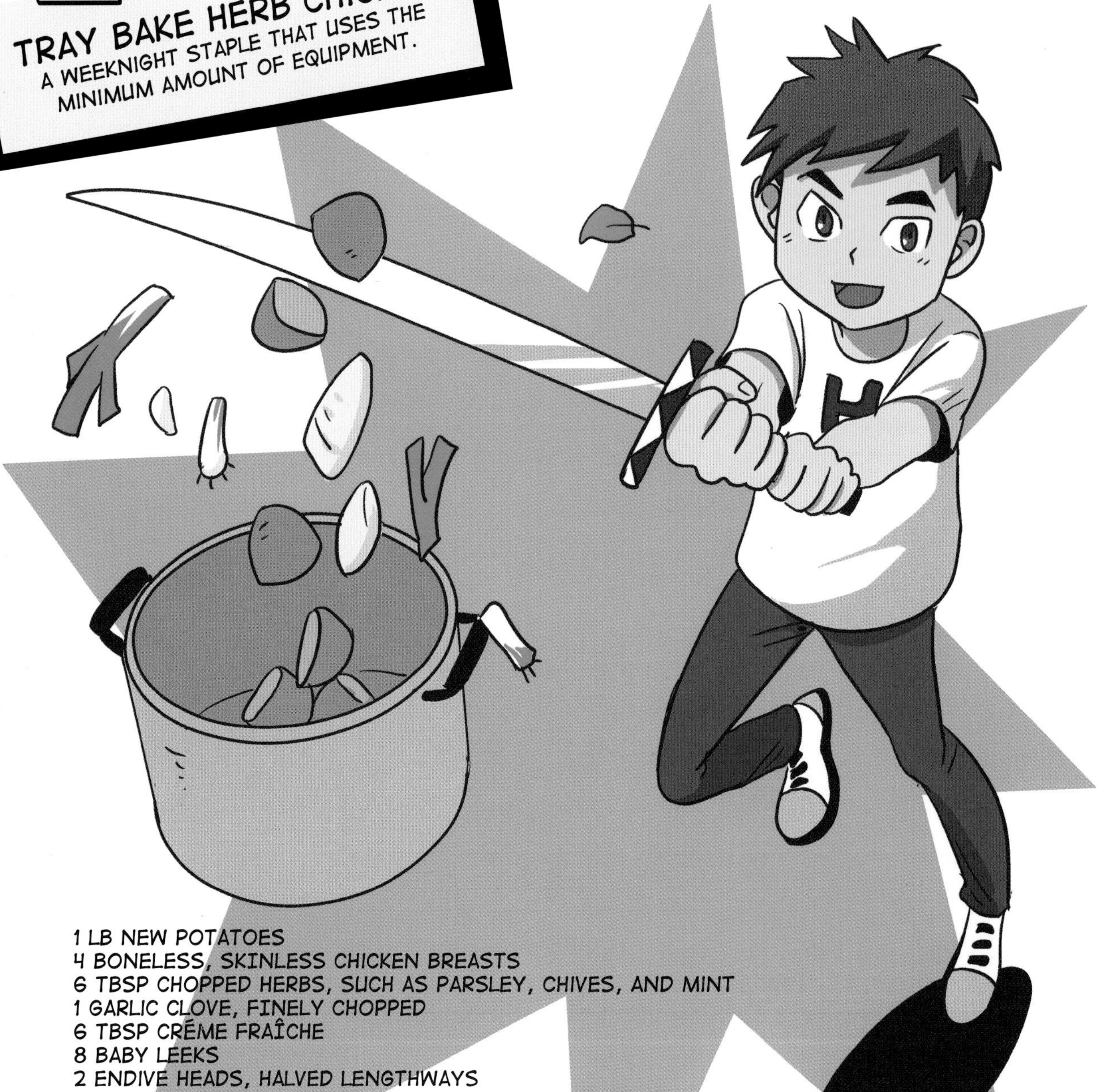

H

1 LB NEW POTATOES
4 BONELESS, SKINLESS CHICKEN BREASTS
6 TBSP CHOPPED HERBS, SUCH AS PARSLEY, CHIVES, AND MINT
1 GARLIC CLOVE, FINELY CHOPPED
6 TBSP CRÉME FRAÎCHE
8 BABY LEEKS
2 ENDIVE HEADS, HALVED LENGTHWAYS
½ PINT CHICKEN STOCK
SALT AND BLACK PEPPER
CRUSTY BREAD, TO SERVE

SERVES 4 WARRIORS
PREP TIME: 10 MINUTES
COOKING TIME: 45 MINUTES

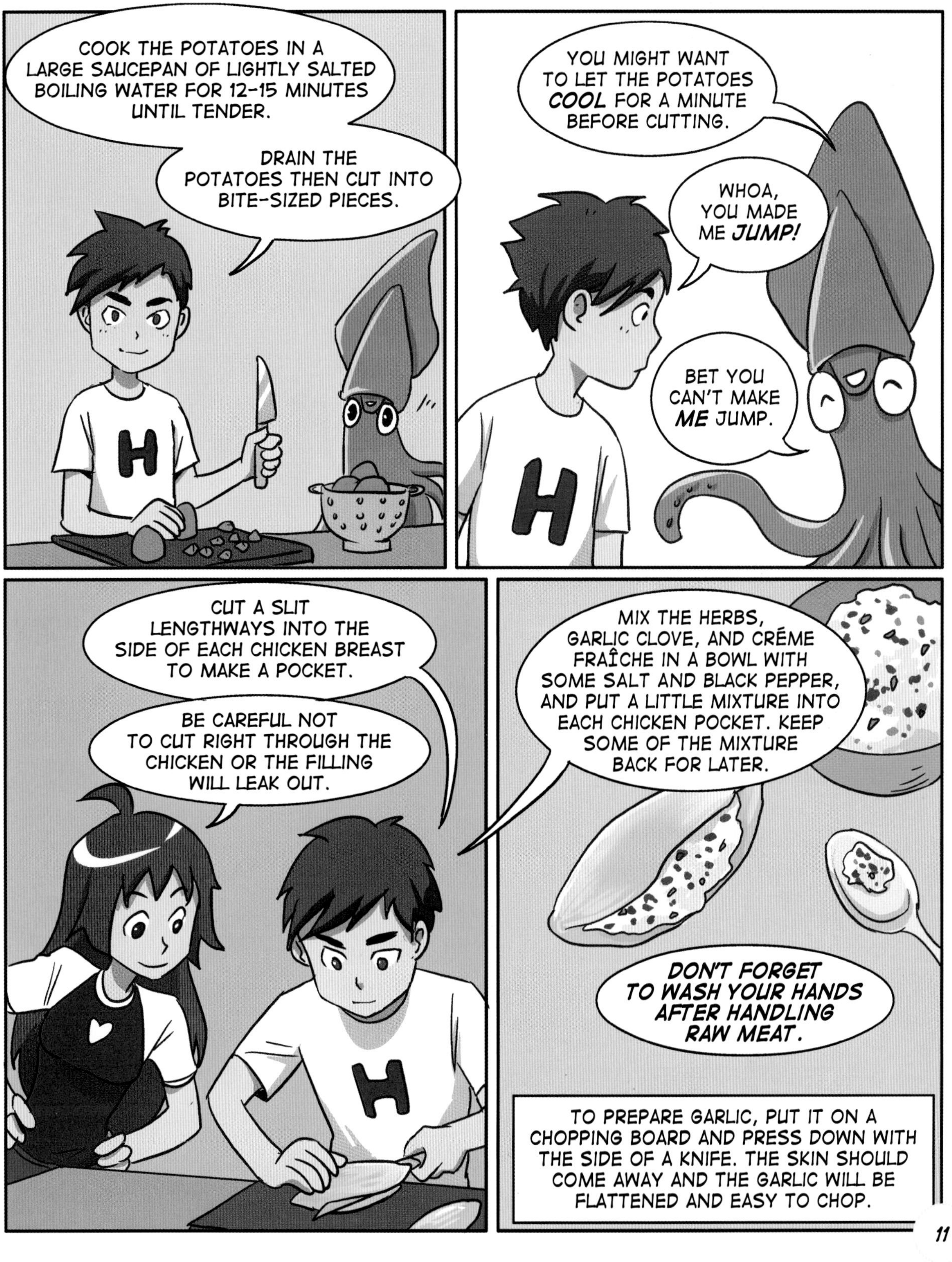
COOK THE POTATOES IN A LARGE SAUCEPAN OF LIGHTLY SALTED BOILING WATER FOR 12-15 MINUTES UNTIL TENDER.
DRAIN THE POTATOES THEN CUT INTO BITE-SIZED PIECES.
YOU MIGHT WANT TO LET THE POTATOES *COOL* FOR A MINUTE BEFORE CUTTING.
WHOA, YOU MADE ME *JUMP!*
BET YOU CAN'T MAKE *ME* JUMP.
CUT A SLIT LENGTHWAYS INTO THE SIDE OF EACH CHICKEN BREAST TO MAKE A POCKET.
BE CAREFUL NOT TO CUT RIGHT THROUGH THE CHICKEN OR THE FILLING WILL LEAK OUT.
MIX THE HERBS, GARLIC CLOVE, AND CRÉME FRAÎCHE IN A BOWL WITH SOME SALT AND BLACK PEPPER, AND PUT A LITTLE MIXTURE INTO EACH CHICKEN POCKET. KEEP SOME OF THE MIXTURE BACK FOR LATER.
DON'T FORGET TO WASH YOUR HANDS AFTER HANDLING RAW MEAT.
TO PREPARE GARLIC, PUT IT ON A CHOPPING BOARD AND PRESS DOWN WITH THE SIDE OF A KNIFE. THE SKIN SHOULD COME AWAY AND THE GARLIC WILL BE FLATTENED AND EASY TO CHOP.

TRAY BAKE HERB CHICKEN

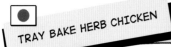

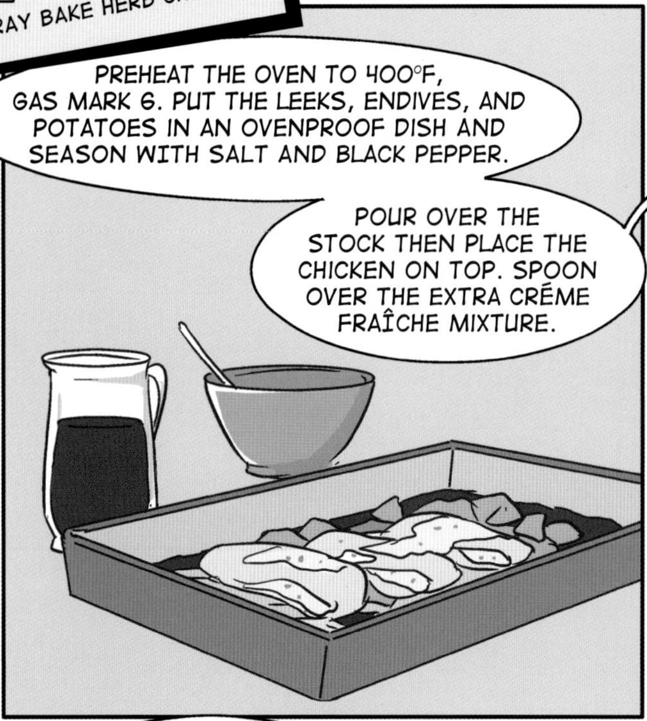
PREHEAT THE OVEN TO 400°F, GAS MARK 6. PUT THE LEEKS, ENDIVES, AND POTATOES IN AN OVENPROOF DISH AND SEASON WITH SALT AND BLACK PEPPER.
POUR OVER THE STOCK THEN PLACE THE CHICKEN ON TOP. SPOON OVER THE EXTRA CRÉME FRAÎCHE MIXTURE.

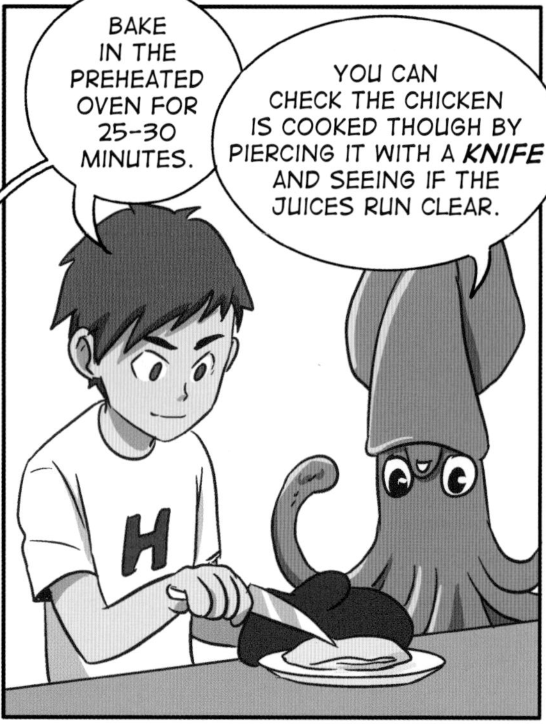
BAKE IN THE PREHEATED OVEN FOR 25–30 MINUTES.
YOU CAN CHECK THE CHICKEN IS COOKED THOUGH BY PIERCING IT WITH A *KNIFE* AND SEEING IF THE JUICES RUN CLEAR.

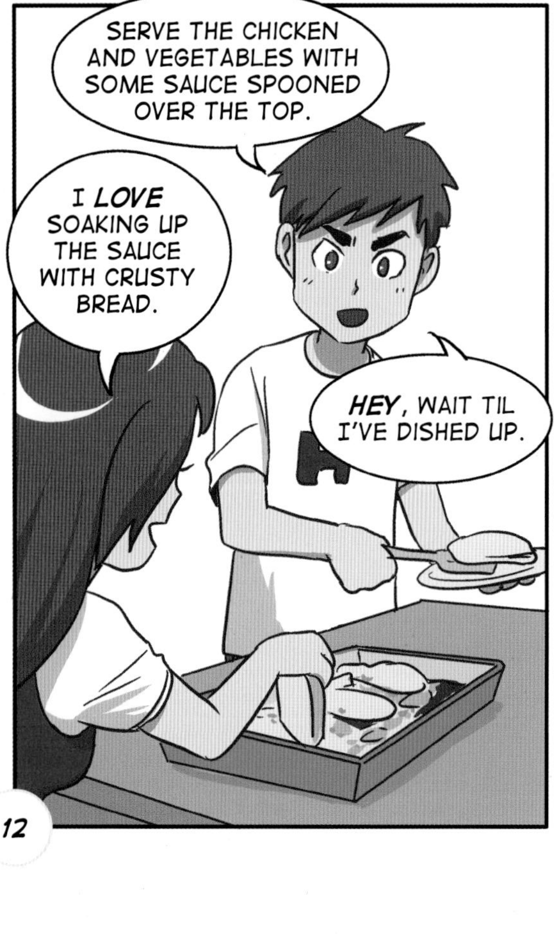
SERVE THE CHICKEN AND VEGETABLES WITH SOME SAUCE SPOONED OVER THE TOP.
I *LOVE* SOAKING UP THE SAUCE WITH CRUSTY BREAD.
HEY, WAIT TIL I'VE DISHED UP.

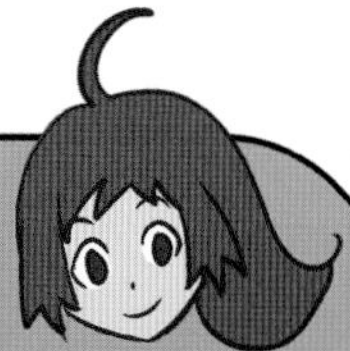

VARIATION

BAKED CHICKEN WITH FENNEL & POTATOES

CUT THE COOKED POTATOES IN HALF (INSTEAD OF CUBES) AND PLACE IN A LARGE OVENPROOF DISH WITH 1 LARGE FENNEL BULB, CUT INTO QUARTERS. YOU DON'T NEED THE LEEKS OR ENDIVES FOR THIS RECIPE. POUR OVER THE STOCK AND BAKE IN A PREHEATED OVEN AT 400°F, GAS MARK 6, FOR 20 MINUTES. REMOVE FROM THE OVEN AND PUT THE PLAIN CHICKEN BREASTS ON THE VEGETABLES. MIX 1 TBSP CHOPPED PARSLEY WITH 1 TBSP MUSTARD AND THE CRÉME FRAÎCHE (NO GARLIC BULB), SEASON WITH SALT AND BLACK PEPPER, AND SPOON OVER THE CHICKEN. BAKE FOR ANOTHER 25–30 MINUTES.

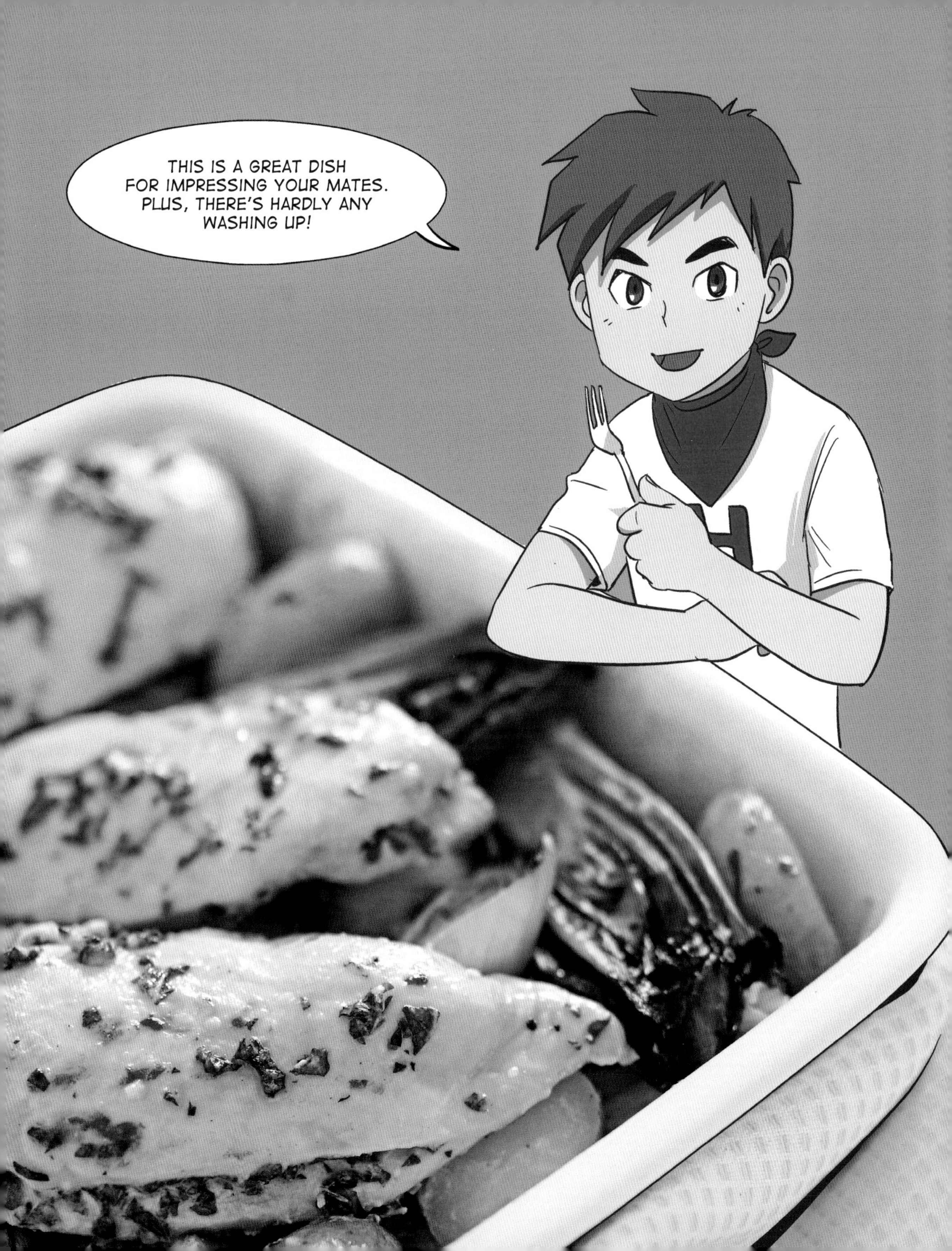
THIS IS A GREAT DISH FOR IMPRESSING YOUR MATES. PLUS, THERE'S HARDLY ANY WASHING UP!

GRILLED CHICKEN SALSA
SPICE UP SUPPERTIME WITH THIS SUPER-EASY CHICKEN DISH.

4 BONELESS, SKINLESS CHICKEN BREASTS
3 TBSP OLIVE OIL
SALT AND BLACK PEPPER
BOILED RICE OR SWEET POTATO MASH, TO SERVE

FOR THE CUCUMBER & TOMATO SALSA:
1 RED ONION, FINELY CHOPPED
2 TOMATOES, DESEEDED AND DICED
1 CUCUMBER, FINELY DICED
1 RED CHILE, FINELY CHOPPED
SMALL HANDFUL OF FRESH CORIANDER, CHOPPED
JUICE OF 1 LIME

SERVES 4 WARRIORS
PREP TIME: 10 MINUTES
COOKING TIME: 10-12 MINUTES

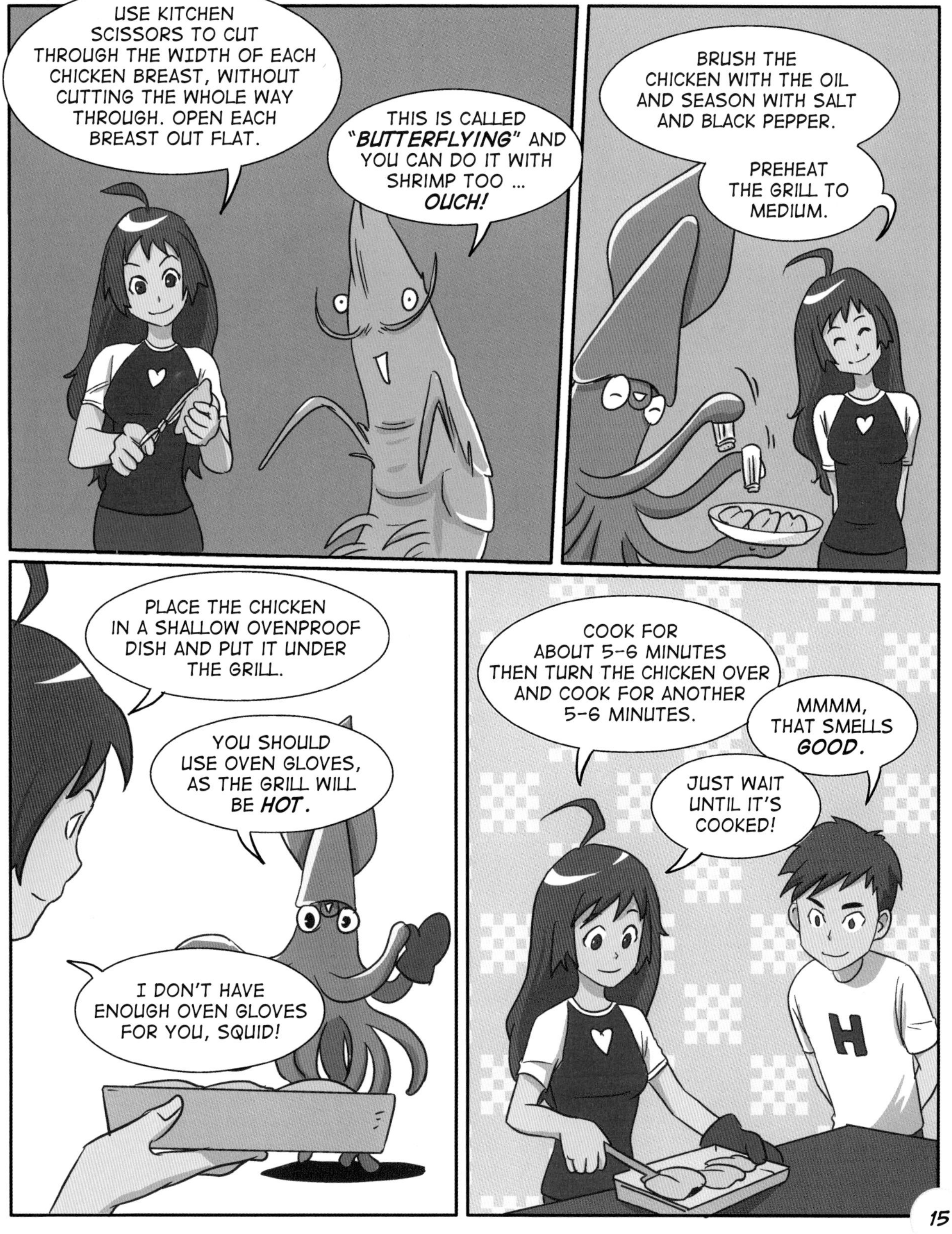
USE KITCHEN SCISSORS TO CUT THROUGH THE WIDTH OF EACH CHICKEN BREAST, WITHOUT CUTTING THE WHOLE WAY THROUGH. OPEN EACH BREAST OUT FLAT.
THIS IS CALLED "*BUTTERFLYING*" AND YOU CAN DO IT WITH SHRIMP TOO ... *OUCH!*
BRUSH THE CHICKEN WITH THE OIL AND SEASON WITH SALT AND BLACK PEPPER.
PREHEAT THE GRILL TO MEDIUM.
PLACE THE CHICKEN IN A SHALLOW OVENPROOF DISH AND PUT IT UNDER THE GRILL.
YOU SHOULD USE OVEN GLOVES, AS THE GRILL WILL BE *HOT*.
I DON'T HAVE ENOUGH OVEN GLOVES FOR YOU, SQUID!
COOK FOR ABOUT 5-6 MINUTES THEN TURN THE CHICKEN OVER AND COOK FOR ANOTHER 5-6 MINUTES.
MMMM, THAT SMELLS *GOOD*.
JUST WAIT UNTIL IT'S COOKED!
H

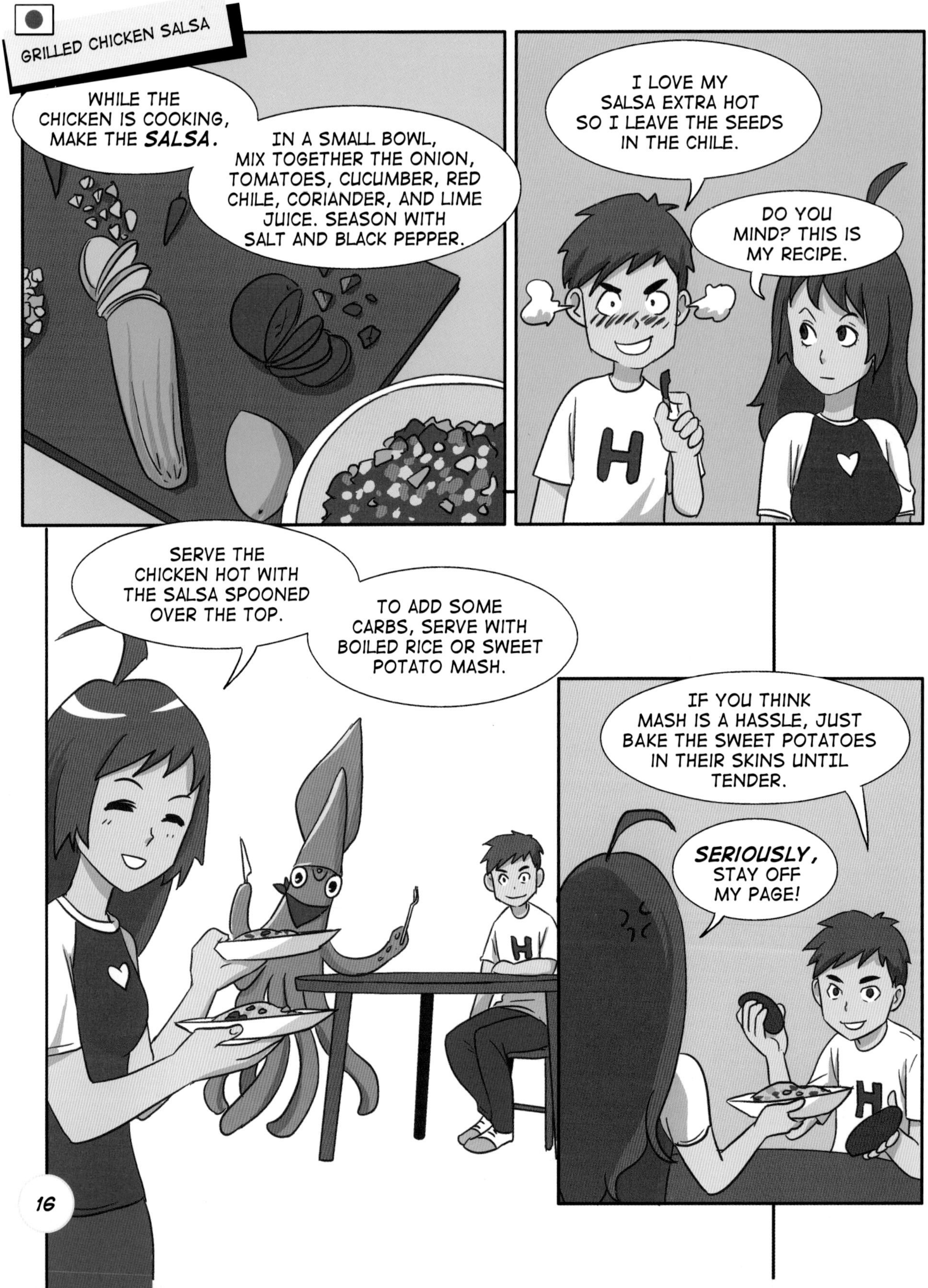
GRILLED CHICKEN SALSA
WHILE THE CHICKEN IS COOKING, MAKE THE SALSA.
IN A SMALL BOWL, MIX TOGETHER THE ONION, TOMATOES, CUCUMBER, RED CHILE, CORIANDER, AND LIME JUICE. SEASON WITH SALT AND BLACK PEPPER.
I LOVE MY SALSA EXTRA HOT SO I LEAVE THE SEEDS IN THE CHILE.
DO YOU MIND? THIS IS MY RECIPE.
SERVE THE CHICKEN HOT WITH THE SALSA SPOONED OVER THE TOP.
TO ADD SOME CARBS, SERVE WITH BOILED RICE OR SWEET POTATO MASH.
IF YOU THINK MASH IS A HASSLE, JUST BAKE THE SWEET POTATOES IN THEIR SKINS UNTIL TENDER.
SERIOUSLY, STAY OFF MY PAGE!

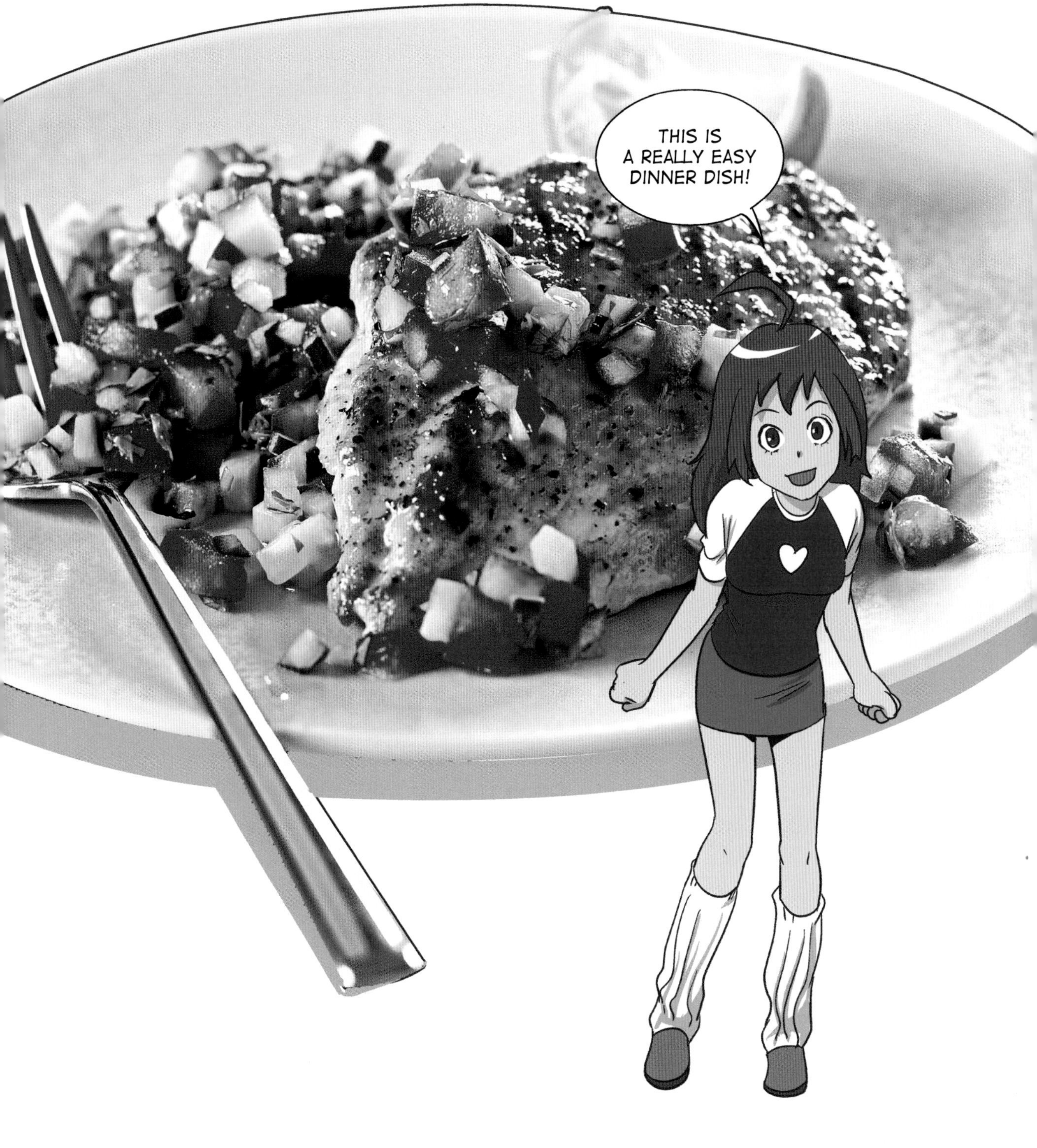
THIS IS A REALLY EASY DINNER DISH!

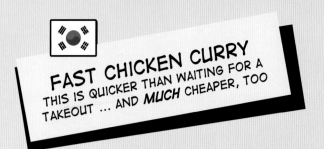

FAST CHICKEN CURRY

THIS IS QUICKER THAN WAITING FOR A TAKEOUT ... AND ***MUCH*** CHEAPER, TOO

3 TBSP OLIVE OIL
1 ONION, FINELY CHOPPED
4 TBSP MEDIUM CURRY PASTE
8 CHICKEN THIGHS, BONED, SKINNED, AND CUT INTO THIN STRIPS
13 OZ CAN DICED TOMATOES
8 OZ BROCCOLI, BROKEN INTO SMALL FLORETS, STALKS PEELED AND SLICED
3½ FL OZ COCONUT MILK
SALT AND BLACK PEPPER

TO SERVE:
BOILED RICE
PAPPADAMS
MANGO CHUTNEY

SERVES 4 WARRIORS
PREP TIME: 5 MINUTES
COOKING TIME: 25 MINUTES

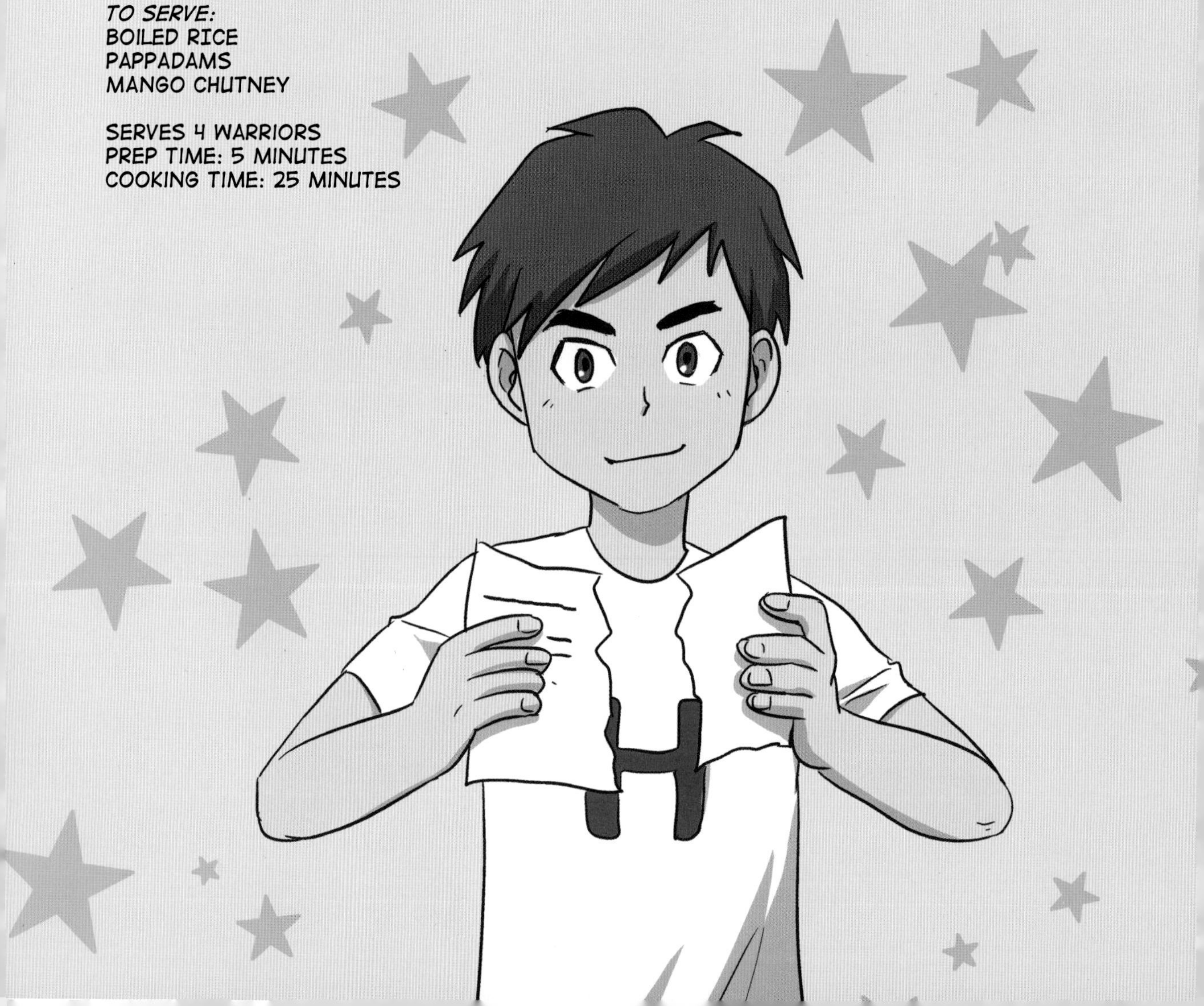

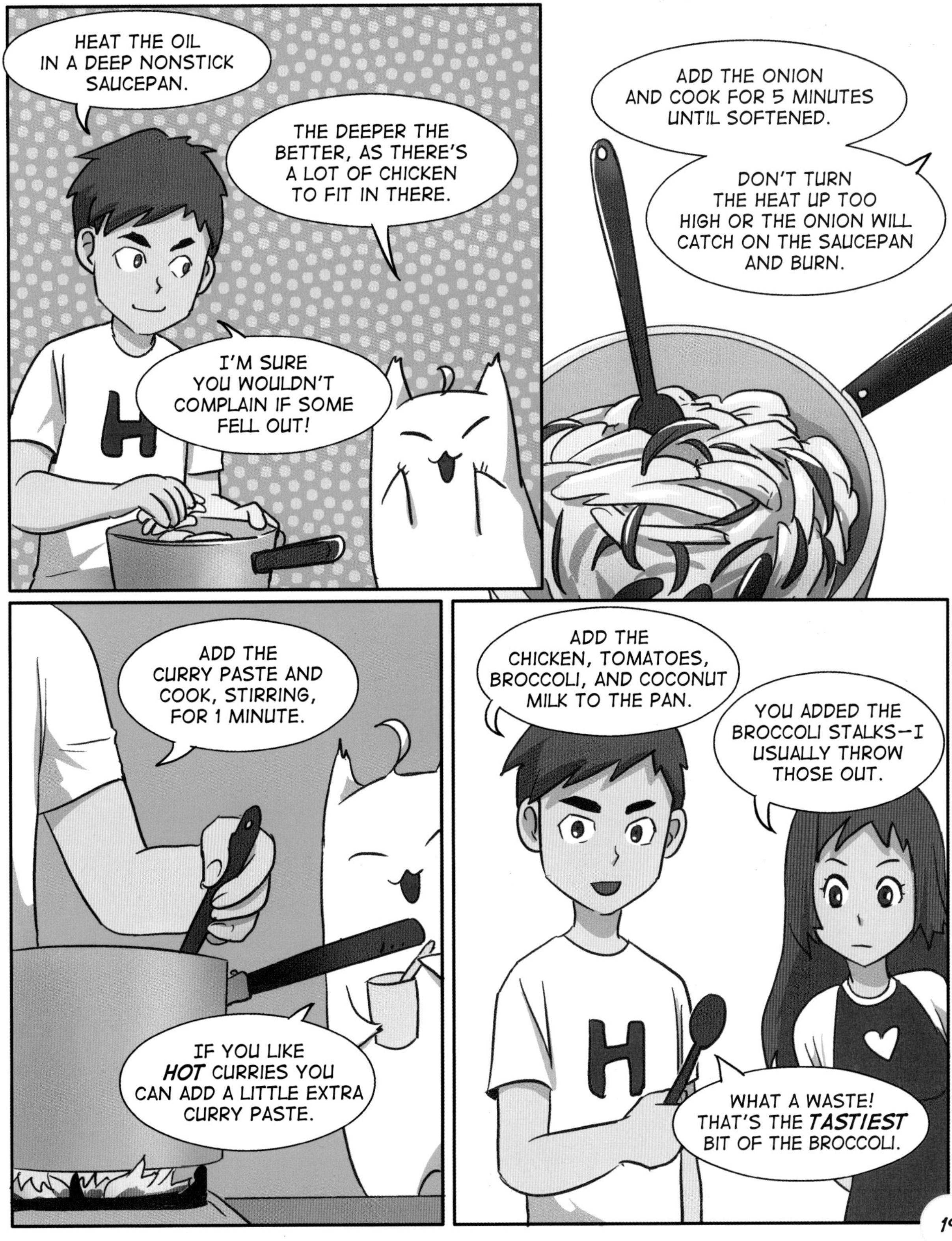
HEAT THE OIL IN A DEEP NONSTICK SAUCEPAN.
THE DEEPER THE BETTER, AS THERE'S A LOT OF CHICKEN TO FIT IN THERE.
I'M SURE YOU WOULDN'T COMPLAIN IF SOME FELL OUT!
ADD THE ONION AND COOK FOR 5 MINUTES UNTIL SOFTENED.
DON'T TURN THE HEAT UP TOO HIGH OR THE ONION WILL CATCH ON THE SAUCEPAN AND BURN.
ADD THE CURRY PASTE AND COOK, STIRRING, FOR 1 MINUTE.
IF YOU LIKE ***HOT*** CURRIES YOU CAN ADD A LITTLE EXTRA CURRY PASTE.
ADD THE CHICKEN, TOMATOES, BROCCOLI, AND COCONUT MILK TO THE PAN.
YOU ADDED THE BROCCOLI STALKS—I USUALLY THROW THOSE OUT.
WHAT A WASTE! THAT'S THE ***TASTIEST*** BIT OF THE BROCCOLI.

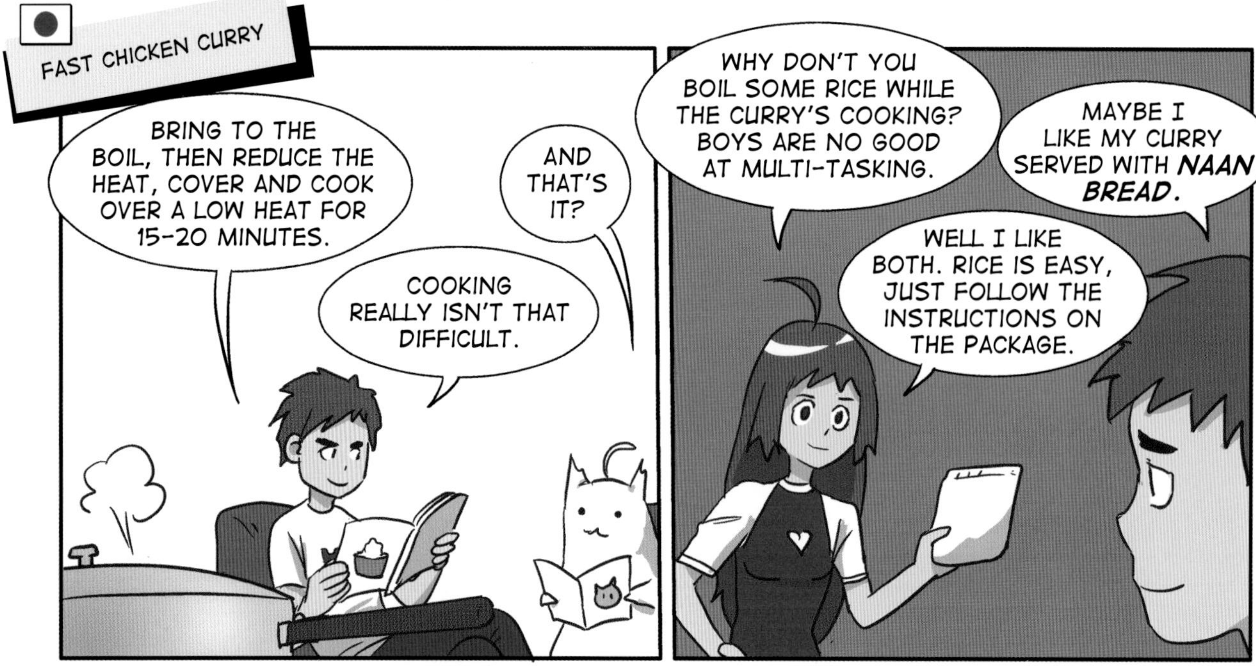
FAST CHICKEN CURRY
BRING TO THE BOIL, THEN REDUCE THE HEAT, COVER AND COOK OVER A LOW HEAT FOR 15–20 MINUTES.
COOKING REALLY ISN'T THAT DIFFICULT.
AND THAT'S IT?
WHY DON'T YOU BOIL SOME RICE WHILE THE CURRY'S COOKING? BOYS ARE NO GOOD AT MULTI-TASKING.
MAYBE I LIKE MY CURRY SERVED WITH NAAN BREAD.
WELL I LIKE BOTH. RICE IS EASY, JUST FOLLOW THE INSTRUCTIONS ON THE PACKAGE.

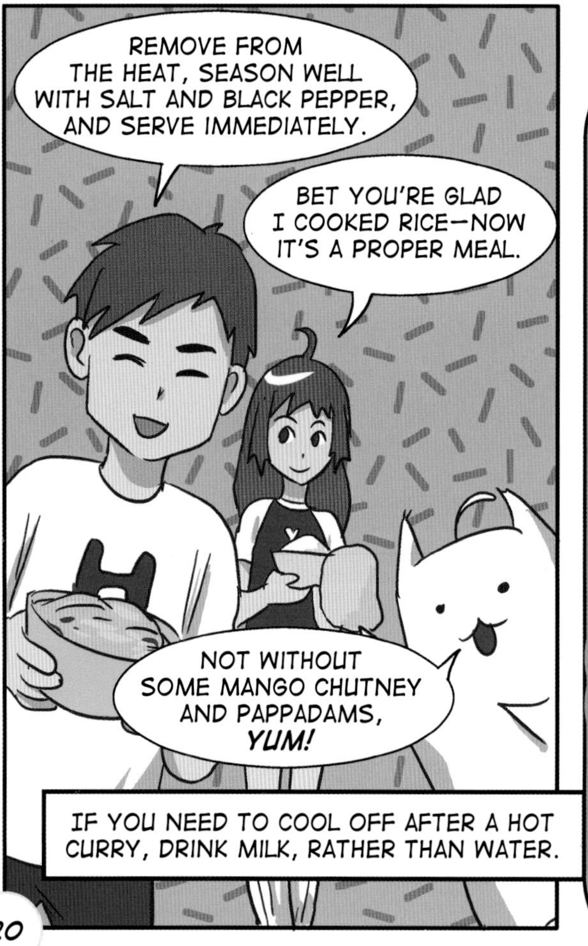
REMOVE FROM THE HEAT, SEASON WELL WITH SALT AND BLACK PEPPER, AND SERVE IMMEDIATELY.
BET YOU'RE GLAD I COOKED RICE—NOW IT'S A PROPER MEAL.
NOT WITHOUT SOME MANGO CHUTNEY AND PAPPADAMS, YUM!
IF YOU NEED TO COOL OFF AFTER A HOT CURRY, DRINK MILK, RATHER THAN WATER.

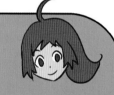

VARIATION

SEAFOOD PATTIES WITH CURRY SAUCE

FOLLOW THE INSTRUCTIONS ABOVE TO COOK THE ONIONS AND CURRY PASTE, THEN ADD THE TOMATOES, 7 OZ BABY SPINACH LEAVES, AND THE COCONUT MILK, AND COOK AS ABOVE.

MEANWHILE, FINELY CHOP 12 OZ WHITE FISH FILLETS AND 6 OZ COOKED PEELED SHRIMP. MIX TOGETHER BY HAND.

TRANSFER TO A BOWL, ADD 4 FINELY CHOPPED SCALLIONS, 2 TBSP CHOPPED CORIANDER LEAVES, 2 OZ FRESH WHITE BREAD CRUMBS, A SQUEEZE OF LEMON JUICE, 1 BEATEN EGG, AND SALT AND BLACK PEPPER.

MIX WELL, THEN FORM INTO 16 PATTIES AND ROLL IN WHITE BREAD CRUMBS TO COAT. HEAT ABOUT 1 CM VEGETABLE OIL IN A LARGE SKILLET, ADD THE PATTIES IN BATCHES, AND COOK FOR 5 MINUTES ON EACH SIDE OR UNTIL GOLDEN BROWN. SERVE WITH THE CURRY SAUCE.

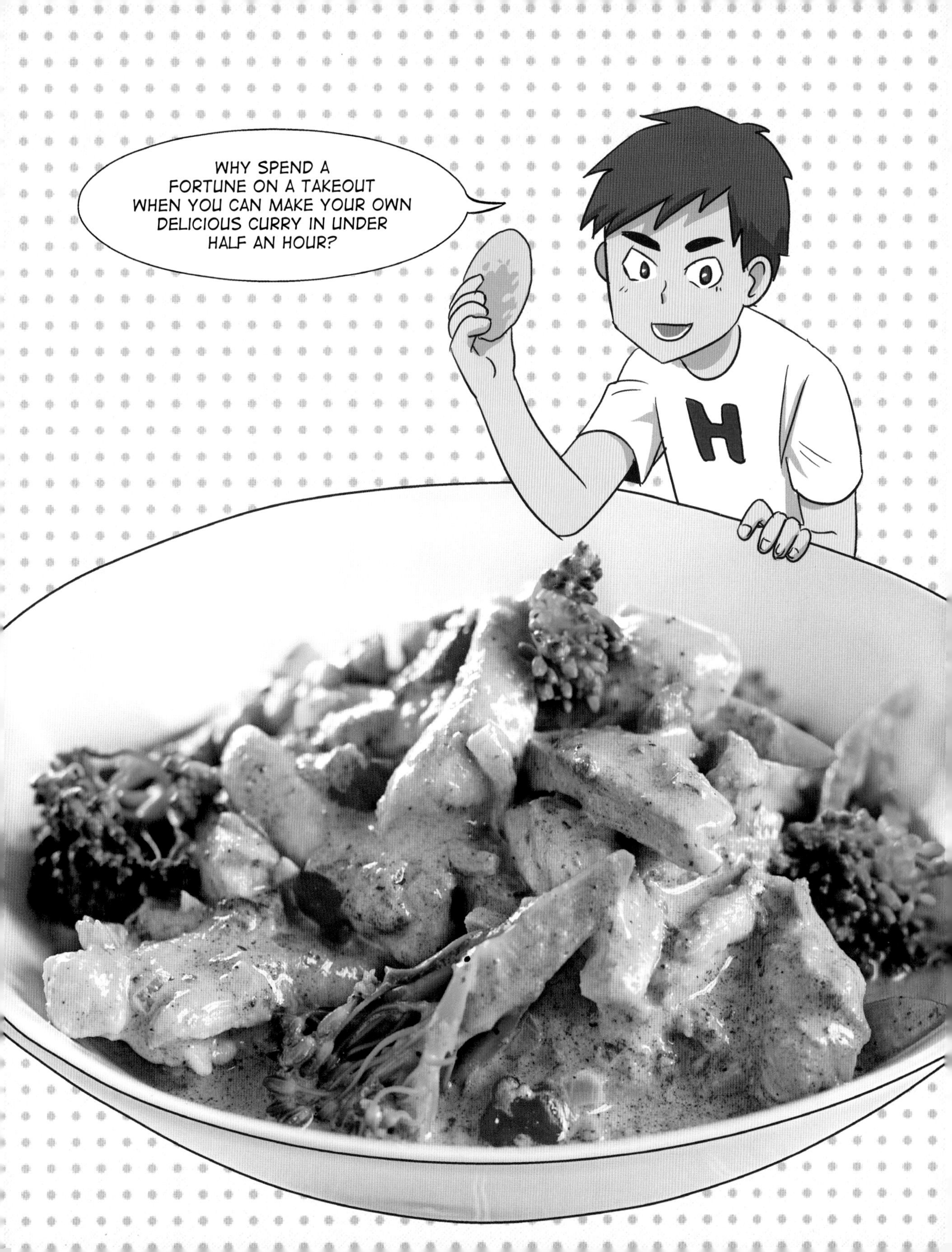
WHY SPEND A FORTUNE ON A TAKEOUT WHEN YOU CAN MAKE YOUR OWN DELICIOUS CURRY IN UNDER HALF AN HOUR?
H

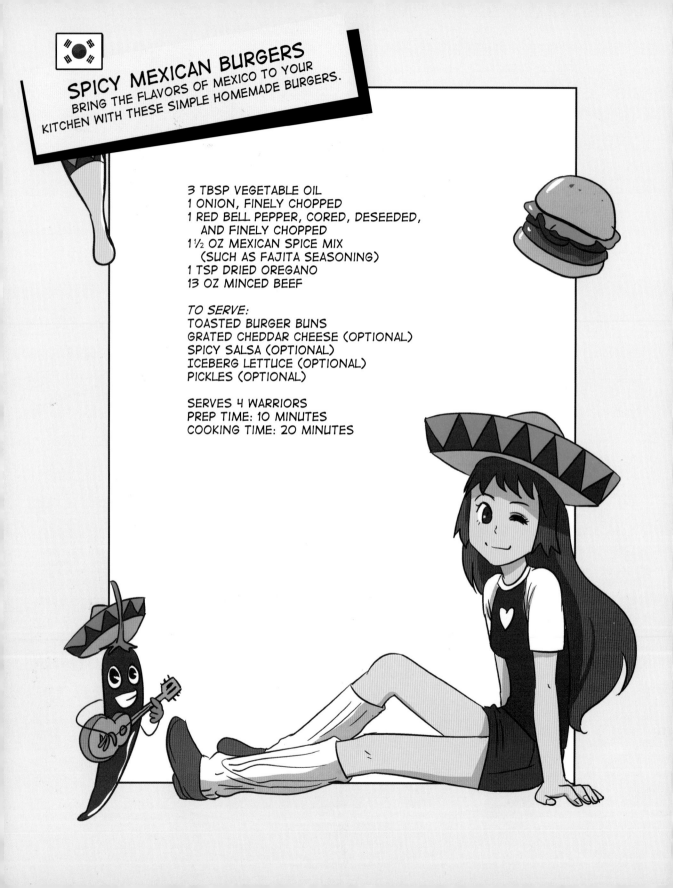

SPICY MEXICAN BURGERS

BRING THE FLAVORS OF MEXICO TO YOUR KITCHEN WITH THESE SIMPLE HOMEMADE BURGERS.

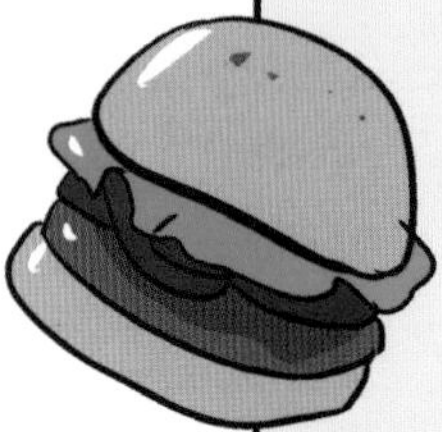

3 TBSP VEGETABLE OIL
1 ONION, FINELY CHOPPED
1 RED BELL PEPPER, CORED, DESEEDED, AND FINELY CHOPPED
1½ OZ MEXICAN SPICE MIX (SUCH AS FAJITA SEASONING)
1 TSP DRIED OREGANO
13 OZ MINCED BEEF

TO SERVE:
TOASTED BURGER BUNS
GRATED CHEDDAR CHEESE (OPTIONAL)
SPICY SALSA (OPTIONAL)
ICEBERG LETTUCE (OPTIONAL)
PICKLES (OPTIONAL)

SERVES 4 WARRIORS
PREP TIME: 10 MINUTES
COOKING TIME: 20 MINUTES

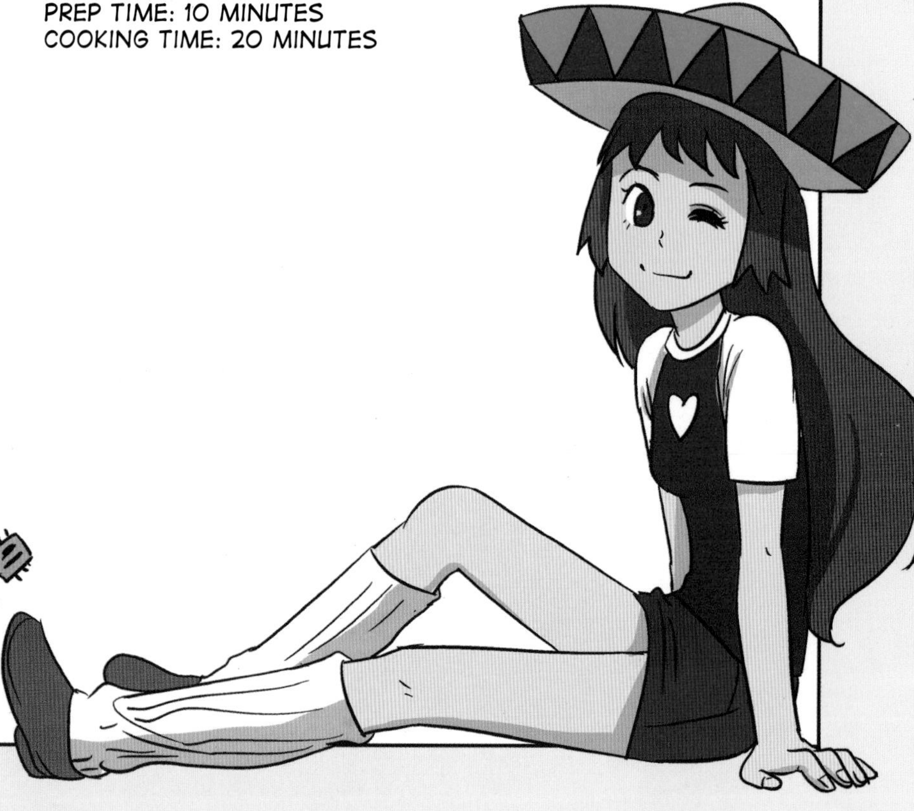

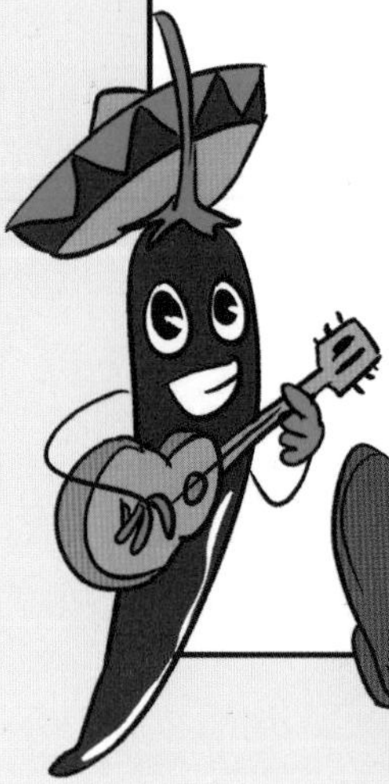

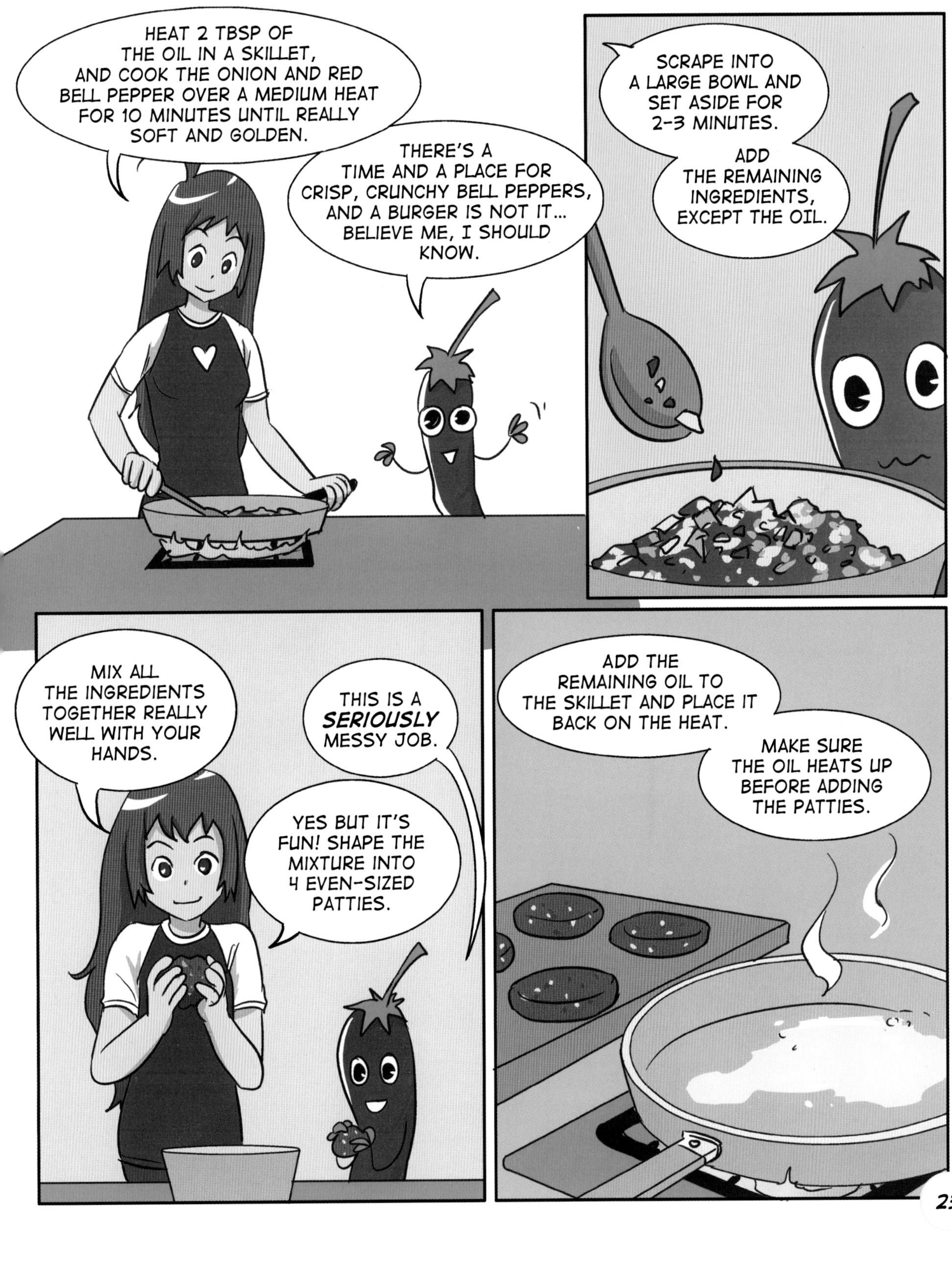
HEAT 2 TBSP OF THE OIL IN A SKILLET, AND COOK THE ONION AND RED BELL PEPPER OVER A MEDIUM HEAT FOR 10 MINUTES UNTIL REALLY SOFT AND GOLDEN.
THERE'S A TIME AND A PLACE FOR CRISP, CRUNCHY BELL PEPPERS, AND A BURGER IS NOT IT... BELIEVE ME, I SHOULD KNOW.
SCRAPE INTO A LARGE BOWL AND SET ASIDE FOR 2-3 MINUTES.
ADD THE REMAINING INGREDIENTS, EXCEPT THE OIL.
MIX ALL THE INGREDIENTS TOGETHER REALLY WELL WITH YOUR HANDS.
THIS IS A *SERIOUSLY* MESSY JOB.
YES BUT IT'S FUN! SHAPE THE MIXTURE INTO 4 EVEN-SIZED PATTIES.
ADD THE REMAINING OIL TO THE SKILLET AND PLACE IT BACK ON THE HEAT.
MAKE SURE THE OIL HEATS UP BEFORE ADDING THE PATTIES.

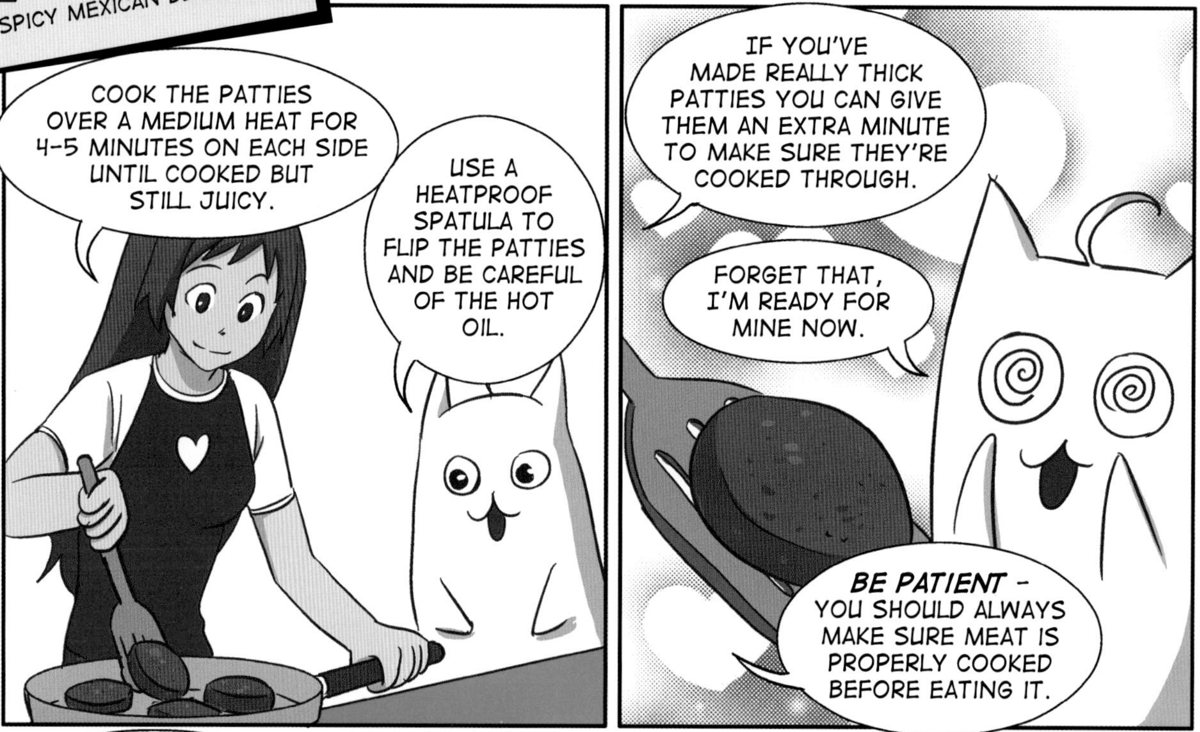
COOK THE PATTIES OVER A MEDIUM HEAT FOR 4-5 MINUTES ON EACH SIDE UNTIL COOKED BUT STILL JUICY.
USE A HEATPROOF SPATULA TO FLIP THE PATTIES AND BE CAREFUL OF THE HOT OIL.
IF YOU'VE MADE REALLY THICK PATTIES YOU CAN GIVE THEM AN EXTRA MINUTE TO MAKE SURE THEY'RE COOKED THROUGH.
FORGET THAT, I'M READY FOR MINE NOW.
BE PATIENT - YOU SHOULD ALWAYS MAKE SURE MEAT IS PROPERLY COOKED BEFORE EATING IT.

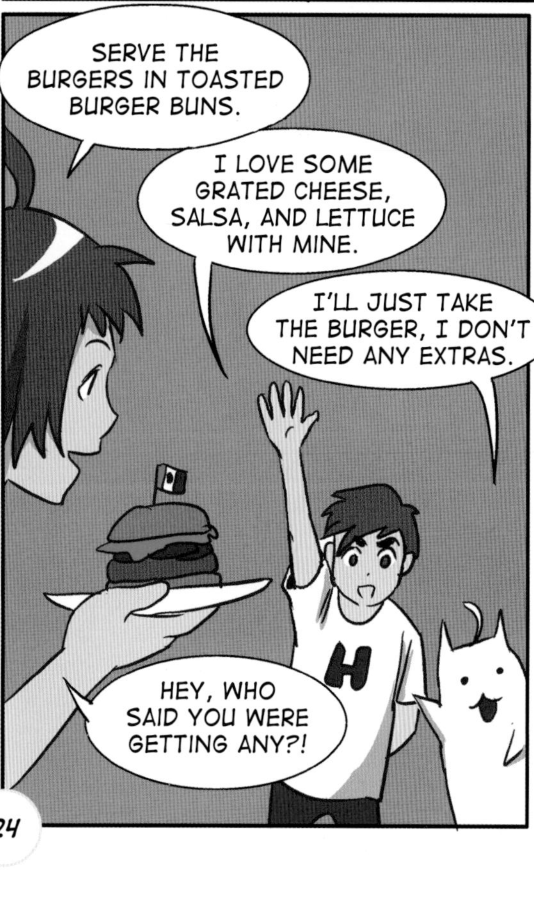
SERVE THE BURGERS IN TOASTED BURGER BUNS.
I LOVE SOME GRATED CHEESE, SALSA, AND LETTUCE WITH MINE.
I'LL JUST TAKE THE BURGER, I DON'T NEED ANY EXTRAS.
HEY, WHO SAID YOU WERE GETTING ANY?!

VARIATION

BEAN TOSTADAS

HEAT A SKILLET AND LIGHTLY TOAST A LARGE SOFT TORTILLA WRAP FOR 1 MINUTE ON EACH SIDE. PUSH INTO A DEEP BOWL AND REPEAT WITH 3 MORE TORTILLAS.

MEANWHILE, MIX A 13 OZ CAN RED KIDNEY BEANS, RINSED AND DRAINED, WITH 1 SMALL FINELY CHOPPED RED ONION, 1 FINELY CHOPPED RED BELL PEPPER, 1 PEELED, PITTED, AND DICED AVOCADO, AND 1 SMALL BUNCH CHOPPED CORIANDER.

DRIZZLE OVER 2 TBSP OIL AND 1 TBSP LIME JUICE, AND SEASON WITH SALT. DROP SOME SHREDDED ICEBERG LETTUCE INTO EACH TORTILLA AND DIVIDE THE BEANS BETWEEN THEM. SERVE WITH GRATED CHEDDAR, SALSA, AND SOUR CREAM.

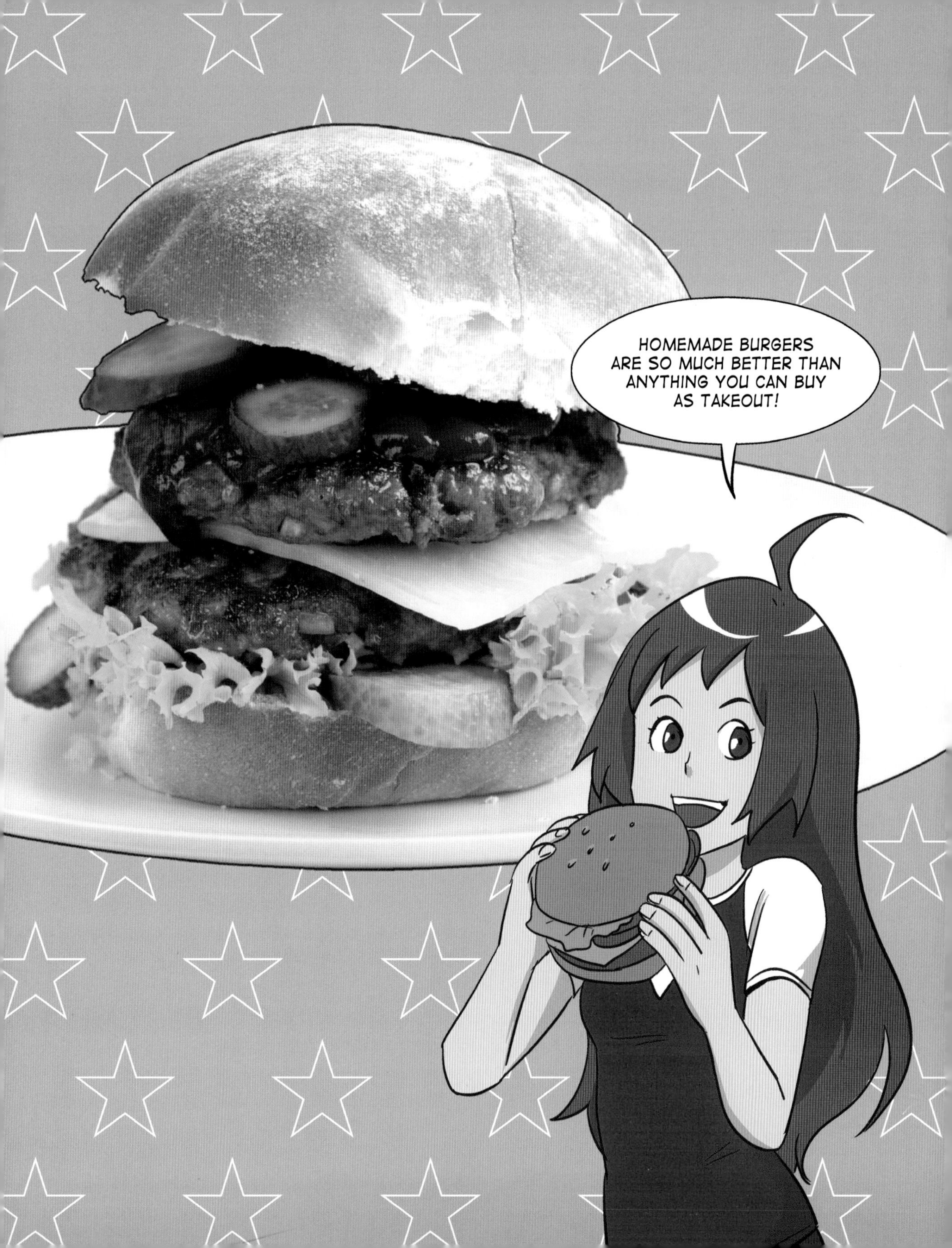
HOMEMADE BURGERS ARE SO MUCH BETTER THAN ANYTHING YOU CAN BUY AS TAKEOUT!

BEEF FAJITAS

THE PERFECT DISH TO SHARE WITH YOUR BUDDIES.

11½ OZ BEEF STIR-FRY STRIPS
1½ OZ PACKET FAJITA SEASONING
4 TBSP VEGETABLE OIL
1 ONION, SLICED
1 RED BELL PEPPER, CORED, DESEEDED, AND SLICED
4 LARGE OR 8 SMALL SOFT TORTILLA WRAPS

TO SERVE:
GRATED CHEDDAR CHEESE (OPTIONAL)
JALEPEÑO CHILES (OPTIONAL)
SOUR CREAM (OPTIONAL)

SERVES 4 WARRIORS
PREP TIME: 10 MINUTES
COOKING TIME: 10 MINUTES

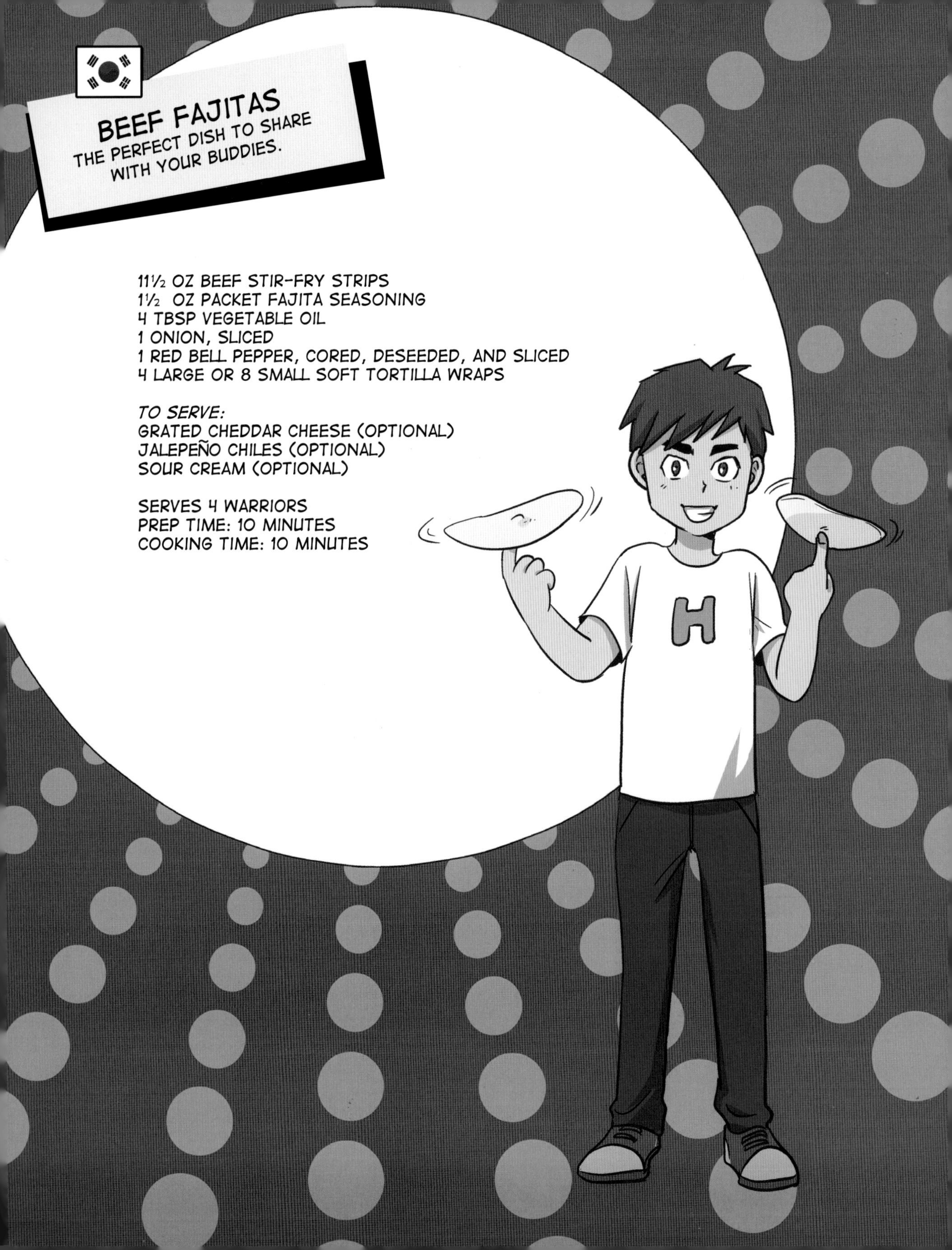
H

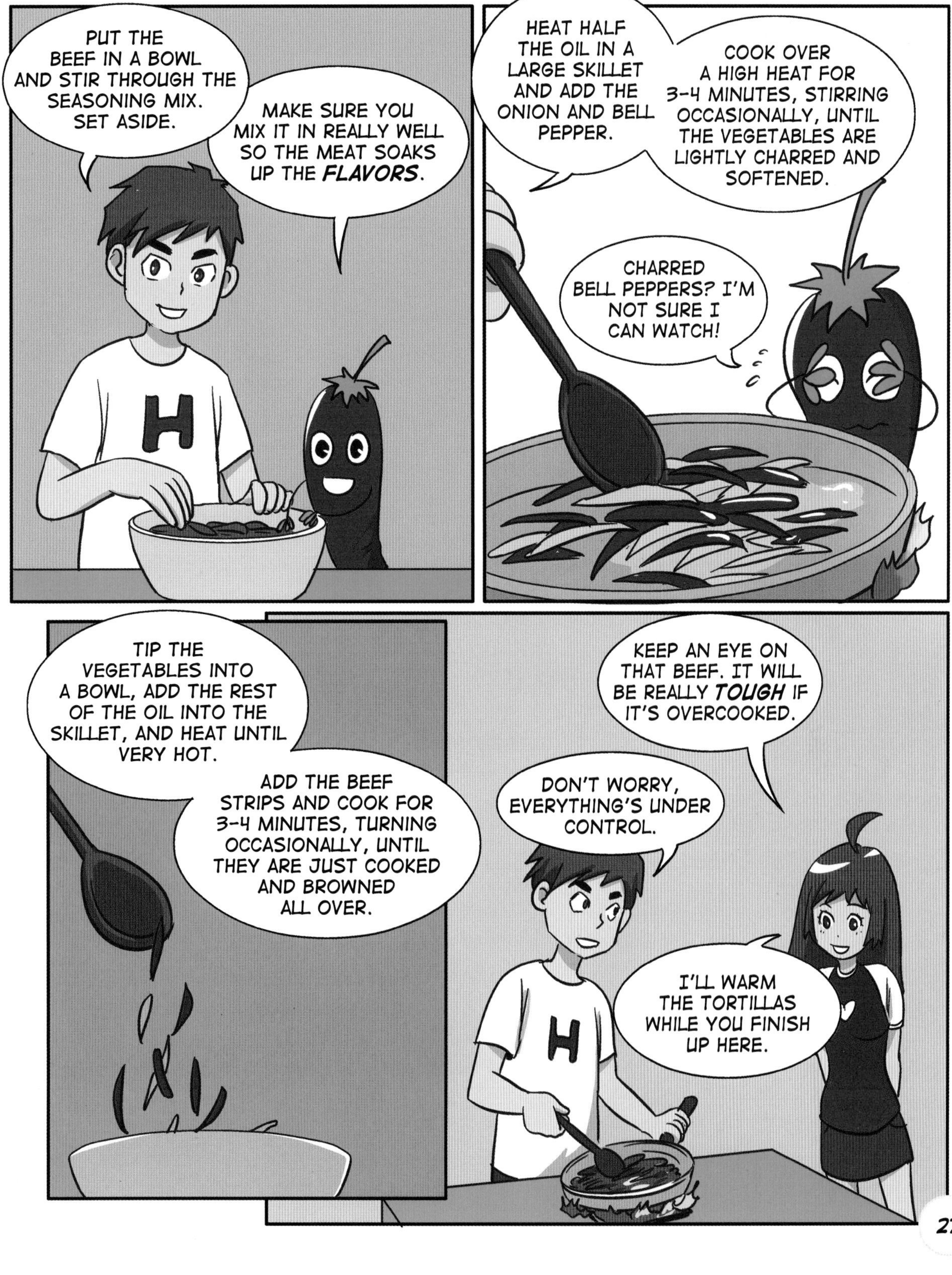

PUT THE BEEF IN A BOWL AND STIR THROUGH THE SEASONING MIX. SET ASIDE.
MAKE SURE YOU MIX IT IN REALLY WELL SO THE MEAT SOAKS UP THE *FLAVORS*.
HEAT HALF THE OIL IN A LARGE SKILLET AND ADD THE ONION AND BELL PEPPER.
COOK OVER A HIGH HEAT FOR 3–4 MINUTES, STIRRING OCCASIONALLY, UNTIL THE VEGETABLES ARE LIGHTLY CHARRED AND SOFTENED.
CHARRED BELL PEPPERS? I'M NOT SURE I CAN WATCH!
TIP THE VEGETABLES INTO A BOWL, ADD THE REST OF THE OIL INTO THE SKILLET, AND HEAT UNTIL VERY HOT.
ADD THE BEEF STRIPS AND COOK FOR 3–4 MINUTES, TURNING OCCASIONALLY, UNTIL THEY ARE JUST COOKED AND BROWNED ALL OVER.
KEEP AN EYE ON THAT BEEF. IT WILL BE REALLY *TOUGH* IF IT'S OVERCOOKED.
DON'T WORRY, EVERYTHING'S UNDER CONTROL.
I'LL WARM THE TORTILLAS WHILE YOU FINISH UP HERE.

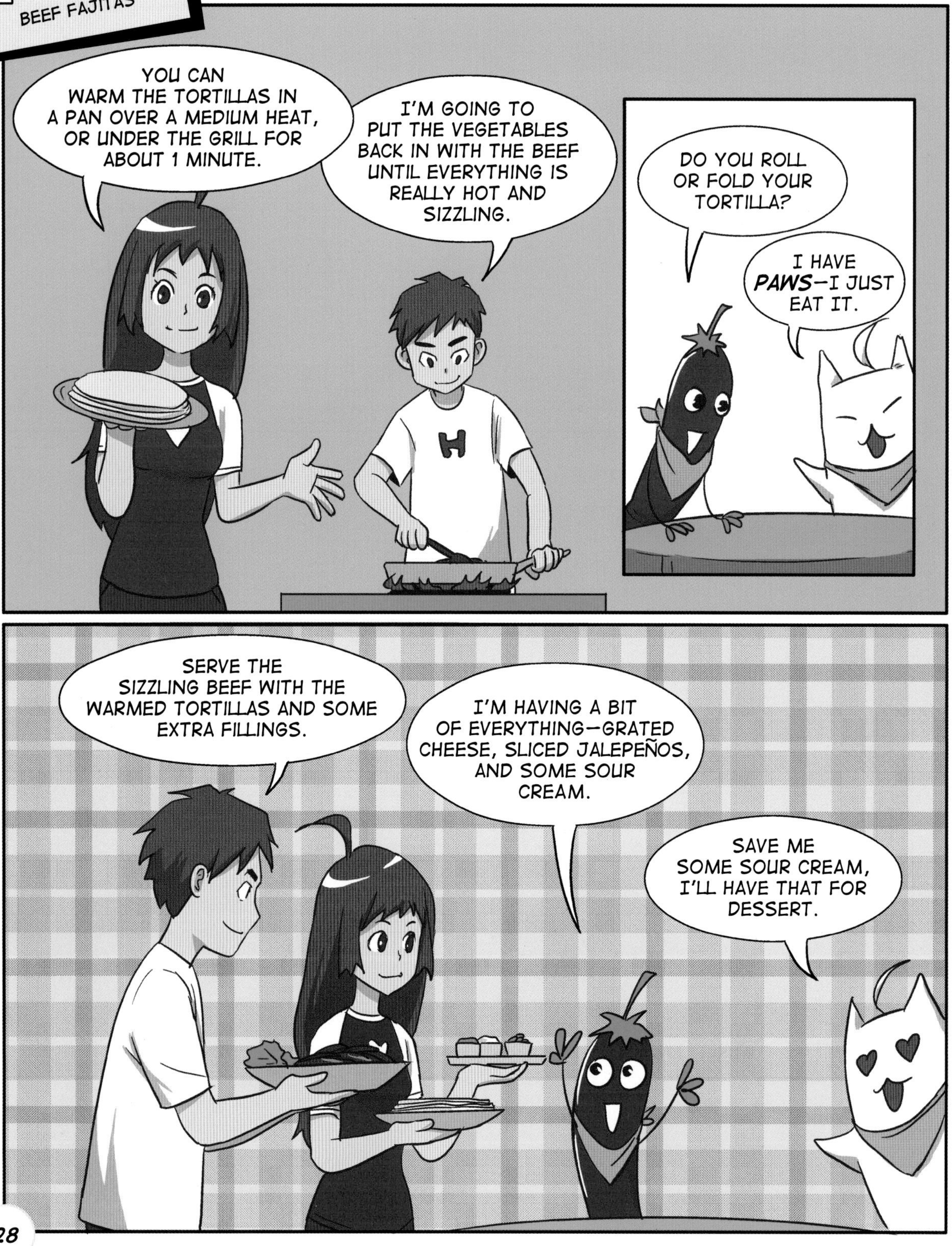
YOU CAN WARM THE TORTILLAS IN A PAN OVER A MEDIUM HEAT, OR UNDER THE GRILL FOR ABOUT 1 MINUTE.
I'M GOING TO PUT THE VEGETABLES BACK IN WITH THE BEEF UNTIL EVERYTHING IS REALLY HOT AND SIZZLING.
DO YOU ROLL OR FOLD YOUR TORTILLA?
I HAVE ***PAWS***—I JUST EAT IT.
SERVE THE SIZZLING BEEF WITH THE WARMED TORTILLAS AND SOME EXTRA FILLINGS.
I'M HAVING A BIT OF EVERYTHING—GRATED CHEESE, SLICED JALEPEÑOS, AND SOME SOUR CREAM.
SAVE ME SOME SOUR CREAM, I'LL HAVE THAT FOR DESSERT.

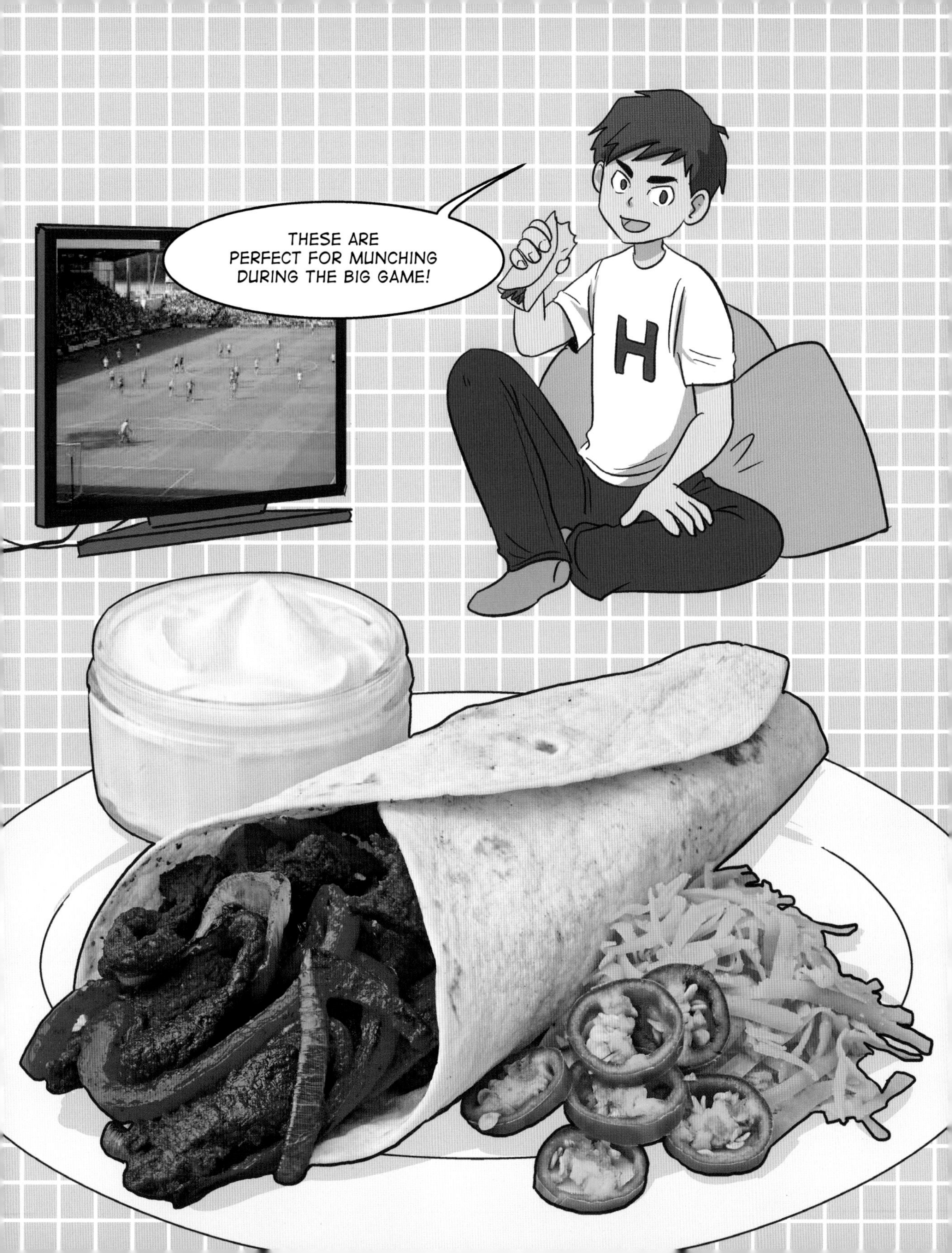
THESE ARE PERFECT FOR MUNCHING DURING THE BIG GAME!

MEATBALL TAGINE

THIS DISH IS FROM MOROCCO WHERE A LOT OF
THE COOKING IS DONE IN A POT CALLED A TAGINE.
BUT DON'T WORRY, IT WILL TASTE JUST AS
GOOD COOKED IN A SAUCEPAN!

2 SMALL ONIONS, FINELY CHOPPED
2 TBSP RAISINS
1½ LB MINCED BEEF
1 TBSP TOMATO PASTE
3 TSP CURRY POWDER
3 TBSP OLIVE OIL
½ TSP GROUND CINNAMON
1¼ LB CANNED DICED TOMATOES
JUICE OF ½ LEMON
2 CELERY STICKS, THICKLY SLICED
1 LARGE OR 2 SMALL ZUCCHINI, COARSELY CHOPPED
6 OZ FROZEN PEAS
SALT AND BLACK PEPPER
CORIANDER & APRICOT COUSCOUS OR PLAIN
   COUSCOUS, TO SERVE

SERVES 4 WARRIORS
PREP TIME: 15 MINUTES
COOKING TIME: 40 MINUTES

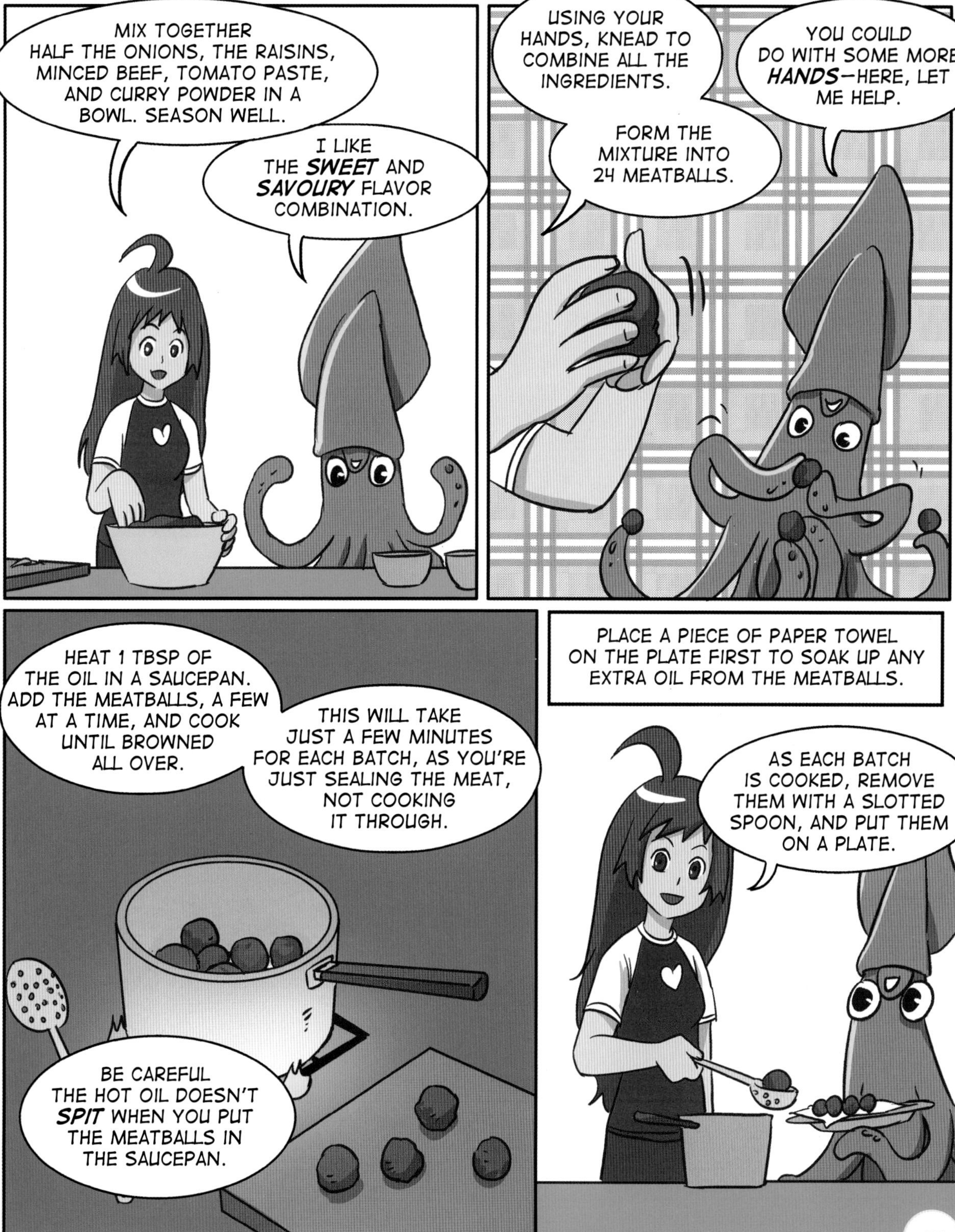
MIX TOGETHER HALF THE ONIONS, THE RAISINS, MINCED BEEF, TOMATO PASTE, AND CURRY POWDER IN A BOWL. SEASON WELL.
I LIKE THE SWEET AND SAVOURY FLAVOR COMBINATION.
USING YOUR HANDS, KNEAD TO COMBINE ALL THE INGREDIENTS.
FORM THE MIXTURE INTO 24 MEATBALLS.
YOU COULD DO WITH SOME MORE HANDS—HERE, LET ME HELP.
HEAT 1 TBSP OF THE OIL IN A SAUCEPAN. ADD THE MEATBALLS, A FEW AT A TIME, AND COOK UNTIL BROWNED ALL OVER.
THIS WILL TAKE JUST A FEW MINUTES FOR EACH BATCH, AS YOU'RE JUST SEALING THE MEAT, NOT COOKING IT THROUGH.
BE CAREFUL THE HOT OIL DOESN'T SPIT WHEN YOU PUT THE MEATBALLS IN THE SAUCEPAN.
PLACE A PIECE OF PAPER TOWEL ON THE PLATE FIRST TO SOAK UP ANY EXTRA OIL FROM THE MEATBALLS.
AS EACH BATCH IS COOKED, REMOVE THEM WITH A SLOTTED SPOON, AND PUT THEM ON A PLATE.

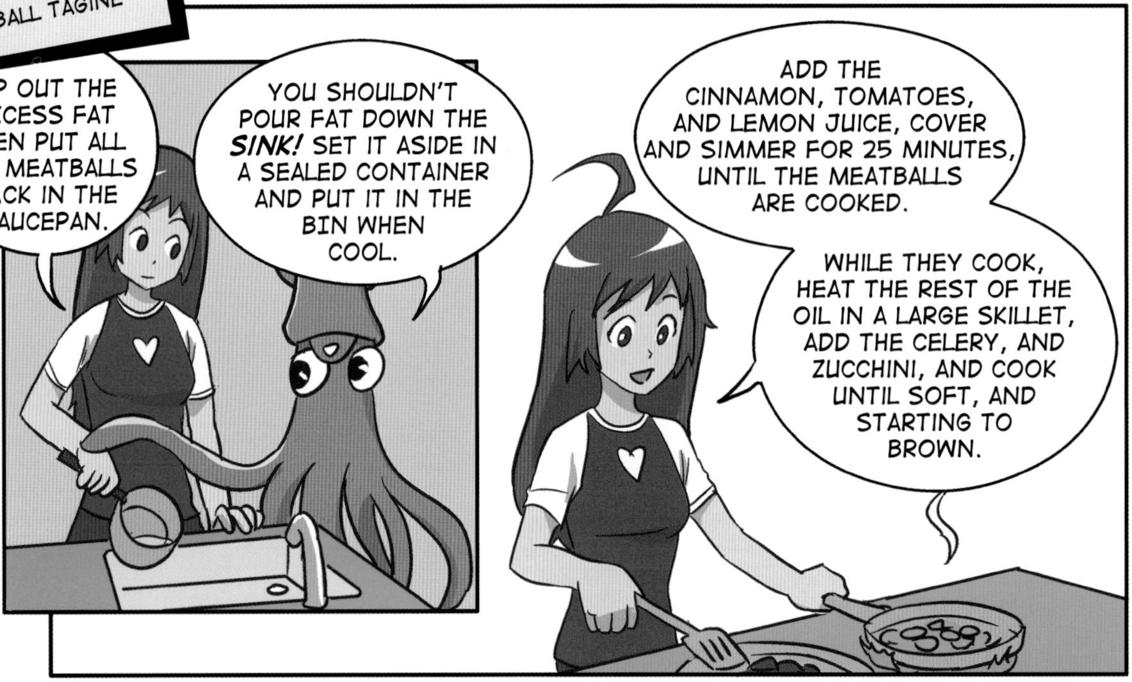
TIP OUT THE EXCESS FAT THEN PUT ALL THE MEATBALLS BACK IN THE SAUCEPAN.
YOU SHOULDN'T POUR FAT DOWN THE ***SINK!*** SET IT ASIDE IN A SEALED CONTAINER AND PUT IT IN THE BIN WHEN COOL.
ADD THE CINNAMON, TOMATOES, AND LEMON JUICE, COVER AND SIMMER FOR 25 MINUTES, UNTIL THE MEATBALLS ARE COOKED.
WHILE THEY COOK, HEAT THE REST OF THE OIL IN A LARGE SKILLET, ADD THE CELERY, AND ZUCCHINI, AND COOK UNTIL SOFT, AND STARTING TO BROWN.

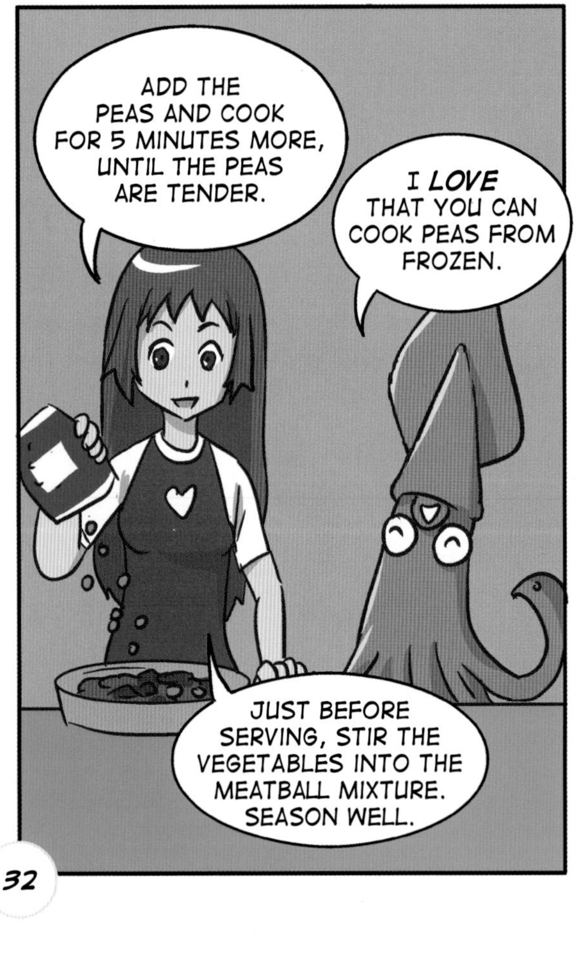
ADD THE PEAS AND COOK FOR 5 MINUTES MORE, UNTIL THE PEAS ARE TENDER.
I ***LOVE*** THAT YOU CAN COOK PEAS FROM FROZEN.
JUST BEFORE SERVING, STIR THE VEGETABLES INTO THE MEATBALL MIXTURE. SEASON WELL.

ACCOMPANIMENT

CORIANDER & APRICOT COUSCOUS

PUT 7 OZ INSTANT COUSCOUS IN A LARGE, HEATPROOF BOWL WITH 2 OZ CHOPPED READY-TO-EAT DRIED APRICOTS. POUR OVER BOILING VEGETABLE STOCK TO JUST COVER THE COUSCOUS. COVER AND LEAVE FOR 10–12 MINUTES UNTIL THE STOCK HAS BEEN ABSORBED.

MEANWHILE, CHOP 2 LARGE, RIPE TOMATOES, AND FINELY CHOP 2 TBSP CORIANDER LEAVES. FLUFF UP THE COUSCOUS WITH A FORK AND TIP INTO A SERVING DISH. STIR IN THE TOMATOES AND CORIANDER WITH 2 TBSP OLIVE OIL. SEASON, MIX WELL, AND SERVE WITH THE TAGINE.

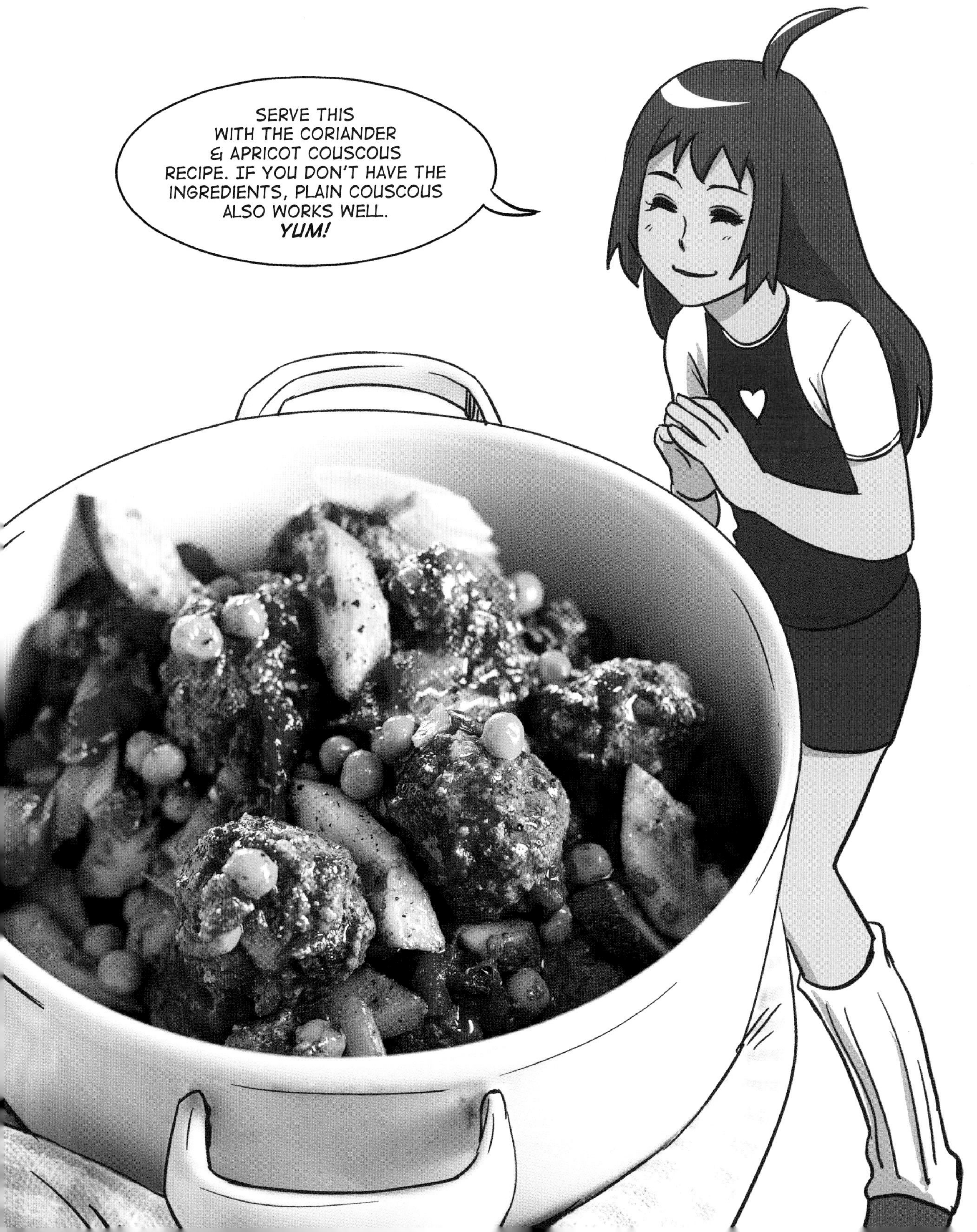
SERVE THIS WITH THE CORIANDER & APRICOT COUSCOUS RECIPE. IF YOU DON'T HAVE THE INGREDIENTS, PLAIN COUSCOUS ALSO WORKS WELL. *YUM!*

CLASSIC BOLOGNESE

EVERYONE NEEDS A BOLOGNESE RECIPE UP THEIR SLEEVE.

2 TBSP UNSALTED BUTTER
1 TBSP OLIVE OIL
1 SMALL ONION, FINELY CHOPPED
2 CELERY STICKS, FINELY CHOPPED
1 CARROT, FINELY CHOPPED
1 BAY LEAF
7 OZ LEAN MINCED BEEF
7 OZ LEAN MINCED PORK
¼ PINT DRY WHITE WINE
2 X 13 OZ CANS DICED TOMATOES
1 PINT CHICKEN STOCK
13 OZ DRIED TAGLIATELLE OR FETTUCCINE
SALT AND BLACK PEPPER

TO SERVE:
FRESHLY GRATED PARMESAN CHEESE
GARLIC BREAD (OPTIONAL)
GREEN SALAD (OPTIONAL)

SERVES 4 WARRIORS
PREP TIME: 10 MINUTES
COOKING TIME: 1¼ HOURS

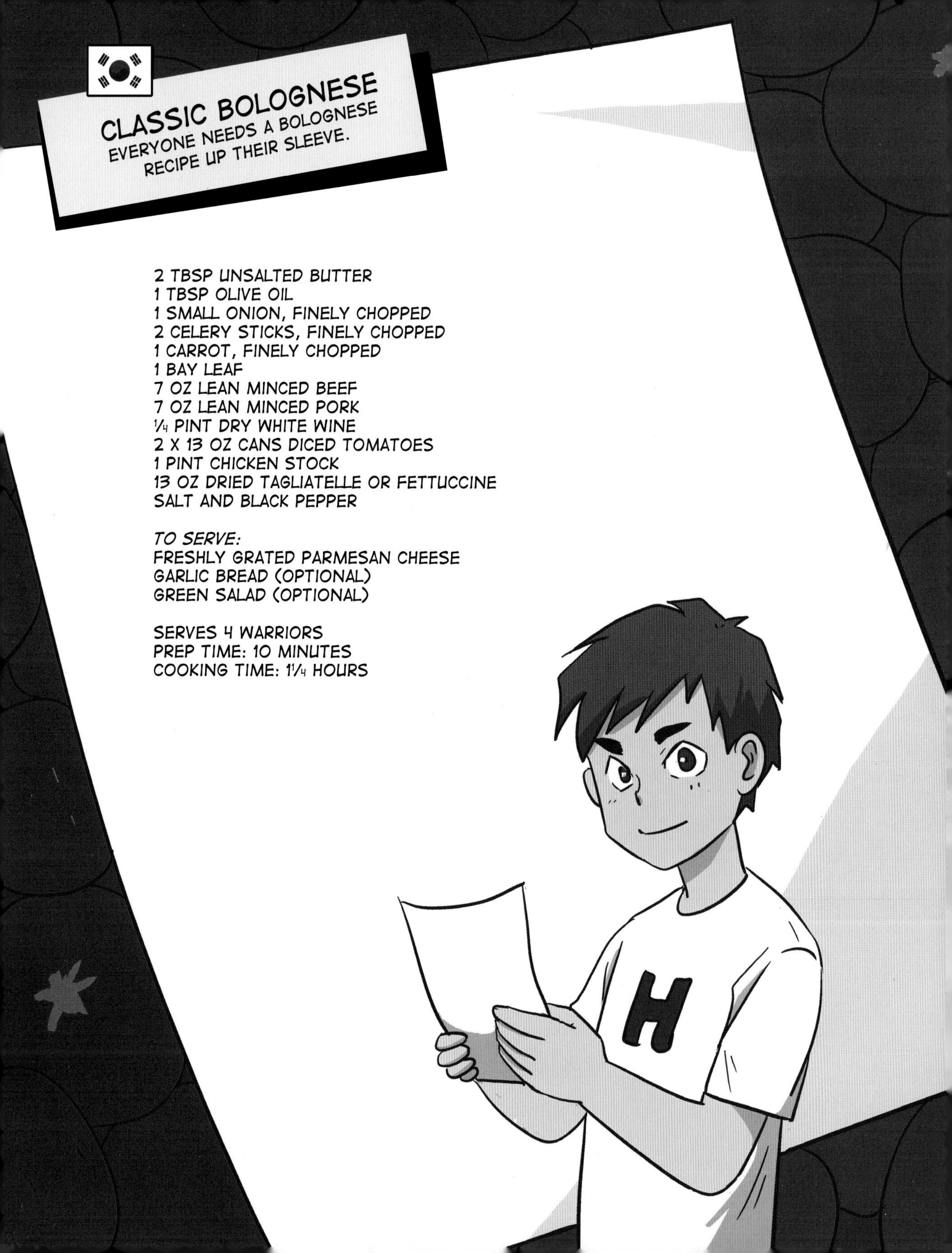
H

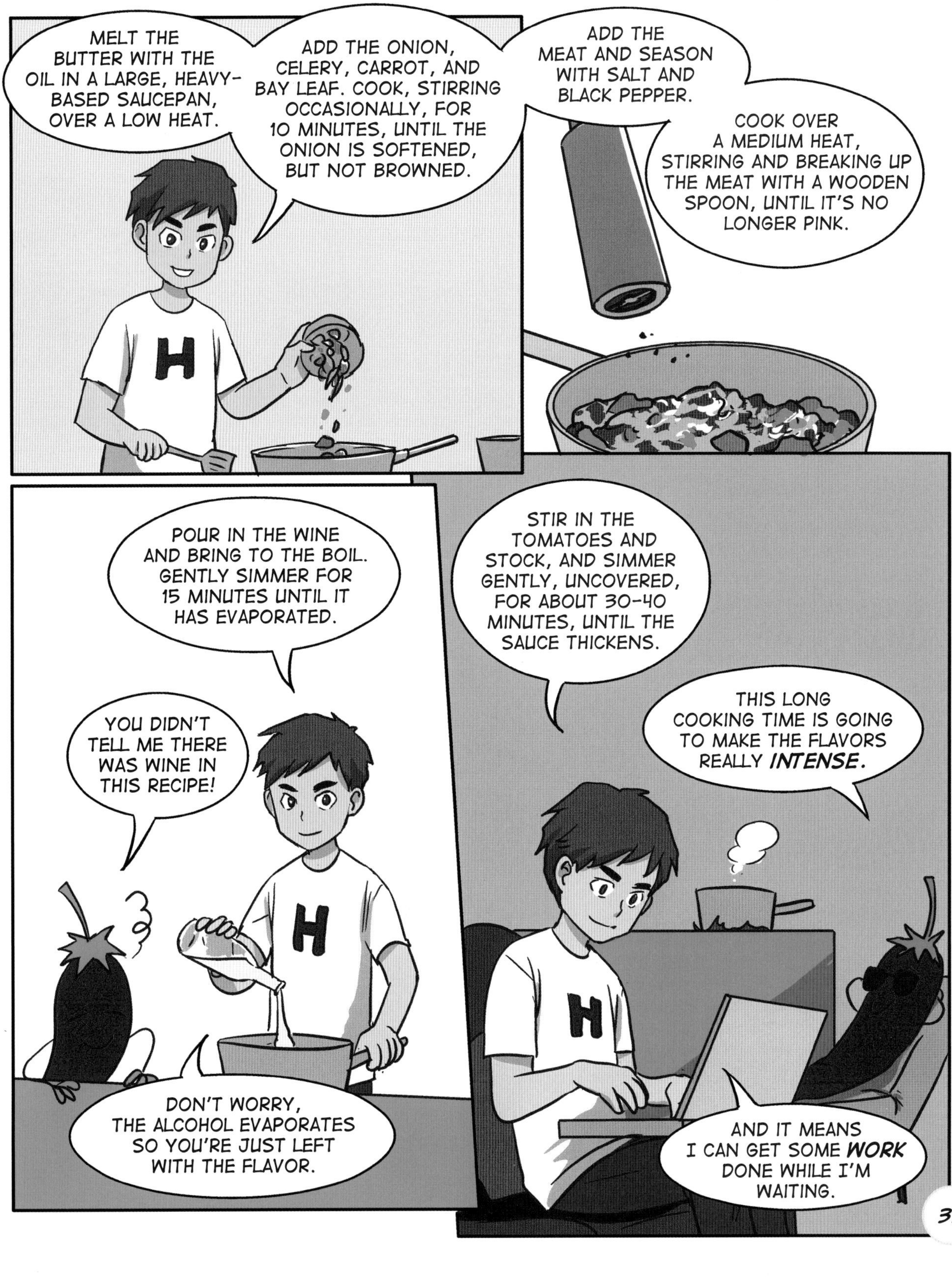

MELT THE BUTTER WITH THE OIL IN A LARGE, HEAVY-BASED SAUCEPAN, OVER A LOW HEAT.
ADD THE ONION, CELERY, CARROT, AND BAY LEAF. COOK, STIRRING OCCASIONALLY, FOR 10 MINUTES, UNTIL THE ONION IS SOFTENED, BUT NOT BROWNED.
ADD THE MEAT AND SEASON WITH SALT AND BLACK PEPPER.
COOK OVER A MEDIUM HEAT, STIRRING AND BREAKING UP THE MEAT WITH A WOODEN SPOON, UNTIL IT'S NO LONGER PINK.
POUR IN THE WINE AND BRING TO THE BOIL. GENTLY SIMMER FOR 15 MINUTES UNTIL IT HAS EVAPORATED.
YOU DIDN'T TELL ME THERE WAS WINE IN THIS RECIPE!
DON'T WORRY, THE ALCOHOL EVAPORATES SO YOU'RE JUST LEFT WITH THE FLAVOR.
STIR IN THE TOMATOES AND STOCK, AND SIMMER GENTLY, UNCOVERED, FOR ABOUT 30-40 MINUTES, UNTIL THE SAUCE THICKENS.
THIS LONG COOKING TIME IS GOING TO MAKE THE FLAVORS REALLY ***INTENSE.***
AND IT MEANS I CAN GET SOME ***WORK*** DONE WHILE I'M WAITING.

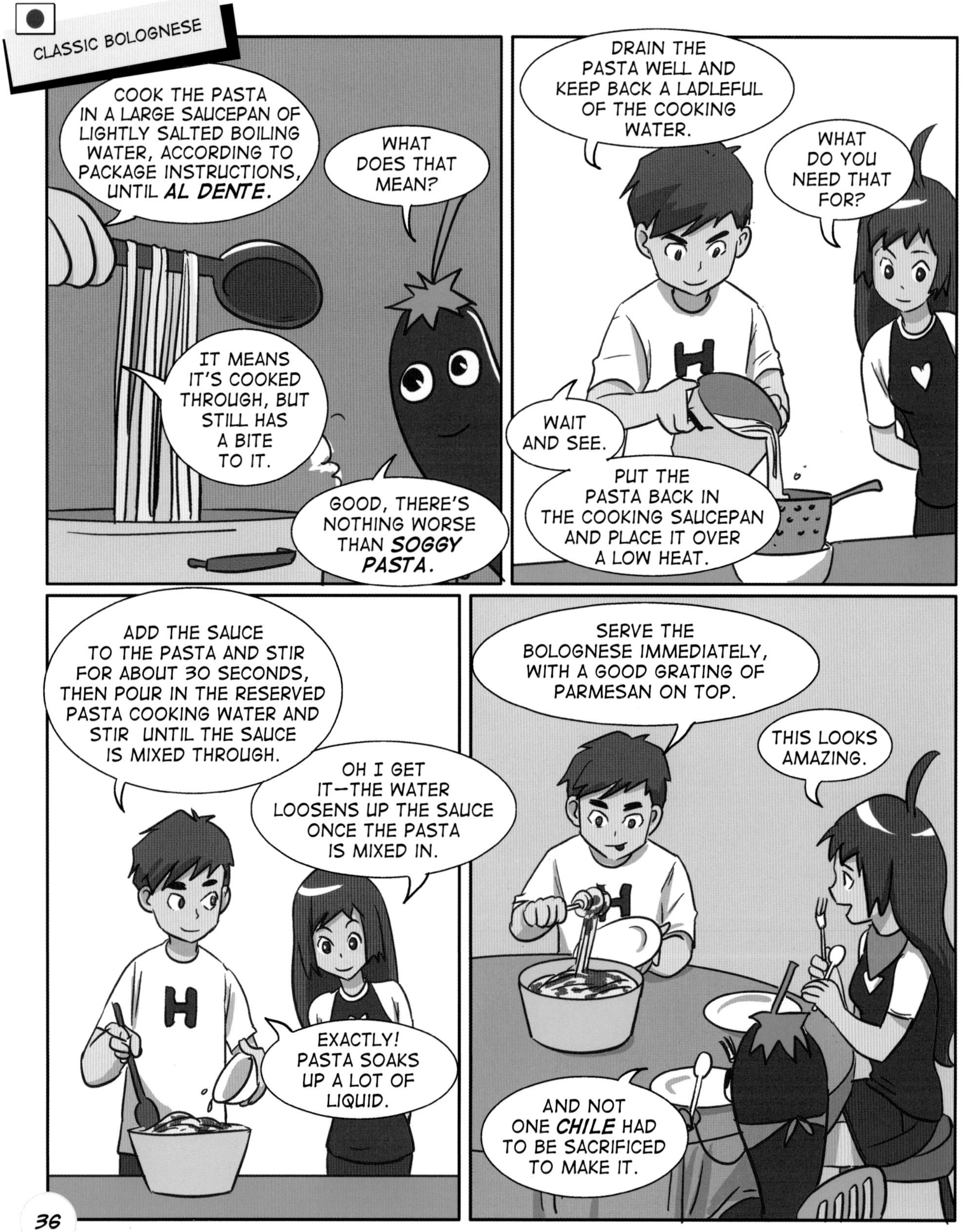
CLASSIC BOLOGNESE
COOK THE PASTA IN A LARGE SAUCEPAN OF LIGHTLY SALTED BOILING WATER, ACCORDING TO PACKAGE INSTRUCTIONS, UNTIL AL DENTE.
WHAT DOES THAT MEAN?
IT MEANS IT'S COOKED THROUGH, BUT STILL HAS A BITE TO IT.
GOOD, THERE'S NOTHING WORSE THAN SOGGY PASTA.
DRAIN THE PASTA WELL AND KEEP BACK A LADLEFUL OF THE COOKING WATER.
WHAT DO YOU NEED THAT FOR?
WAIT AND SEE.
PUT THE PASTA BACK IN THE COOKING SAUCEPAN AND PLACE IT OVER A LOW HEAT.
ADD THE SAUCE TO THE PASTA AND STIR FOR ABOUT 30 SECONDS, THEN POUR IN THE RESERVED PASTA COOKING WATER AND STIR UNTIL THE SAUCE IS MIXED THROUGH.
OH I GET IT—THE WATER LOOSENS UP THE SAUCE ONCE THE PASTA IS MIXED IN.
EXACTLY! PASTA SOAKS UP A LOT OF LIQUID.
SERVE THE BOLOGNESE IMMEDIATELY, WITH A GOOD GRATING OF PARMESAN ON TOP.
THIS LOOKS AMAZING.
AND NOT ONE CHILE HAD TO BE SACRIFICED TO MAKE IT.

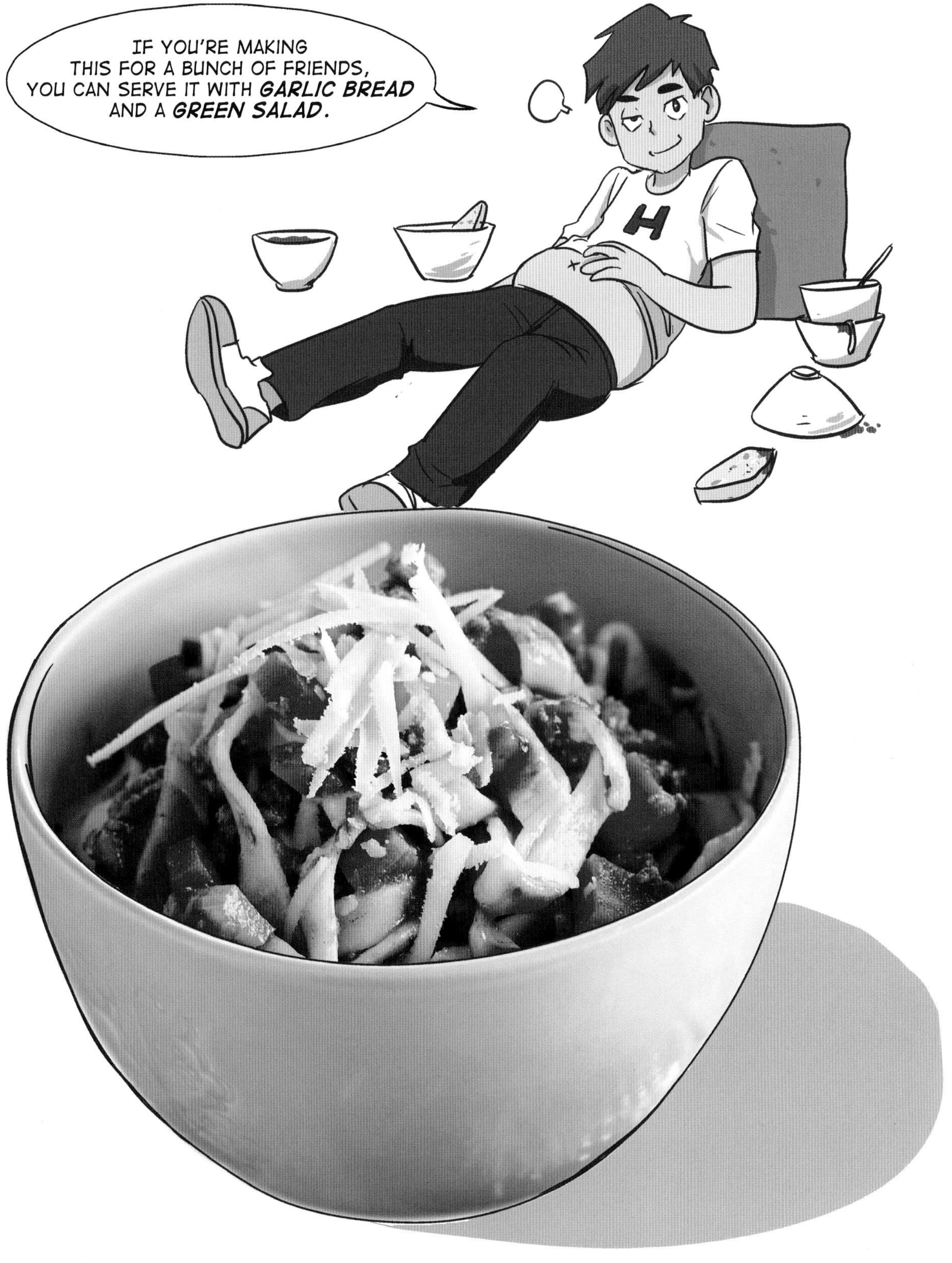
IF YOU'RE MAKING THIS FOR A BUNCH OF FRIENDS, YOU CAN SERVE IT WITH GARLIC BREAD AND A GREEN SALAD.

SHEPHERD'S PIE
THE PERFECT MEAL FOR A
CHILLY WINTER EVENING.

1 TBSP OLIVE OIL
1 ONION, FINELY CHOPPED
1 CARROT, DICED
1 CELERY STICK, DICED
1 TBSP CHOPPED THYME
1 LB MINCED LAMB
13 OZ CAN DICED TOMATOES
4 TBSP TOMATO PASTE
1½ LB FLOURY POTATOES,
    PEELED AND CUBED
3½ TBSP BUTTER
3 TBSP MILK
3 OZ CHEDDAR CHEESE, GRATED
SALT AND BLACK PEPPER

SERVES 4-6 WARRIORS
PREP TIME: 20 MINUTES
COOKING TIME: 1½ HOURS

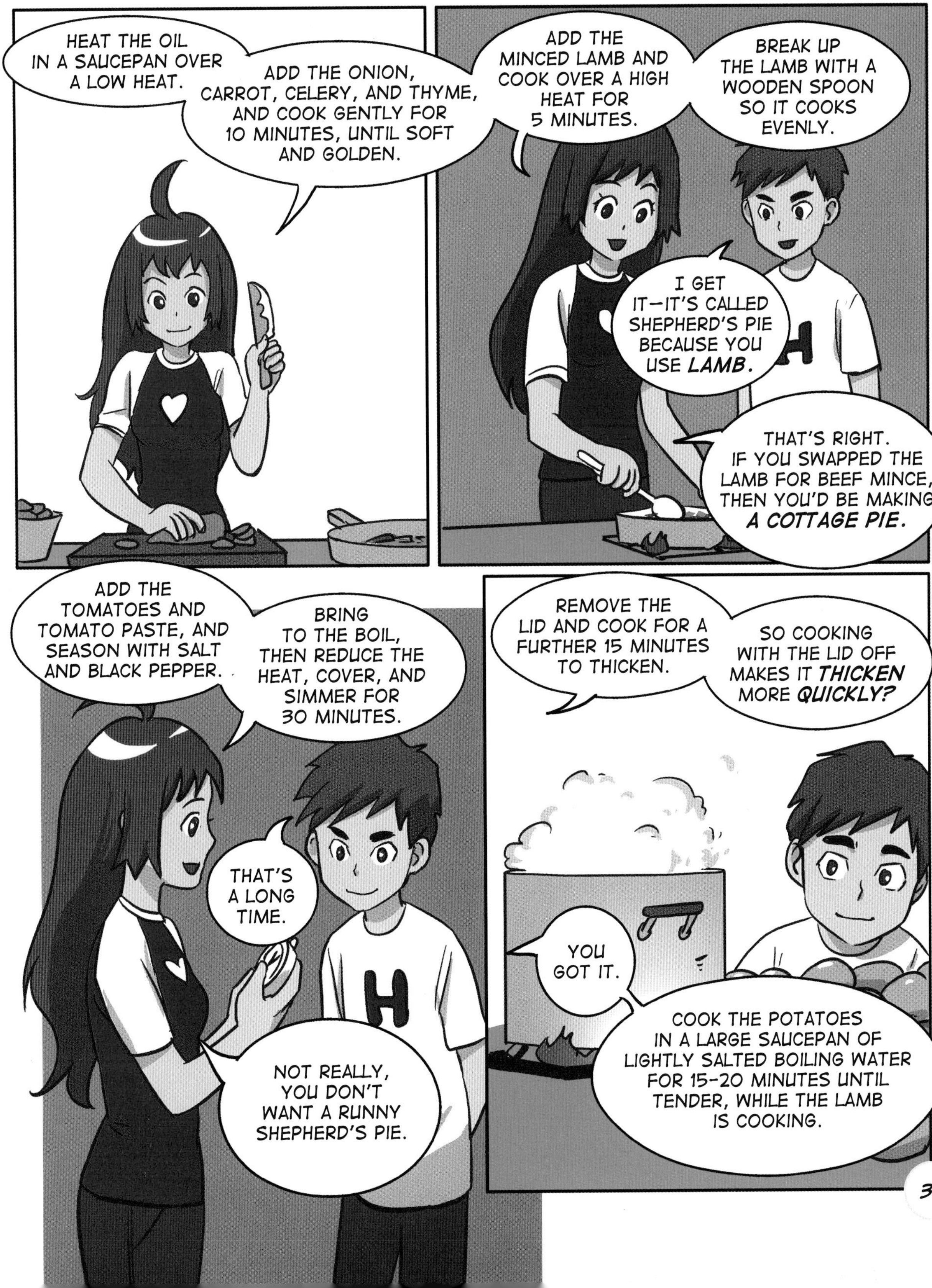
HEAT THE OIL IN A SAUCEPAN OVER A LOW HEAT.
ADD THE ONION, CARROT, CELERY, AND THYME, AND COOK GENTLY FOR 10 MINUTES, UNTIL SOFT AND GOLDEN.
ADD THE MINCED LAMB AND COOK OVER A HIGH HEAT FOR 5 MINUTES.
BREAK UP THE LAMB WITH A WOODEN SPOON SO IT COOKS EVENLY.
I GET IT—IT'S CALLED SHEPHERD'S PIE BECAUSE YOU USE ***LAMB***.
THAT'S RIGHT. IF YOU SWAPPED THE LAMB FOR BEEF MINCE, THEN YOU'D BE MAKING ***A COTTAGE PIE***.
ADD THE TOMATOES AND TOMATO PASTE, AND SEASON WITH SALT AND BLACK PEPPER.
BRING TO THE BOIL, THEN REDUCE THE HEAT, COVER, AND SIMMER FOR 30 MINUTES.
THAT'S A LONG TIME.
NOT REALLY, YOU DON'T WANT A RUNNY SHEPHERD'S PIE.
REMOVE THE LID AND COOK FOR A FURTHER 15 MINUTES TO THICKEN.
SO COOKING WITH THE LID OFF MAKES IT ***THICKEN*** MORE ***QUICKLY?***
YOU GOT IT.
COOK THE POTATOES IN A LARGE SAUCEPAN OF LIGHTLY SALTED BOILING WATER FOR 15-20 MINUTES UNTIL TENDER, WHILE THE LAMB IS COOKING.

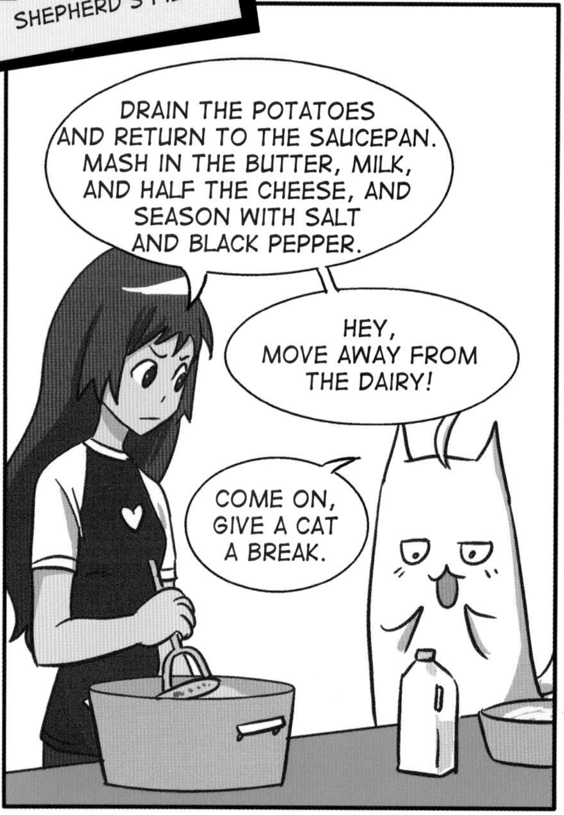
DRAIN THE POTATOES AND RETURN TO THE SAUCEPAN. MASH IN THE BUTTER, MILK, AND HALF THE CHEESE, AND SEASON WITH SALT AND BLACK PEPPER.
HEY, MOVE AWAY FROM THE DAIRY!
COME ON, GIVE A CAT A BREAK.

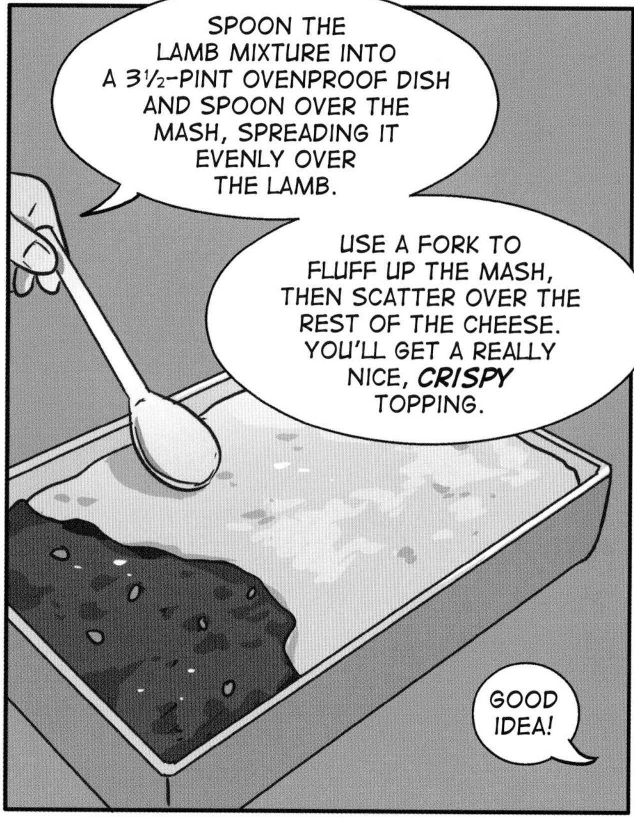
SPOON THE LAMB MIXTURE INTO A 3½-PINT OVENPROOF DISH AND SPOON OVER THE MASH, SPREADING IT EVENLY OVER THE LAMB.
USE A FORK TO FLUFF UP THE MASH, THEN SCATTER OVER THE REST OF THE CHEESE. YOU'LL GET A REALLY NICE, *CRISPY* TOPPING.
GOOD IDEA!

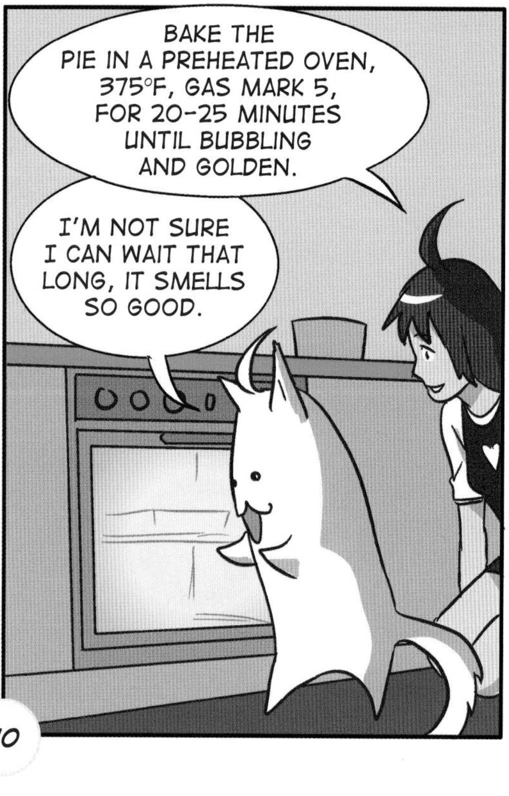
BAKE THE PIE IN A PREHEATED OVEN, 375°F, GAS MARK 5, FOR 20–25 MINUTES UNTIL BUBBLING AND GOLDEN.
I'M NOT SURE I CAN WAIT THAT LONG, IT SMELLS SO GOOD.

VARIATION

CURRIED LAMB PHYLLO PIES

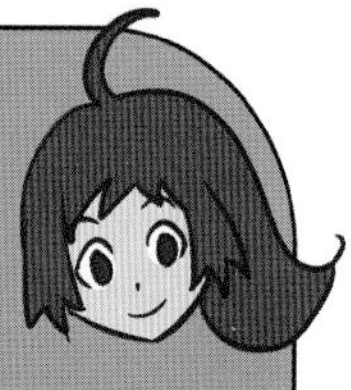

PREPARE AND COOK THE MINCED MEAT MIXTURE AS ABOVE, ADDING 1 TBSP MEDIUM CURRY PASTE WITH THE TOMATOES AND TOMATO PASTE.

SPOON THE FILLING INTO SIX ½-PINT OVENPROOF DISHES. INSTEAD OF THE POTATO TOPPING, LAYER 4 SHEETS OF PHYLLO PASTRY, ONE ON TOP OF THE OTHER, BRUSHING EACH ONE WITH MELTED BUTTER. CUT THE STACK INTO 6 PIECES AND SCRUNCH EACH ONE OVER A DISH TO COVER THE MEAT.

BAKE IN A PREHEATED OVEN, 375°F, GAS MARK 5, FOR 20 MINUTES UNTIL THE PASTRY IS LIGHTLY GOLDEN.

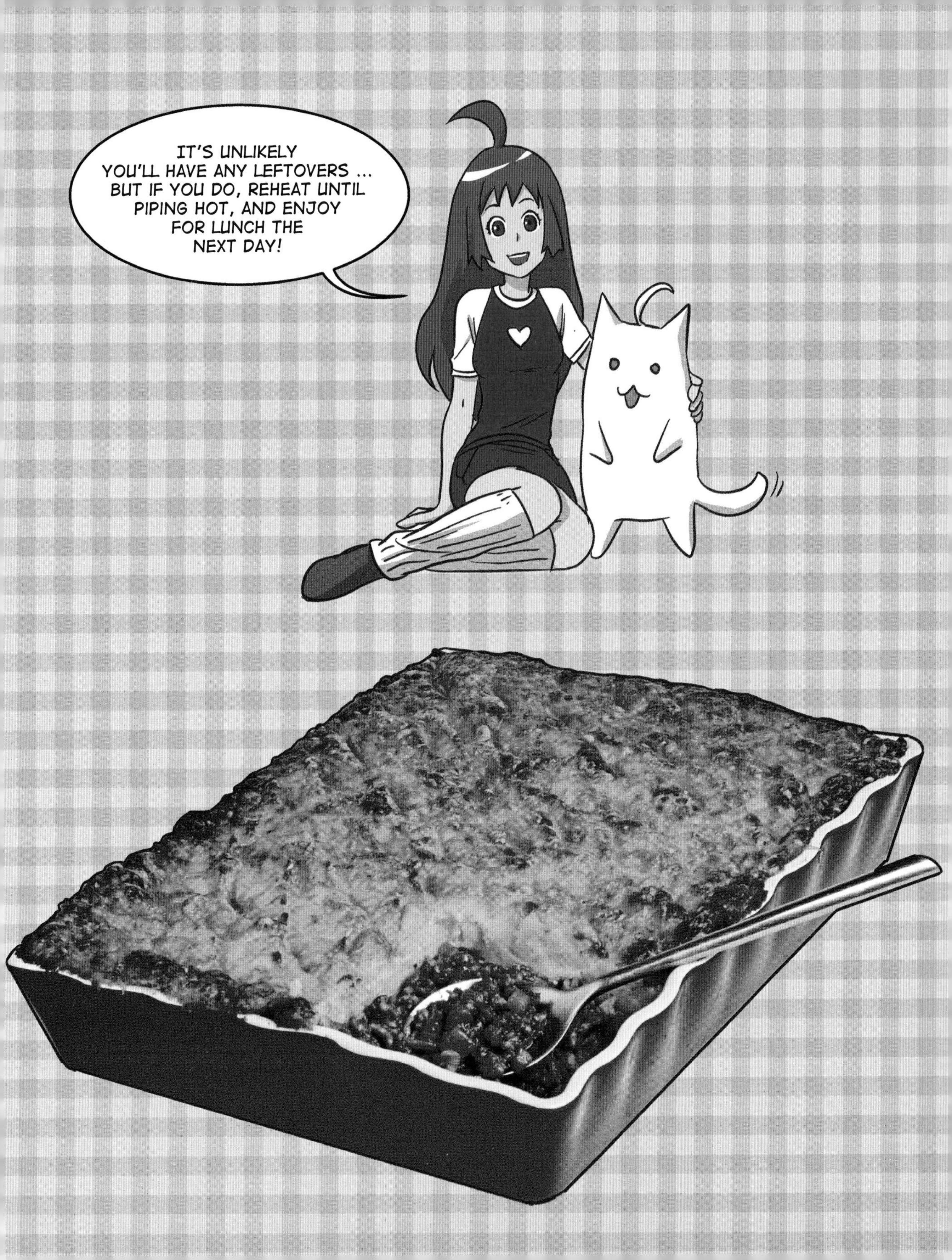
IT'S UNLIKELY YOU'LL HAVE ANY LEFTOVERS ... BUT IF YOU DO, REHEAT UNTIL PIPING HOT, AND ENJOY FOR LUNCH THE NEXT DAY!

SWEET & SOUR PORK

ANOTHER MONEY-SAVING ALTERNATIVE TO TAKEOUT—AND IT WILL TASTE EVEN BETTER, AS YOU MADE IT YOURSELF!

3 TBSP VEGETABLE OIL
11½ OZ CUBED PORK
1 LARGE ONION, CUT INTO BITE-SIZED PIECES
1 RED OR YELLOW BELL PEPPER, CORED, DESEEDED, AND CUT INTO BITE-SIZED PIECES
5 OZ KETCHUP (ABOUT 8 TBSP)
3 TBSP DARK SOFT BROWN SUGAR
7½ OZ CAN PINEAPPLE CHUNKS IN JUICE
3 TBSP MALT VINEGAR
1 TBSP LIGHT SOY SAUCE
BOILED RICE, TO SERVE

SERVES 4 WARRIORS
PREP TIME: 10 MINUTES
COOKING TIME: 25 MINUTES

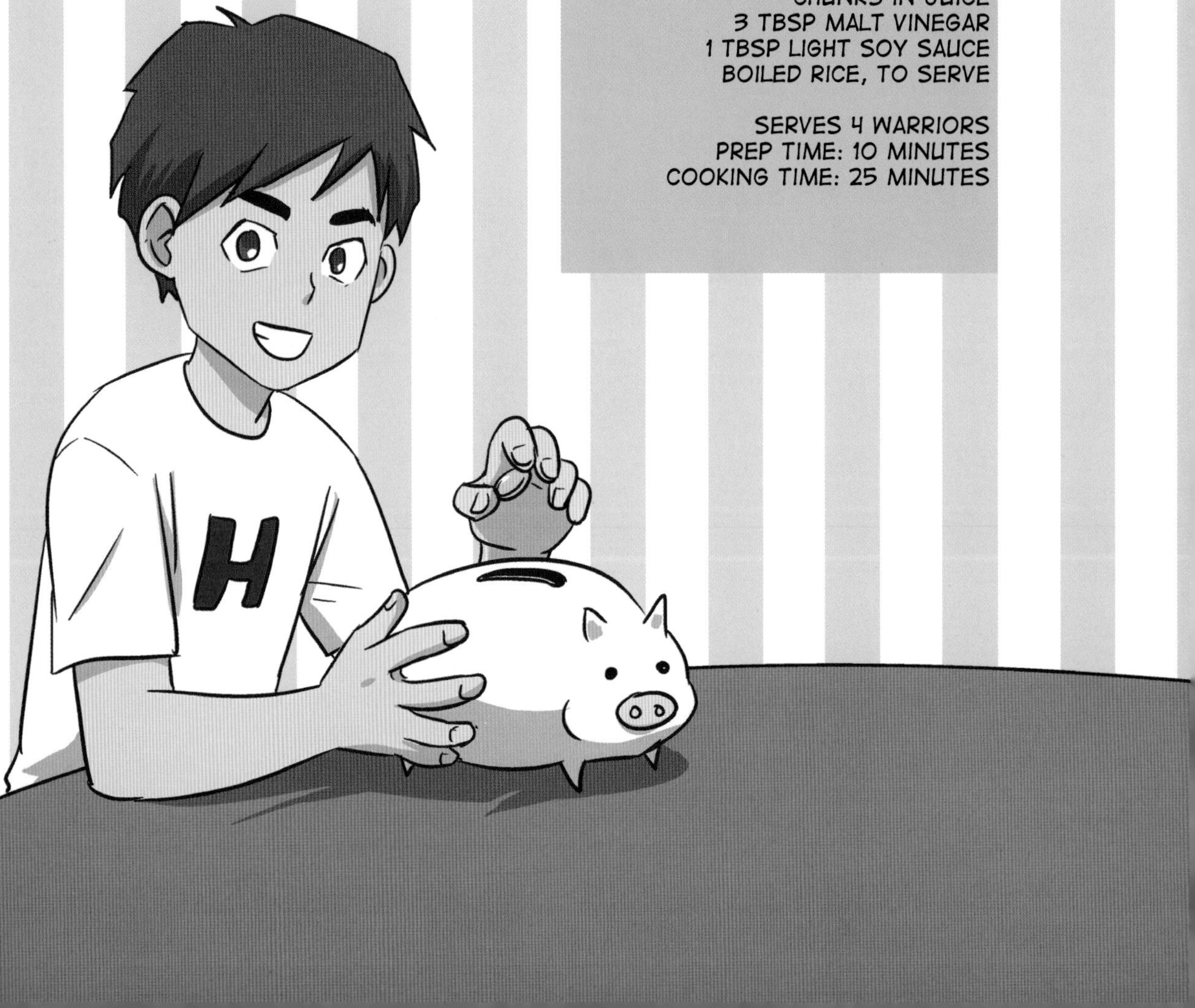

H

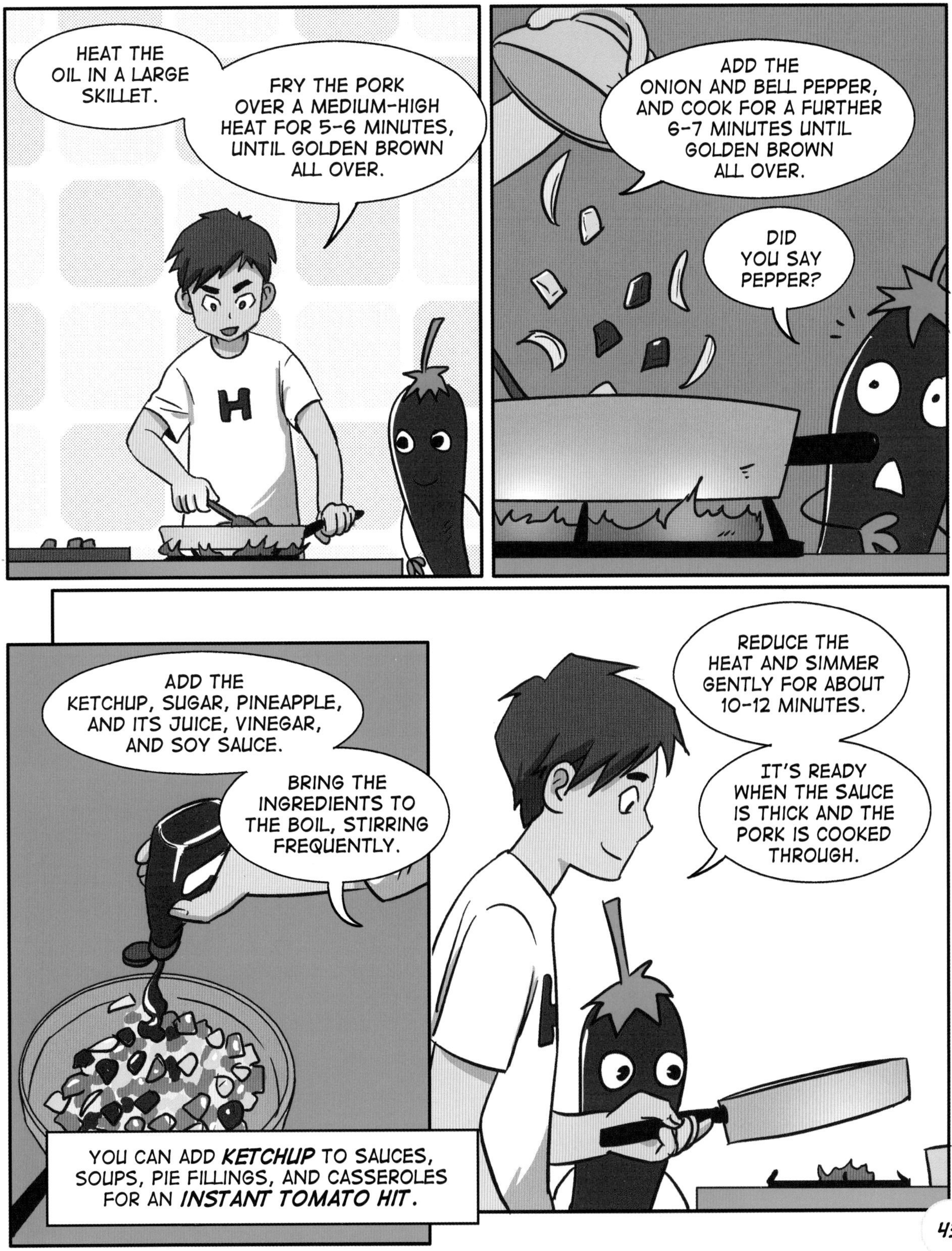

HEAT THE OIL IN A LARGE SKILLET.
FRY THE PORK OVER A MEDIUM-HIGH HEAT FOR 5-6 MINUTES, UNTIL GOLDEN BROWN ALL OVER.
ADD THE ONION AND BELL PEPPER, AND COOK FOR A FURTHER 6-7 MINUTES UNTIL GOLDEN BROWN ALL OVER.
DID YOU SAY PEPPER?
ADD THE KETCHUP, SUGAR, PINEAPPLE, AND ITS JUICE, VINEGAR, AND SOY SAUCE.
BRING THE INGREDIENTS TO THE BOIL, STIRRING FREQUENTLY.
YOU CAN ADD ***KETCHUP*** TO SAUCES, SOUPS, PIE FILLINGS, AND CASSEROLES FOR AN ***INSTANT TOMATO HIT***.
REDUCE THE HEAT AND SIMMER GENTLY FOR ABOUT 10-12 MINUTES.
IT'S READY WHEN THE SAUCE IS THICK AND THE PORK IS COOKED THROUGH.

SWEET & SOUR PORK

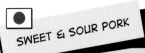

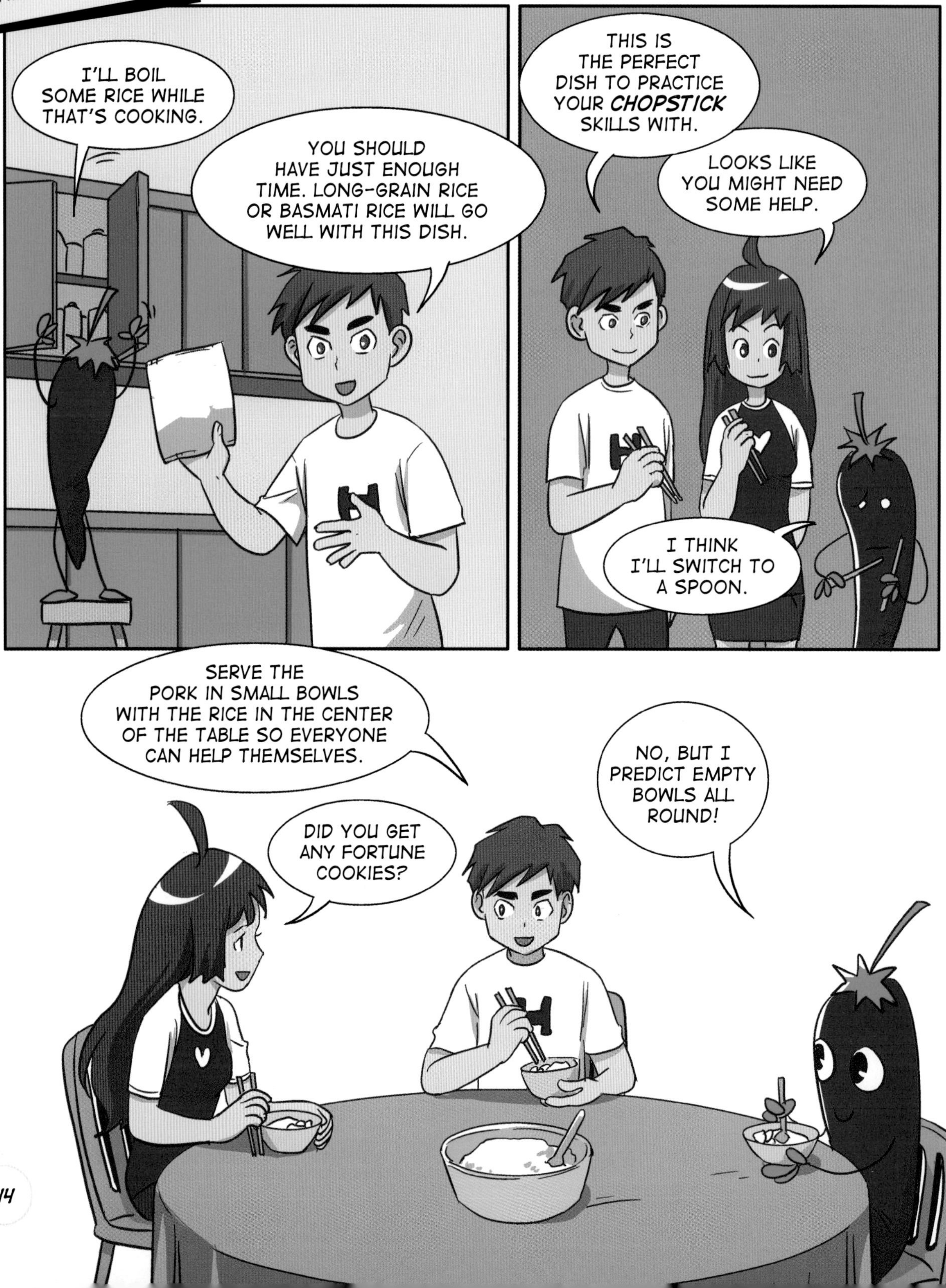
I'LL BOIL SOME RICE WHILE THAT'S COOKING.
YOU SHOULD HAVE JUST ENOUGH TIME. LONG-GRAIN RICE OR BASMATI RICE WILL GO WELL WITH THIS DISH.
THIS IS THE PERFECT DISH TO PRACTICE YOUR ***CHOPSTICK*** SKILLS WITH.
LOOKS LIKE YOU MIGHT NEED SOME HELP.
I THINK I'LL SWITCH TO A SPOON.
SERVE THE PORK IN SMALL BOWLS WITH THE RICE IN THE CENTER OF THE TABLE SO EVERYONE CAN HELP THEMSELVES.
DID YOU GET ANY FORTUNE COOKIES?
NO, BUT I PREDICT EMPTY BOWLS ALL ROUND!

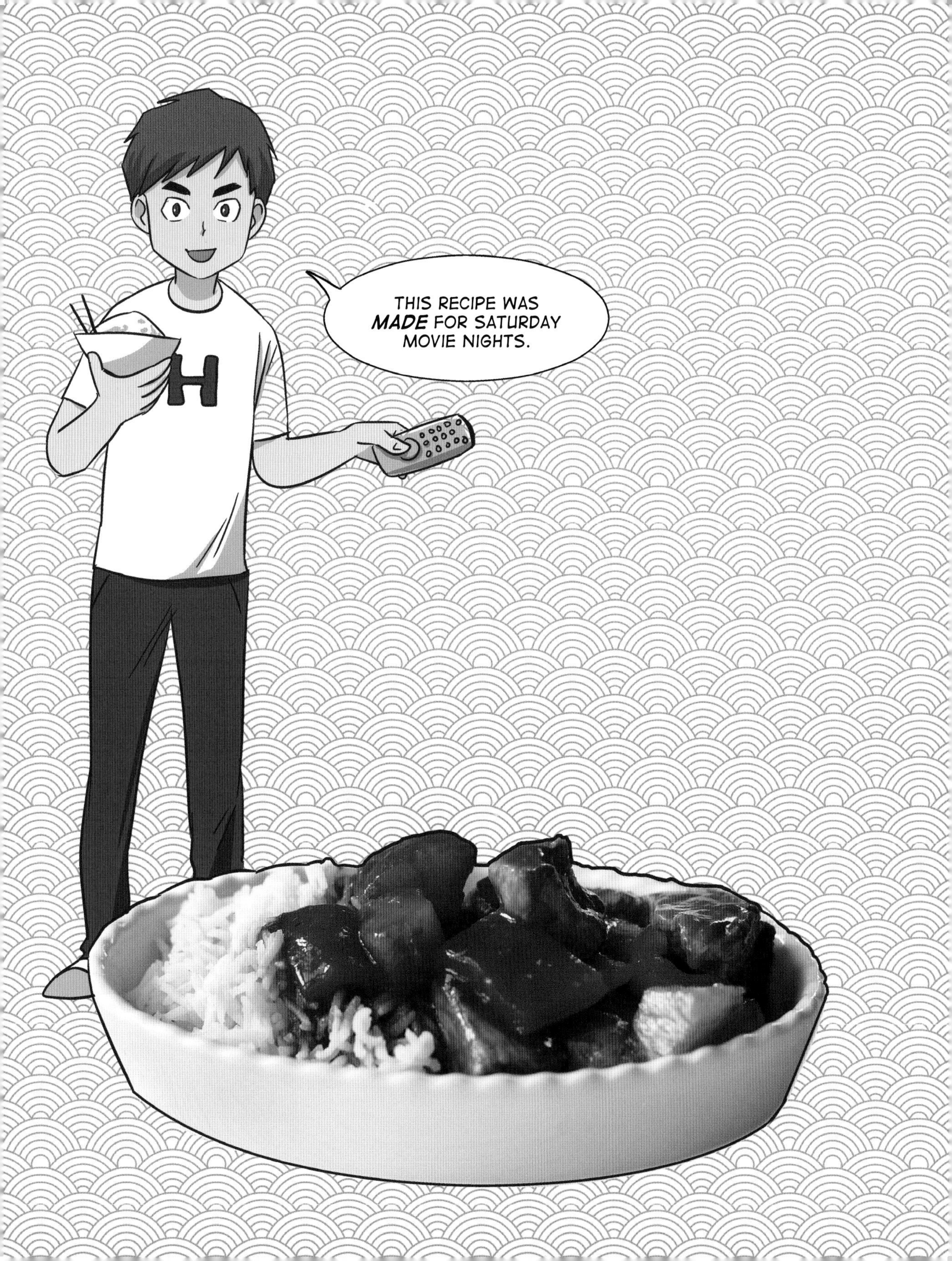
THIS RECIPE WAS *MADE* FOR SATURDAY MOVIE NIGHTS.

PORK & RED BELL PEPPER CHILLI

THIS IS HOT, SPICY COMFORT FOOD THAT'S PERFECT FOR SHARING.

2 TBSP OLIVE OIL
1 LARGE ONION, CHOPPED
1 RED BELL PEPPER, CORED, DESEEDED, AND DICED
2 GARLIC CLOVES, FINELY CHOPPED
14 ½ OZ MINCED PORK
1 FRESH RED CHILE, DESEEDED, AND FINELY CHOPPED
1 TSP DRIED OREGANO
1 LB PUREE (SIEVED TOMATOES)
13 OZ CAN RED KIDNEY BEANS, RINSED, AND DRAINED
SALT AND BLACK PEPPER
COARSELY CHOPPED BASIL, TO GARNISH

TO SERVE:
SOUR CREAM
BOILED RICE AND/OR BREAD

SERVES 4 WARRIORS
PREP TIME: 10 MINUTES
COOKING TIME: 30 MINUTES

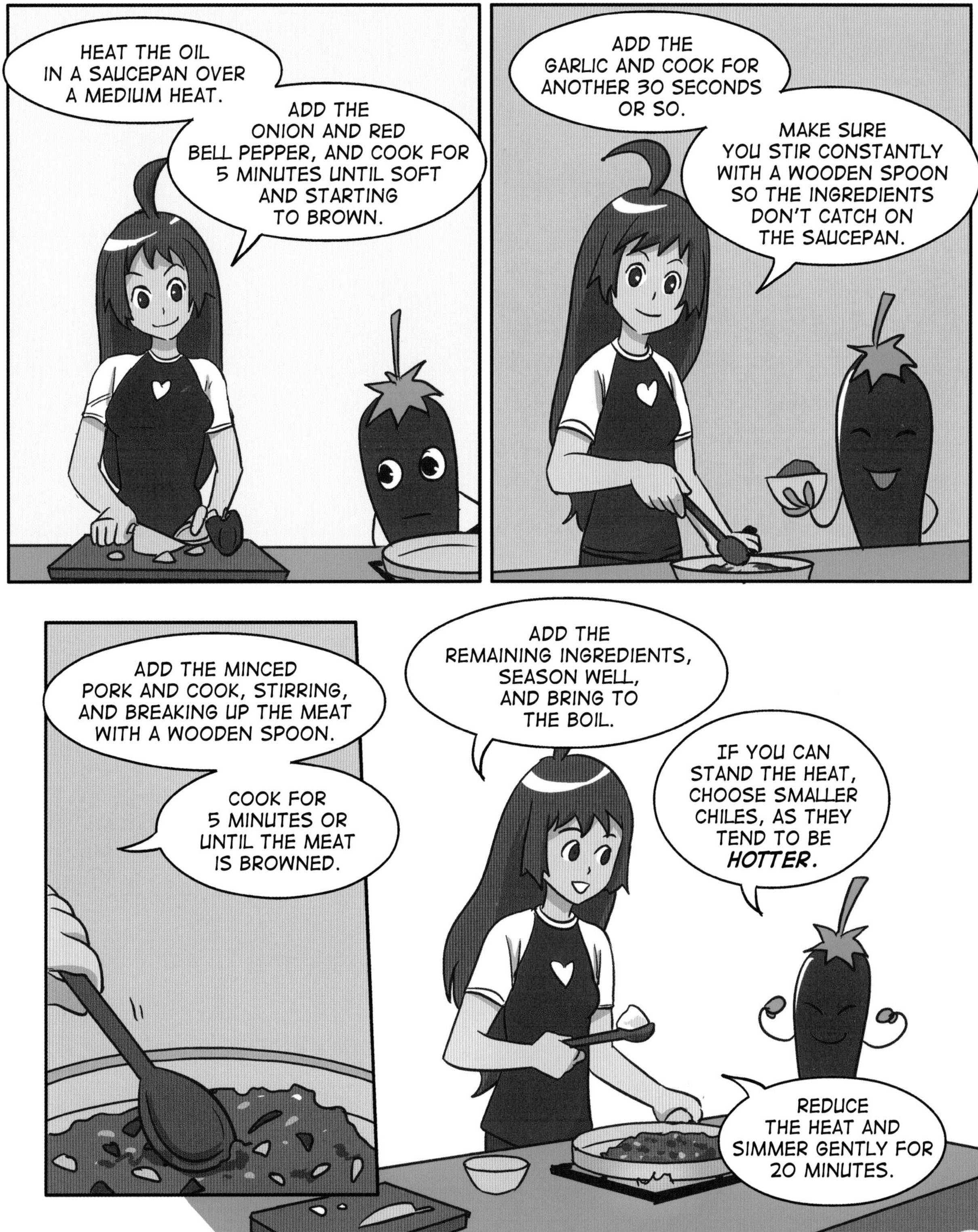
HEAT THE OIL IN A SAUCEPAN OVER A MEDIUM HEAT.
ADD THE ONION AND RED BELL PEPPER, AND COOK FOR 5 MINUTES UNTIL SOFT AND STARTING TO BROWN.
ADD THE GARLIC AND COOK FOR ANOTHER 30 SECONDS OR SO.
MAKE SURE YOU STIR CONSTANTLY WITH A WOODEN SPOON SO THE INGREDIENTS DON'T CATCH ON THE SAUCEPAN.
ADD THE MINCED PORK AND COOK, STIRRING, AND BREAKING UP THE MEAT WITH A WOODEN SPOON.
COOK FOR 5 MINUTES OR UNTIL THE MEAT IS BROWNED.
ADD THE REMAINING INGREDIENTS, SEASON WELL, AND BRING TO THE BOIL.
IF YOU CAN STAND THE HEAT, CHOOSE SMALLER CHILES, AS THEY TEND TO BE ***HOTTER***.
REDUCE THE HEAT AND SIMMER GENTLY FOR 20 MINUTES.

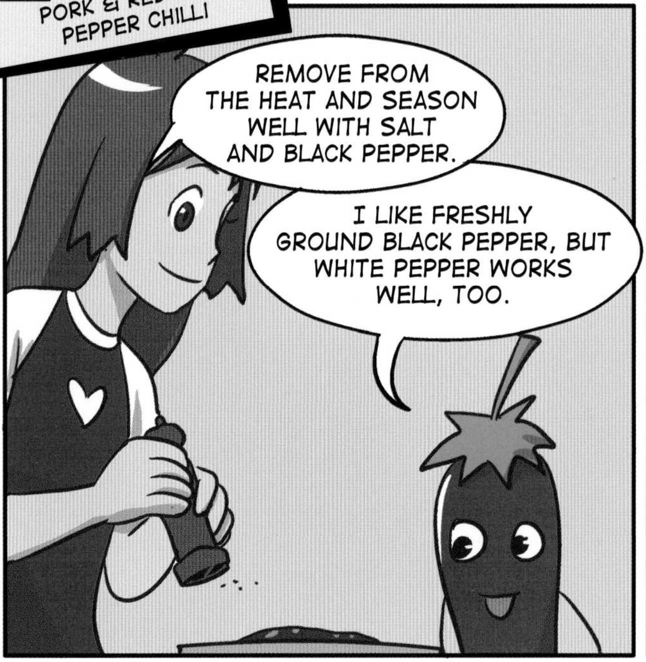
REMOVE FROM THE HEAT AND SEASON WELL WITH SALT AND BLACK PEPPER.
I LIKE FRESHLY GROUND BLACK PEPPER, BUT WHITE PEPPER WORKS WELL, TOO.

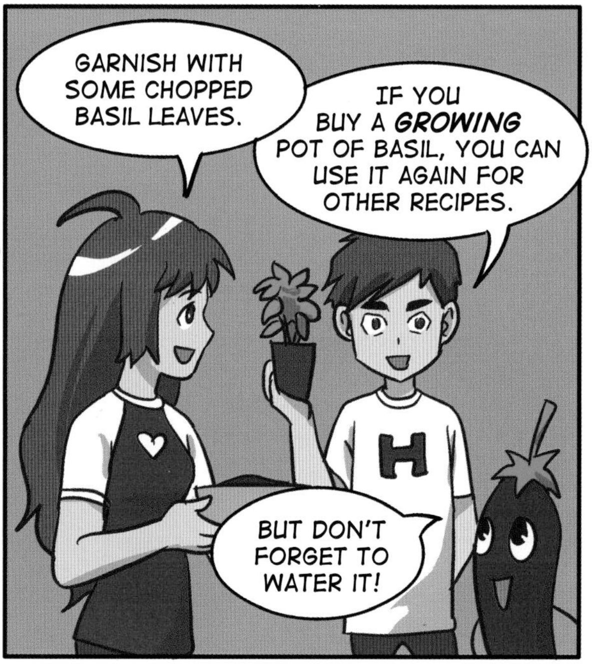
GARNISH WITH SOME CHOPPED BASIL LEAVES.
IF YOU BUY A ***GROWING*** POT OF BASIL, YOU CAN USE IT AGAIN FOR OTHER RECIPES.
BUT DON'T FORGET TO WATER IT!

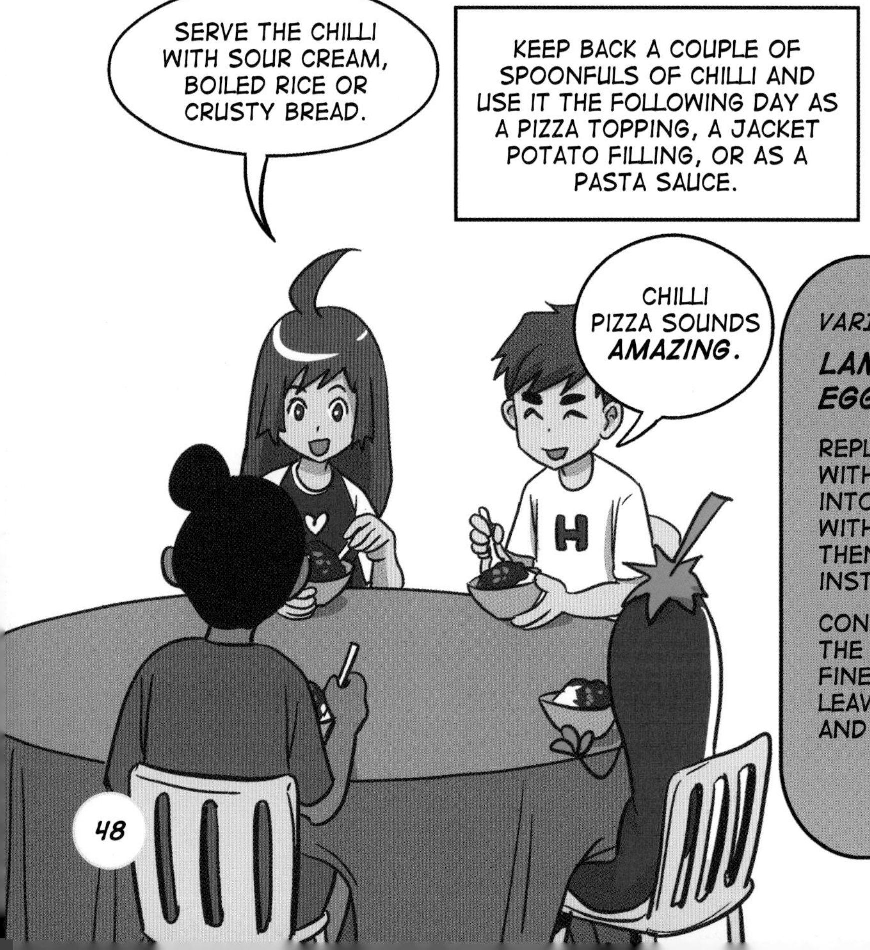
SERVE THE CHILLI WITH SOUR CREAM, BOILED RICE OR CRUSTY BREAD.
KEEP BACK A COUPLE OF SPOONFULS OF CHILLI AND USE IT THE FOLLOWING DAY AS A PIZZA TOPPING, A JACKET POTATO FILLING, OR AS A PASTA SAUCE.
CHILLI PIZZA SOUNDS ***AMAZING***.

VARIATION

LAMB & EGG PLANT CHILLI

REPLACE THE RED BELL PEPPER WITH 1 MEDIUM EGG PLANT, CUT INTO SMALL CUBES. FRY AS ABOVE WITH THE ONION AND GARLIC, THEN ADD 14¼ OZ MINCED LAMB INSTEAD OF THE PORK.

CONTINUE AS ABOVE. SPRINKLE THE FINISHED DISH WITH 2 TBSP FINELY CHOPPED MINT LEAVES, LEAVE OUT THE SOUR CREAM, AND SERVE WITH BOILED RICE.

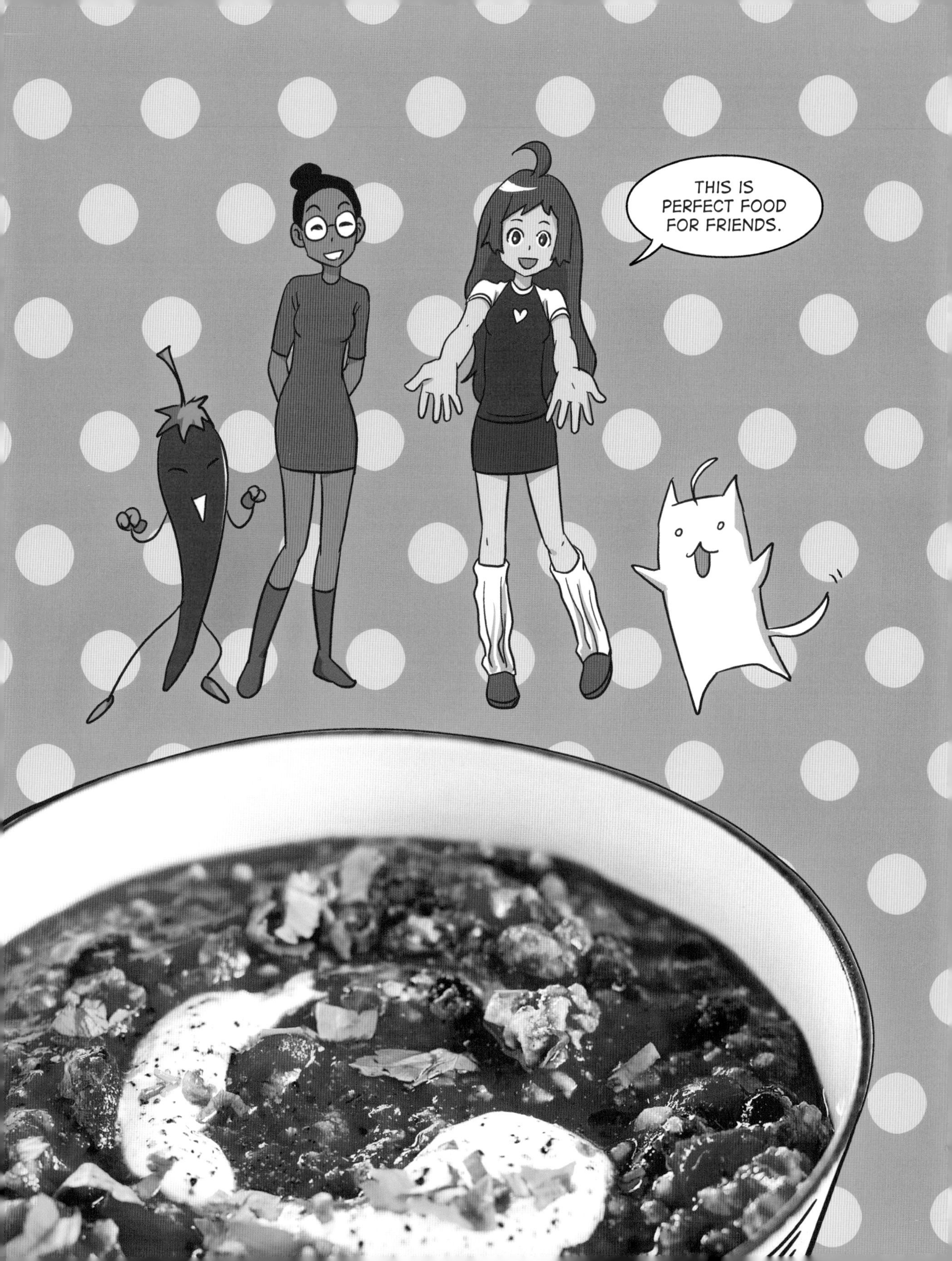
THIS IS PERFECT FOOD FOR FRIENDS.

SPICY PEA & HAM RISOTTO
THIS IS A HEARTY MEAL THAT'S EASY ON THE WALLET AND TASTES GREAT, TOO.

1 TBSP OLIVE OIL
2 TBSP BUTTER
1 ONION, CHOPPED
1 RED CHILE, DESEEDED, AND FINELY CHOPPED
2 GARLIC CLOVES, FINELY CHOPPED
8 OZ RISOTTO RICE, SUCH AS
   CARNAROLI OR ARBORIO
1½ PINTS HOT CHICKEN STOCK
7 OZ FROZEN PEAS
3½ OZ PARMESAN CHEESE, GRATED
10 OZ COOKED HAM, DICED
BUNCH OF PARSLEY, FINELY CHOPPED
SALT AND BLACK PEPPER

SERVES 4 WARRIORS
PREP TIME: 10 MINUTES
COOKING TIME: 30 MINUTES

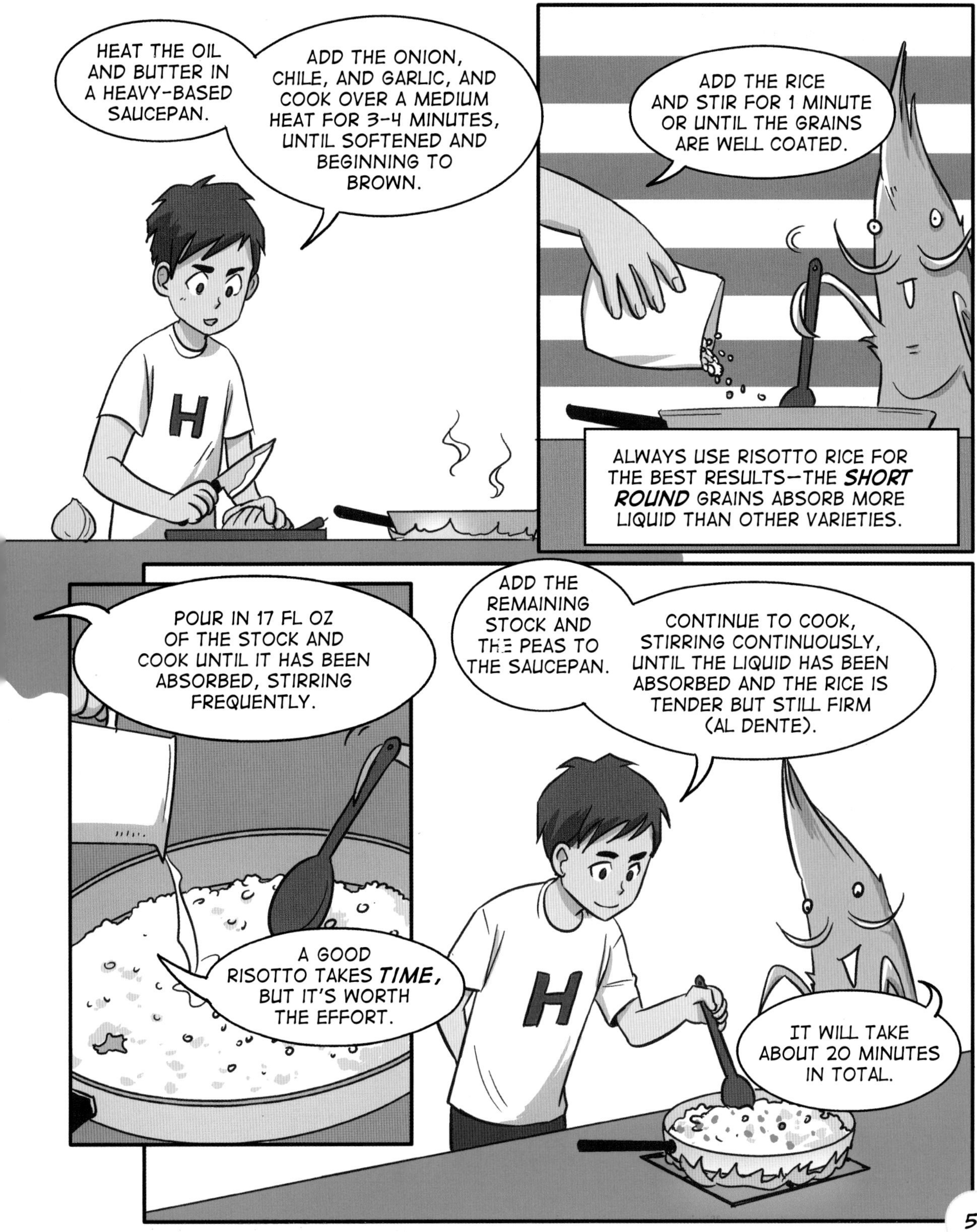
HEAT THE OIL AND BUTTER IN A HEAVY-BASED SAUCEPAN.
ADD THE ONION, CHILE, AND GARLIC, AND COOK OVER A MEDIUM HEAT FOR 3-4 MINUTES, UNTIL SOFTENED AND BEGINNING TO BROWN.
ADD THE RICE AND STIR FOR 1 MINUTE OR UNTIL THE GRAINS ARE WELL COATED.
ALWAYS USE RISOTTO RICE FOR THE BEST RESULTS—THE ***SHORT ROUND*** GRAINS ABSORB MORE LIQUID THAN OTHER VARIETIES.
POUR IN 17 FL OZ OF THE STOCK AND COOK UNTIL IT HAS BEEN ABSORBED, STIRRING FREQUENTLY.
A GOOD RISOTTO TAKES ***TIME,*** BUT IT'S WORTH THE EFFORT.
ADD THE REMAINING STOCK AND THE PEAS TO THE SAUCEPAN.
CONTINUE TO COOK, STIRRING CONTINUOUSLY, UNTIL THE LIQUID HAS BEEN ABSORBED AND THE RICE IS TENDER BUT STILL FIRM (AL DENTE).
IT WILL TAKE ABOUT 20 MINUTES IN TOTAL.

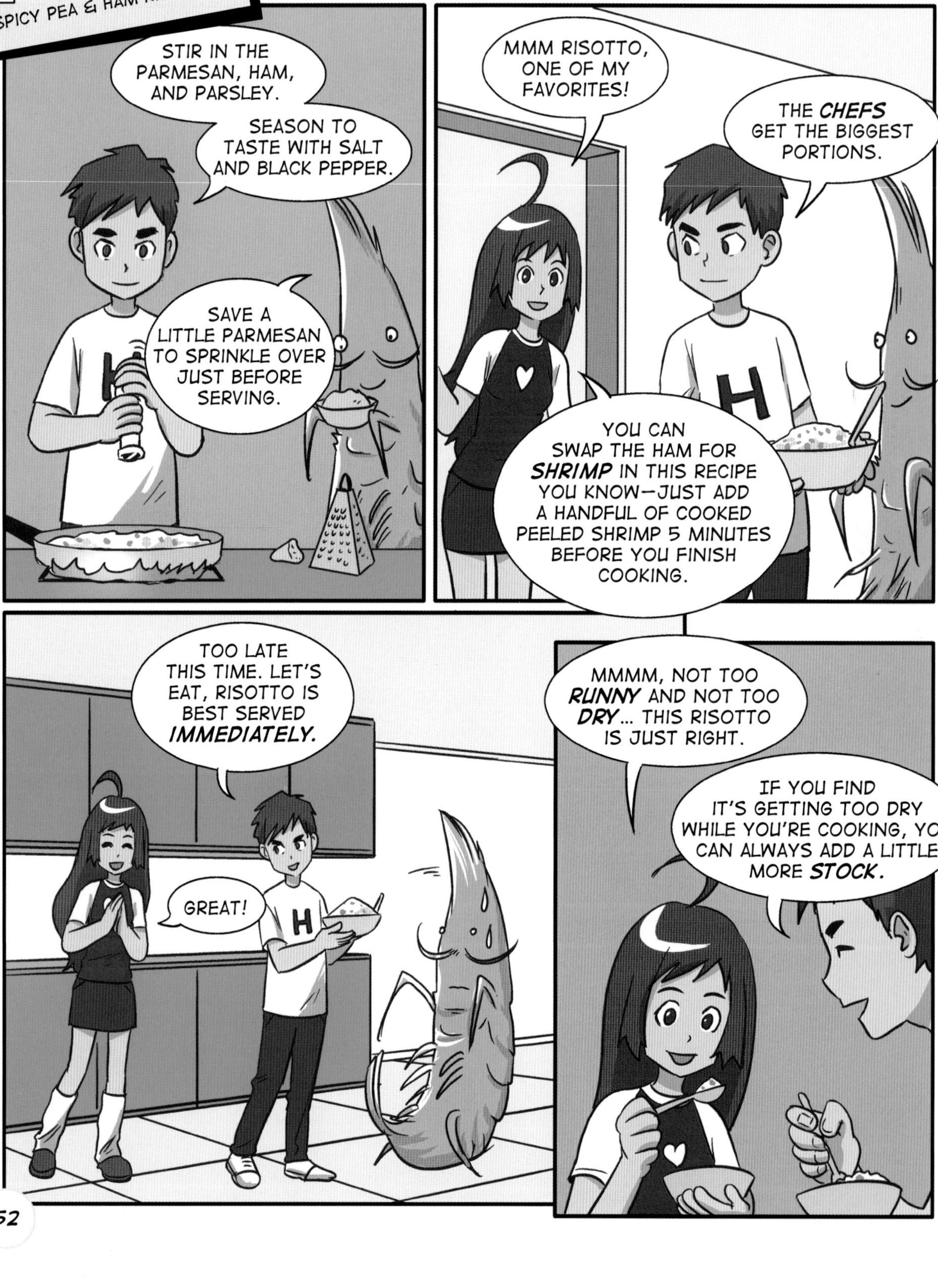
STIR IN THE PARMESAN, HAM, AND PARSLEY.
SEASON TO TASTE WITH SALT AND BLACK PEPPER.
SAVE A LITTLE PARMESAN TO SPRINKLE OVER JUST BEFORE SERVING.
MMM RISOTTO, ONE OF MY FAVORITES!
THE CHEFS GET THE BIGGEST PORTIONS.
YOU CAN SWAP THE HAM FOR SHRIMP IN THIS RECIPE YOU KNOW—JUST ADD A HANDFUL OF COOKED PEELED SHRIMP 5 MINUTES BEFORE YOU FINISH COOKING.
TOO LATE THIS TIME. LET'S EAT, RISOTTO IS BEST SERVED IMMEDIATELY.
GREAT!
MMMM, NOT TOO RUNNY AND NOT TOO DRY... THIS RISOTTO IS JUST RIGHT.
IF YOU FIND IT'S GETTING TOO DRY WHILE YOU'RE COOKING, YOU CAN ALWAYS ADD A LITTLE MORE STOCK.

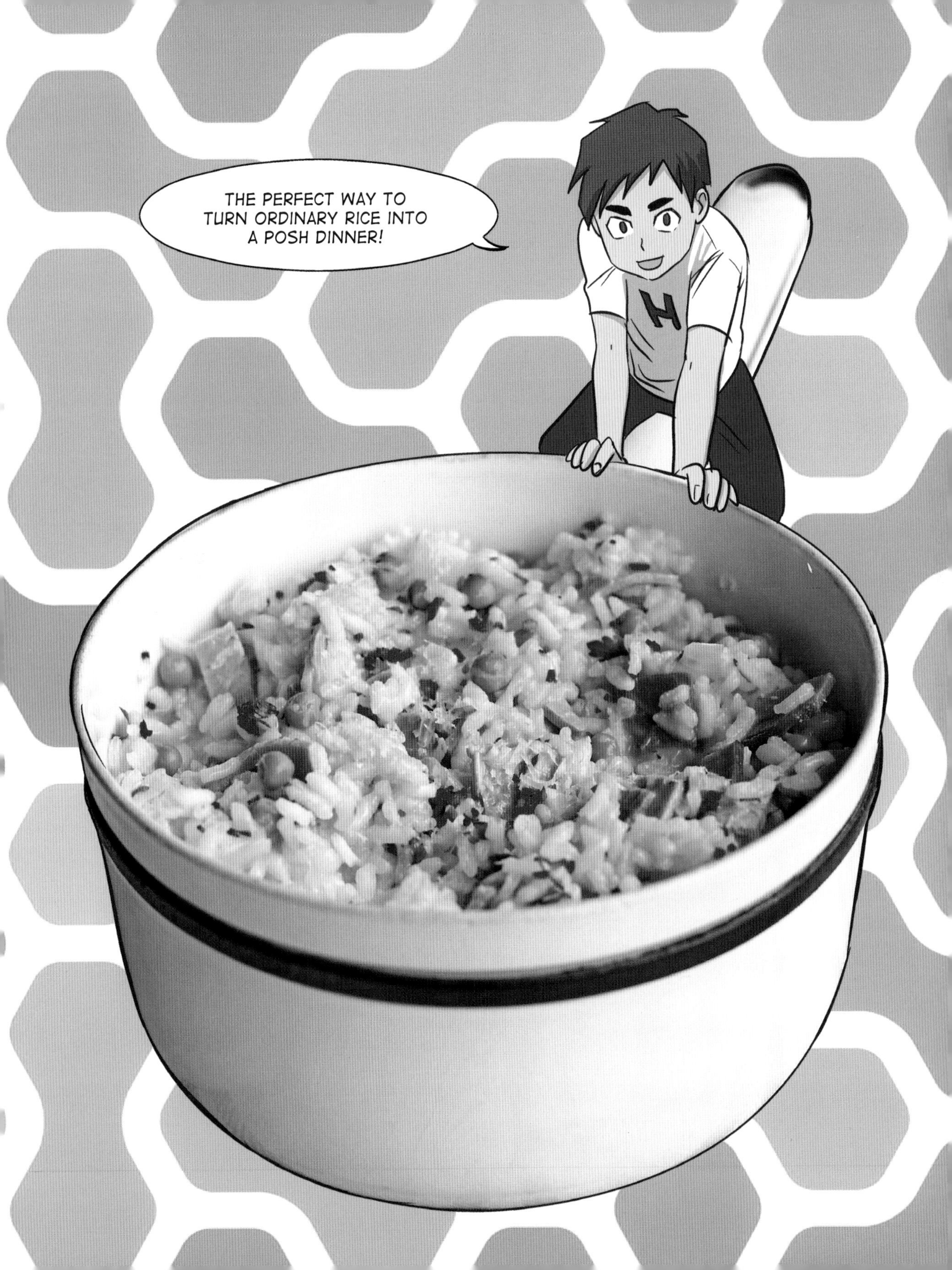
THE PERFECT WAY TO TURN ORDINARY RICE INTO A POSH DINNER!

POTATO & BACON PATTIES
GIVE YOUR POTATOES A FACELIFT
WITH THIS EASY DINNER DISH.

2 LB POTATOES, PEELED, AND CUT INTO CHUNKS
1 TBSP VEGETABLE OIL
6 SCALLIONS, SLICED
7 OZ BACK BACON, CHOPPED
2 TBSP CHOPPED PARSLEY
PLAIN FLOUR, FOR COATING
2 TBSP BUTTER
SALT AND BLACK PEPPER
STEAMED GREEN VEGETABLES, TO SERVE

FOR THE CREAMY TOMATO SAUCE:
7 FL OZ CRÉME FRAÎCHE
2 TBSP CHOPPED BASIL
2 TBSP CHOPPED TOMATOES

SERVES 4 WARRIORS
PREP TIME: 15 MINUTES, PLUS CHILLING
COOKING TIME: ABOUT 45 MINUTES

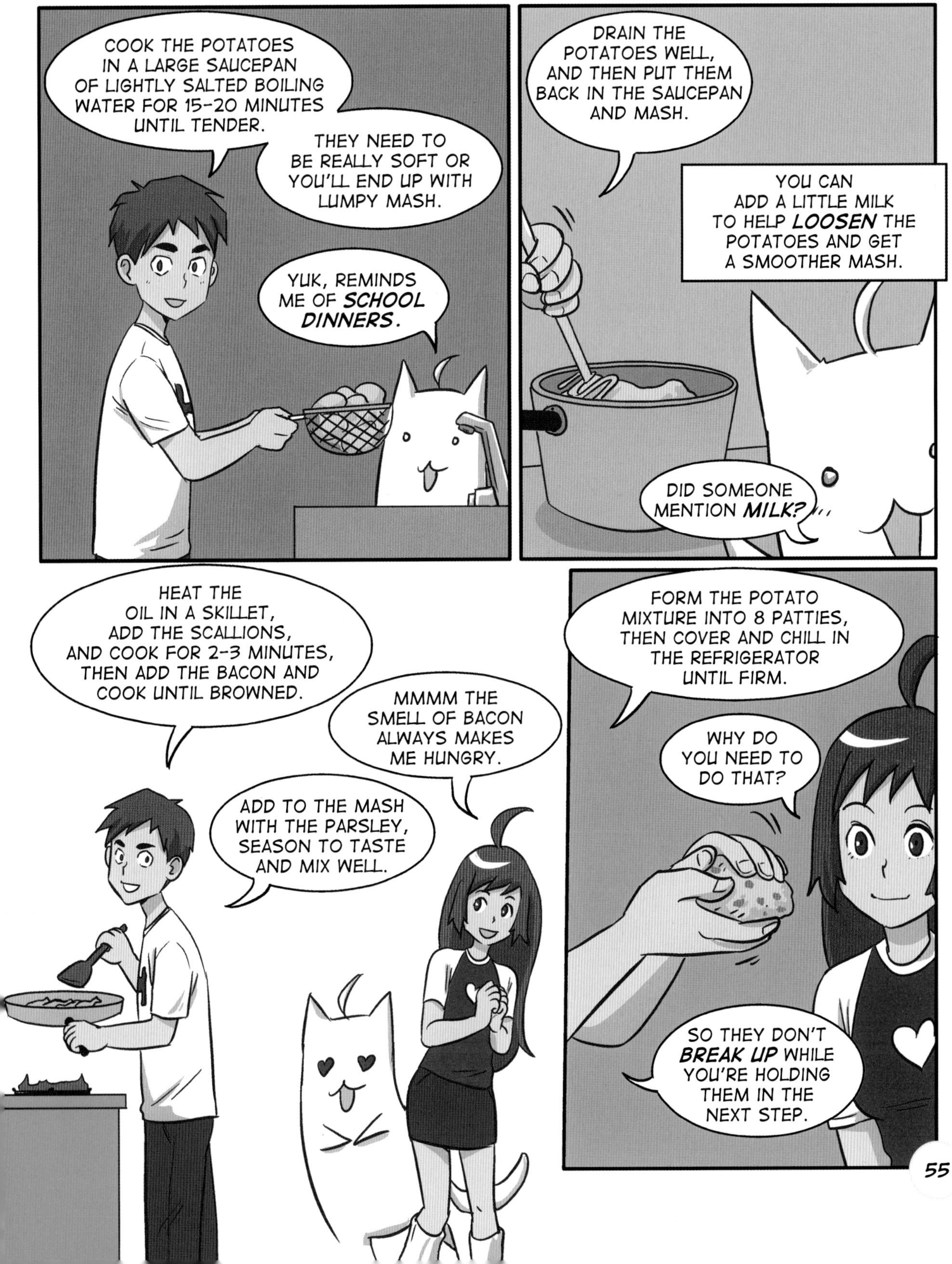

COOK THE POTATOES IN A LARGE SAUCEPAN OF LIGHTLY SALTED BOILING WATER FOR 15-20 MINUTES UNTIL TENDER.
THEY NEED TO BE REALLY SOFT OR YOU'LL END UP WITH LUMPY MASH.
YUK, REMINDS ME OF *SCHOOL DINNERS*.
DRAIN THE POTATOES WELL, AND THEN PUT THEM BACK IN THE SAUCEPAN AND MASH.
YOU CAN ADD A LITTLE MILK TO HELP *LOOSEN* THE POTATOES AND GET A SMOOTHER MASH.
DID SOMEONE MENTION *MILK?*
HEAT THE OIL IN A SKILLET, ADD THE SCALLIONS, AND COOK FOR 2-3 MINUTES, THEN ADD THE BACON AND COOK UNTIL BROWNED.
MMMM THE SMELL OF BACON ALWAYS MAKES ME HUNGRY.
ADD TO THE MASH WITH THE PARSLEY, SEASON TO TASTE AND MIX WELL.
FORM THE POTATO MIXTURE INTO 8 PATTIES, THEN COVER AND CHILL IN THE REFRIGERATOR UNTIL FIRM.
WHY DO YOU NEED TO DO THAT?
SO THEY DON'T *BREAK UP* WHILE YOU'RE HOLDING THEM IN THE NEXT STEP.

POTATO & BACON PATTIES

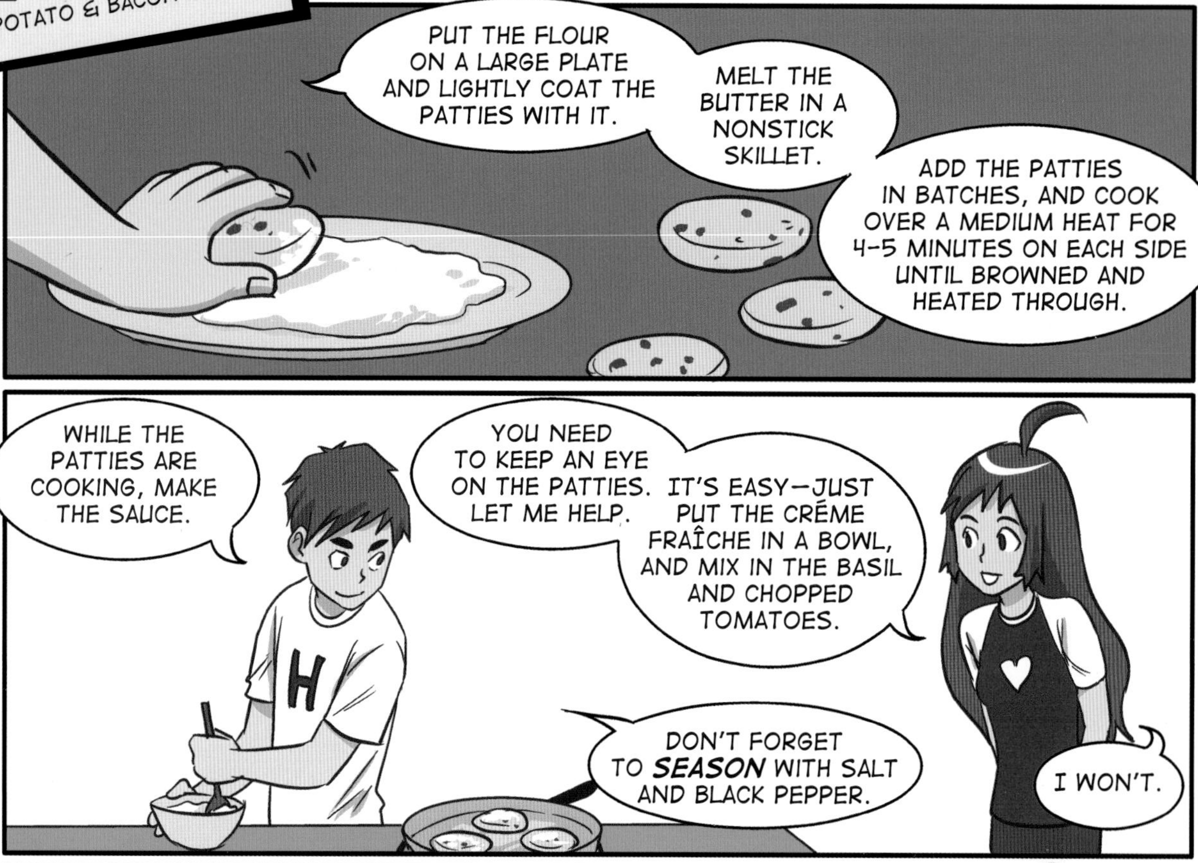
PUT THE FLOUR ON A LARGE PLATE AND LIGHTLY COAT THE PATTIES WITH IT.
MELT THE BUTTER IN A NONSTICK SKILLET.
ADD THE PATTIES IN BATCHES, AND COOK OVER A MEDIUM HEAT FOR 4-5 MINUTES ON EACH SIDE UNTIL BROWNED AND HEATED THROUGH.
WHILE THE PATTIES ARE COOKING, MAKE THE SAUCE.
YOU NEED TO KEEP AN EYE ON THE PATTIES. LET ME HELP.
IT'S EASY—JUST PUT THE CRÊME FRAÎCHE IN A BOWL, AND MIX IN THE BASIL AND CHOPPED TOMATOES.
DON'T FORGET TO SEASON WITH SALT AND BLACK PEPPER.
I WON'T.
H

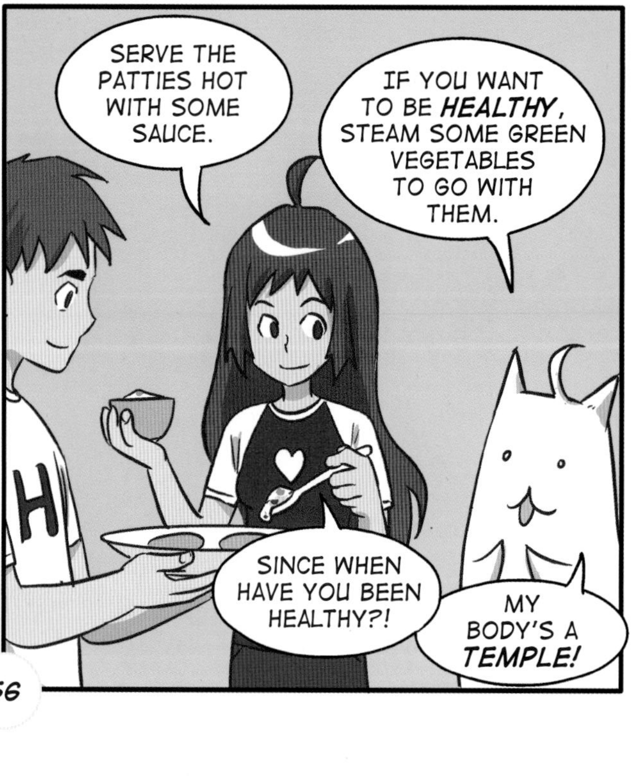
SERVE THE PATTIES HOT WITH SOME SAUCE.
IF YOU WANT TO BE HEALTHY, STEAM SOME GREEN VEGETABLES TO GO WITH THEM.
SINCE WHEN HAVE YOU BEEN HEALTHY?!
MY BODY'S A TEMPLE!
H

VARIATION

SALMON FISHCAKES WITH SOUR CREAM & MUSHROOM SAUCE

USE A 7 OZ CAN RED SALMON INSTEAD OF THE BACON. DRAIN AND FLAKE THE SALMON INTO THE MASHED POTATO MIXTURE. FORM INTO CAKES AND COOK AS ABOVE.

MEANWHILE, MELT 2 TBSP BUTTER IN A SAUCEPAN, ADD 3½ OZ SLICED BUTTON MUSHROOMS AND COOK FOR 1 MINUTE.

STIR IN 7 FL OZ SOUR CREAM AND ¼ TSP PAPRIKA AND SEASON. HEAT THROUGH GENTLY AND SERVE WITH THE FISHCAKES.

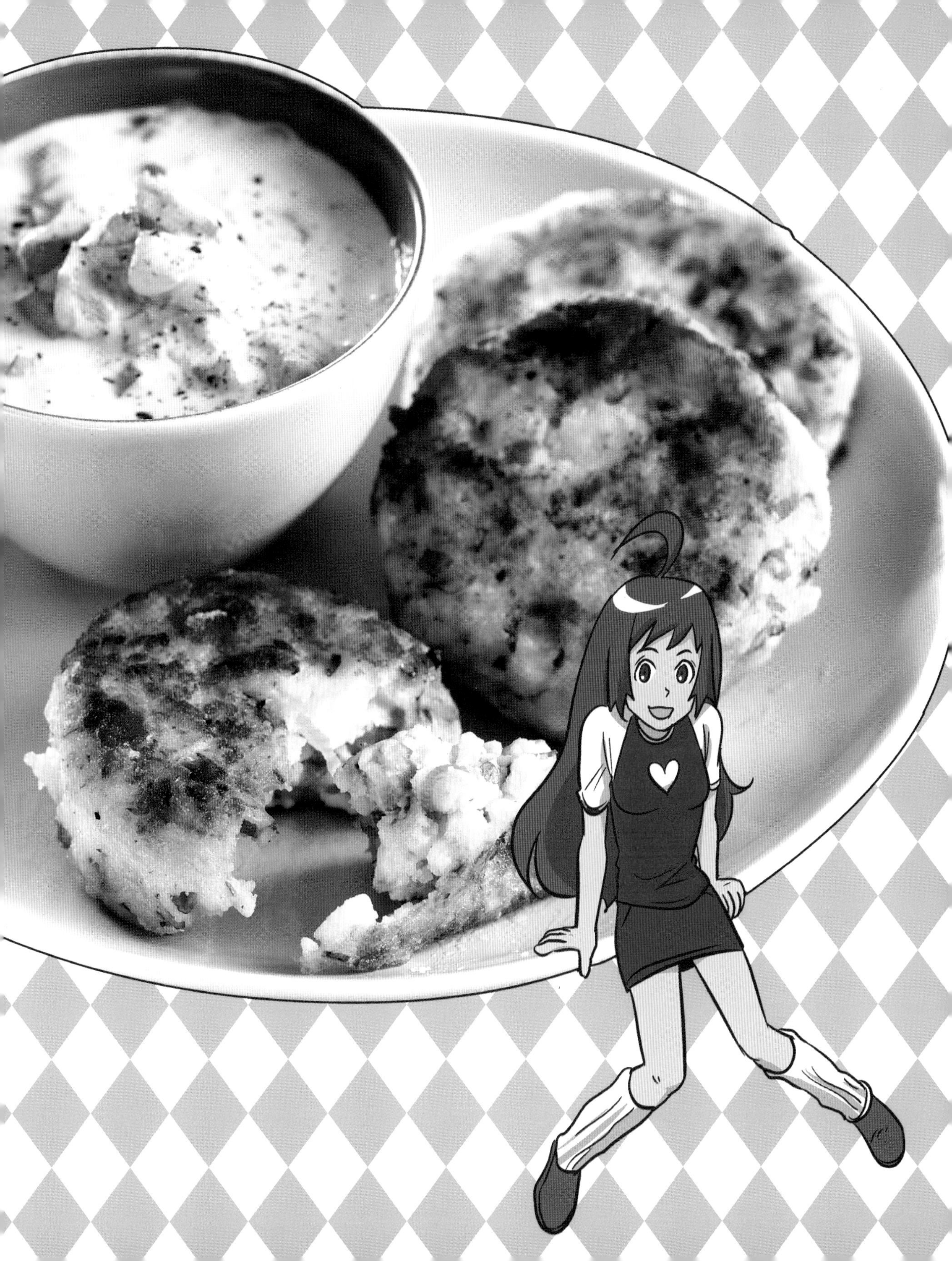

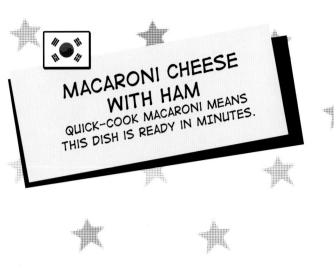

MACARONI CHEESE WITH HAM

QUICK-COOK MACARONI MEANS THIS DISH IS READY IN MINUTES.

11½ OZ DRIED QUICK-COOK MACARONI
8 OZ MASCARPONE CHEESE
3½ OZ CHEDDAR CHEESE, GRATED
3½ FL OZ MILK
2 TSP DIJON MUSTARD
13 OZ CAN PREMIUM CURED HAM, CUT INTO SMALL CUBES
SALT AND BLACK PEPPER
CHOPPED PARSLEY, TO GARNISH
SPINACH WITH OLIVE OIL & LEMON DRESSING, TO SERVE

SERVES 4 WARRIORS
PREP TIME: 5 MINUTES
COOKING TIME: 15 MINUTES

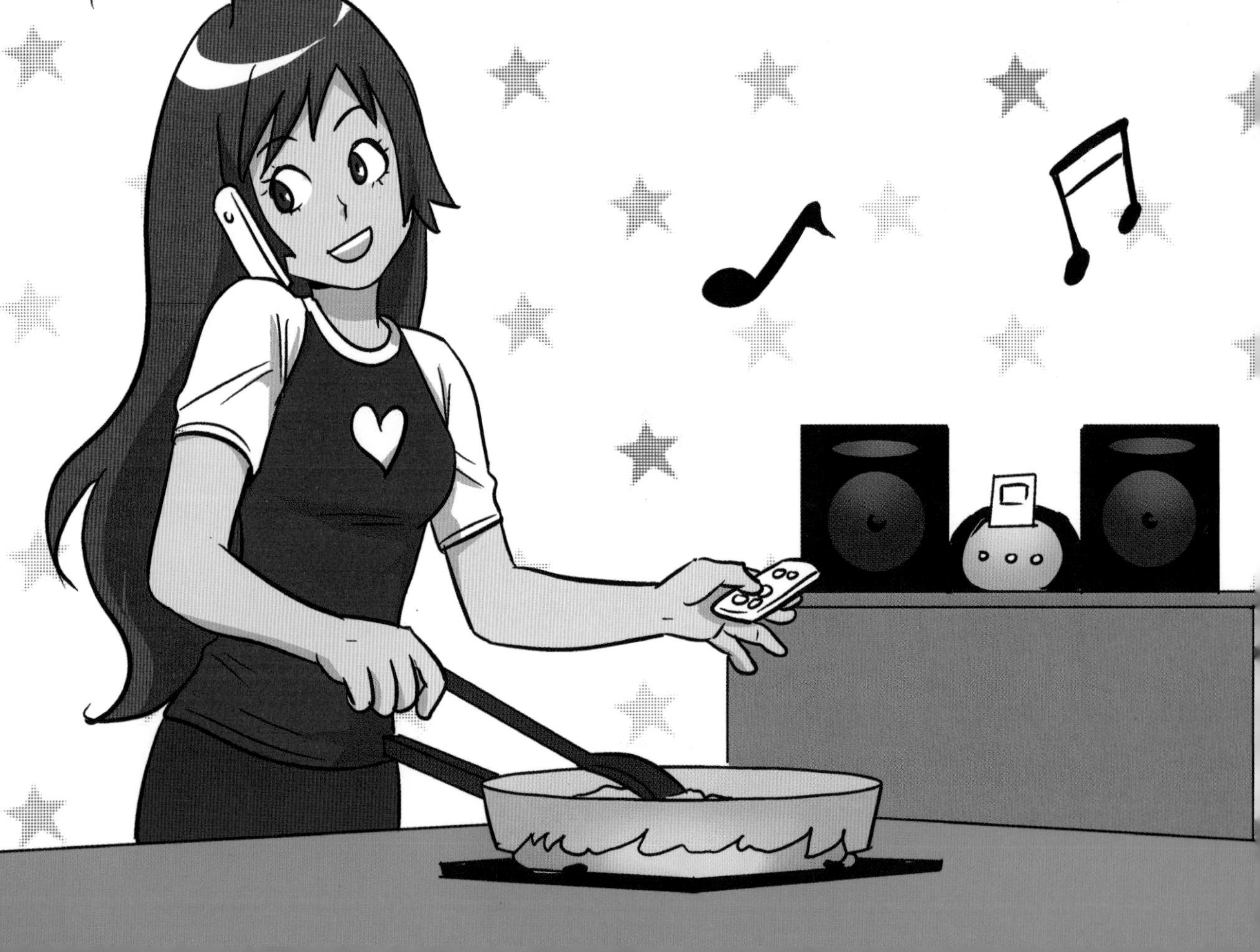

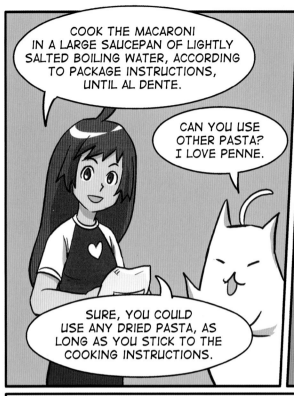

COOK THE MACARONI IN A LARGE SAUCEPAN OF LIGHTLY SALTED BOILING WATER, ACCORDING TO PACKAGE INSTRUCTIONS, UNTIL AL DENTE.

CAN YOU USE OTHER PASTA? I LOVE PENNE.

SURE, YOU COULD USE ANY DRIED PASTA, AS LONG AS YOU STICK TO THE COOKING INSTRUCTIONS.

DRAIN THE PASTA AND PUT IT IN A WARMED SERVING BOWL. COVER AND KEEP WARM.

HOW DO YOU WARM A SERVING BOWL?

YOU CAN PUT IT IN A WARM OVEN FOR A FEW MINUTES OR POUR SOME REALLY HOT WATER IN IT, LEAVE IT FOR A FEW MINUTES, AND TIP THE WATER OUT.

GENTLY HEAT THE MASCARPONE, CHEDDAR, MILK, AND MUSTARD IN A SAUCEPAN UNTIL MELTED INTO A SAUCE.

MUSTARD COMES IN DIFFERENT STRENGTHS—CHOOSE AMERICAN FOR A *MILD* FLAVOR, FRENCH FOR AN *UNDERTONE* OF HEAT, AND ENGLISH TO *KNOCK YOUR SOCKS OFF*.

STIR IN THE HAM AND COOK GENTLY FOR 1-2 MINUTES.

SEASON TO TASTE WITH SALT AND BLACK PEPPER.

IT'S HOTTER THAN I THOUGHT.

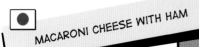

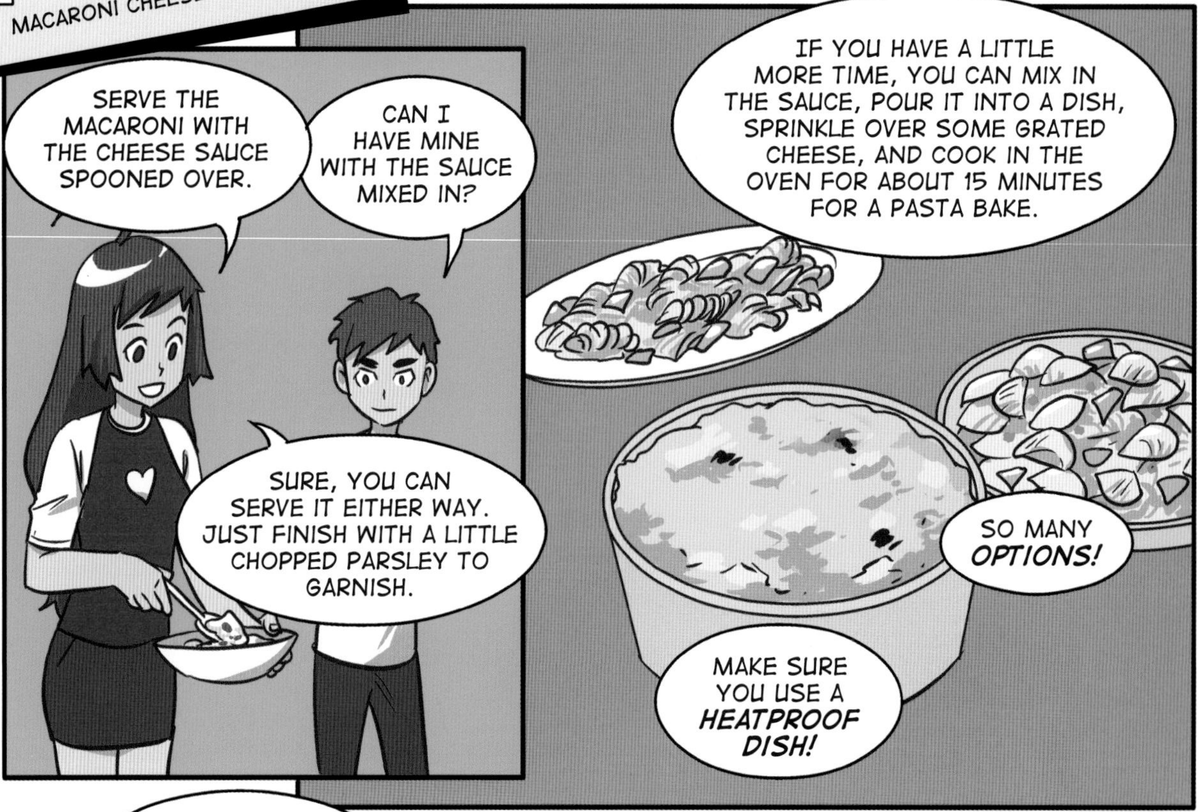
SERVE THE MACARONI WITH THE CHEESE SAUCE SPOONED OVER.
CAN I HAVE MINE WITH THE SAUCE MIXED IN?
SURE, YOU CAN SERVE IT EITHER WAY. JUST FINISH WITH A LITTLE CHOPPED PARSLEY TO GARNISH.
IF YOU HAVE A LITTLE MORE TIME, YOU CAN MIX IN THE SAUCE, POUR IT INTO A DISH, SPRINKLE OVER SOME GRATED CHEESE, AND COOK IN THE OVEN FOR ABOUT 15 MINUTES FOR A PASTA BAKE.
SO MANY OPTIONS!
MAKE SURE YOU USE A HEATPROOF DISH!

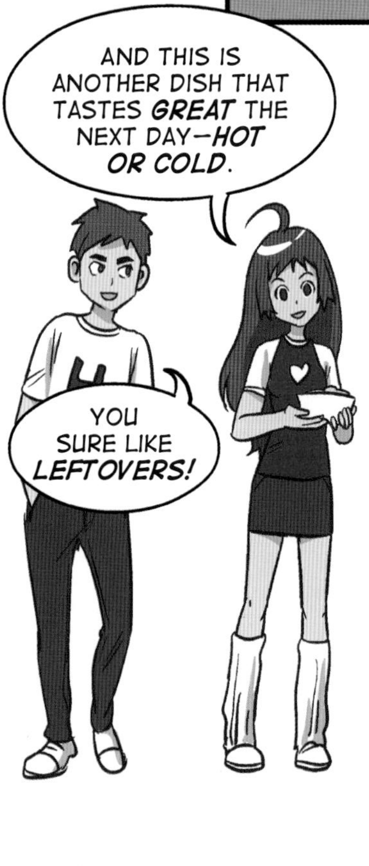
AND THIS IS ANOTHER DISH THAT TASTES GREAT THE NEXT DAY—HOT OR COLD.
YOU SURE LIKE LEFTOVERS!

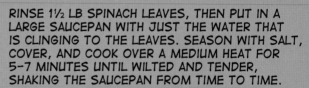

ACCOMPANIMENT

SPINACH WITH OLIVE OIL & LEMON DRESSING

RINSE 1½ LB SPINACH LEAVES, THEN PUT IN A LARGE SAUCEPAN WITH JUST THE WATER THAT IS CLINGING TO THE LEAVES. SEASON WITH SALT, COVER, AND COOK OVER A MEDIUM HEAT FOR 5–7 MINUTES UNTIL WILTED AND TENDER, SHAKING THE SAUCEPAN FROM TIME TO TIME.

DRAIN IN A COLANDER, THEN RETURN TO THE SAUCEPAN, AND TOSS OVER A HIGH HEAT UNTIL ANY REMAINING WATER HAS EVAPORATED. ADD 2 TBSP BUTTER AND 2 FINELY CHOPPED GARLIC CLOVES, AND MIX WITH THE SPINACH. TRANSFER TO A SERVING DISH, DRIZZLE OVER 4 TBSP OLIVE OIL, AND 2 TBSP LEMON JUICE, AND SERVE WITH THE MACARONI.

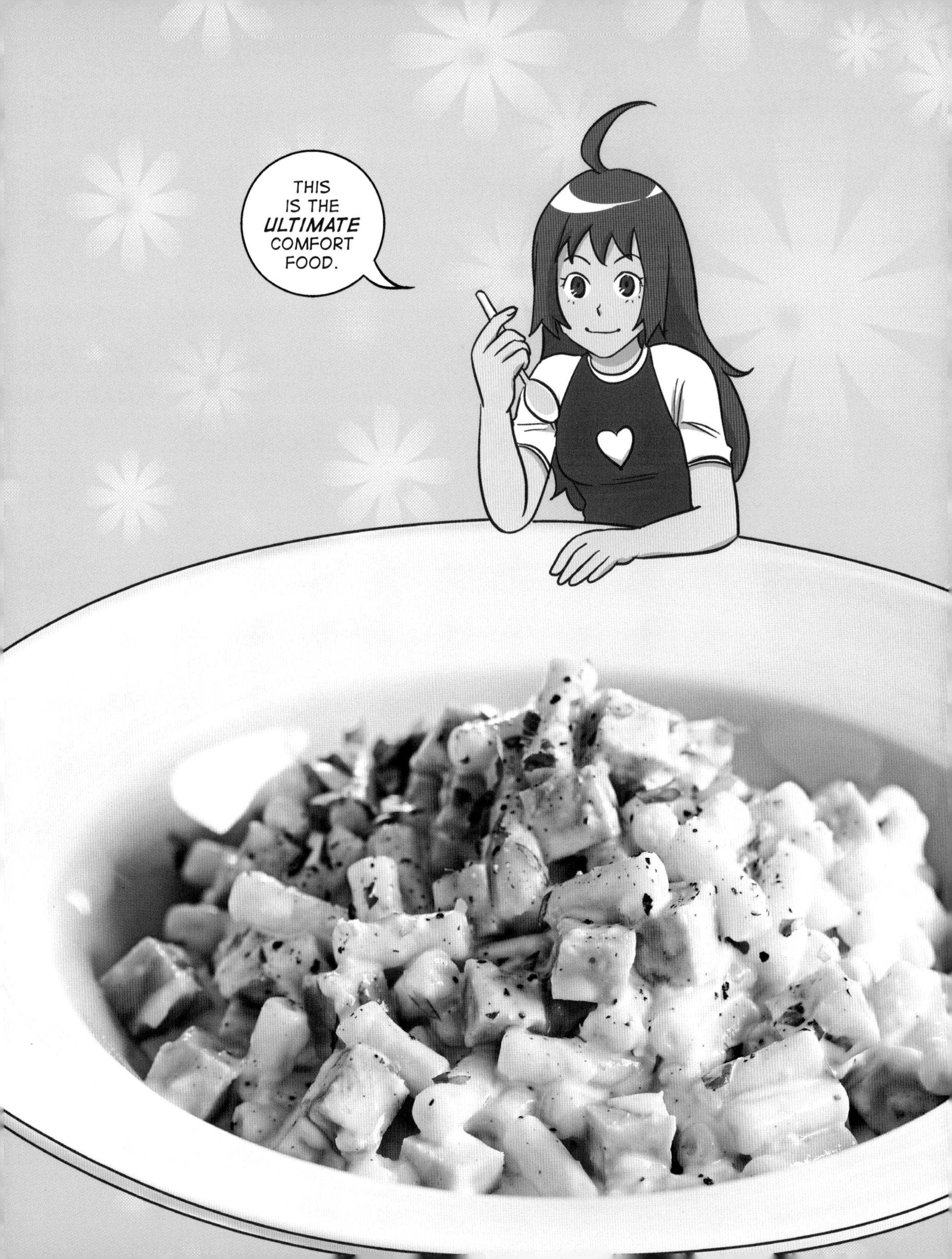
THIS IS THE ULTIMATE COMFORT FOOD.

QUICK SAUSAGE & BEAN CASSEROLE
CASSEROLES USUALLY TAKE AGES TO COOK,
BUT THIS ONE IS QUICK AND EASY.

2 TBSP OLIVE OIL
16 COCKTAIL SAUSAGES
2 GARLIC CLOVES, FINELY CHOPPED
13 OZ CAN DICED TOMATOES
13 OZ CAN BAKED BEANS
7 OZ CAN MIXED BEANS, DRAINED, AND RINSED
½ TSP DRIED THYME
SALT AND BLACK PEPPER
3 TBSP CHOPPED PARSLEY, TO GARNISH
MUSTARD MASH, TO SERVE

SERVES 4 WARRIORS
PREP TIME: 5 MINUTES
COOKING TIME: 25 MINUTES

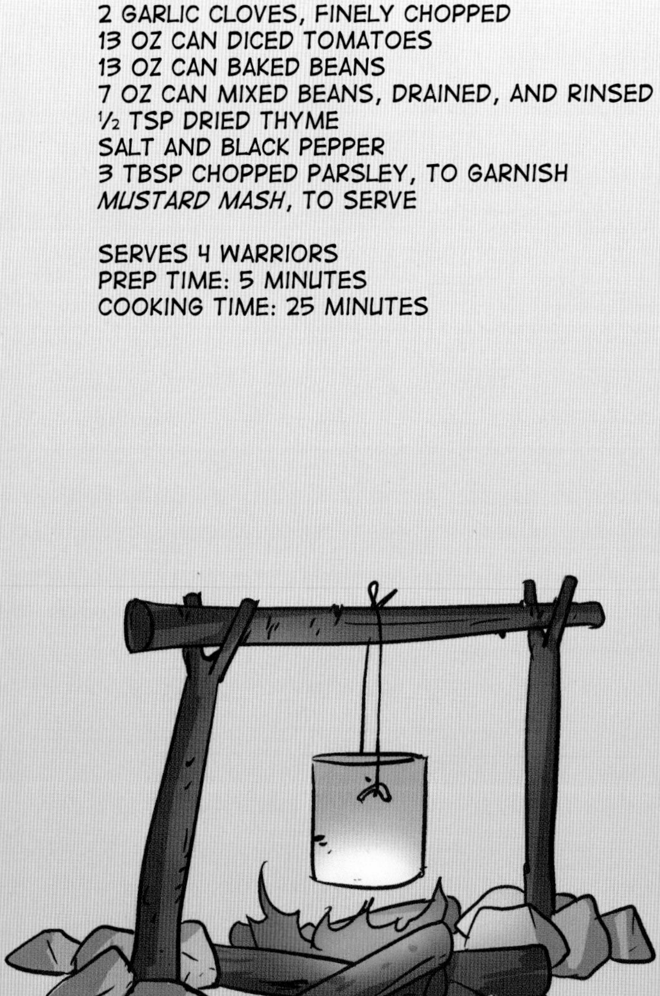

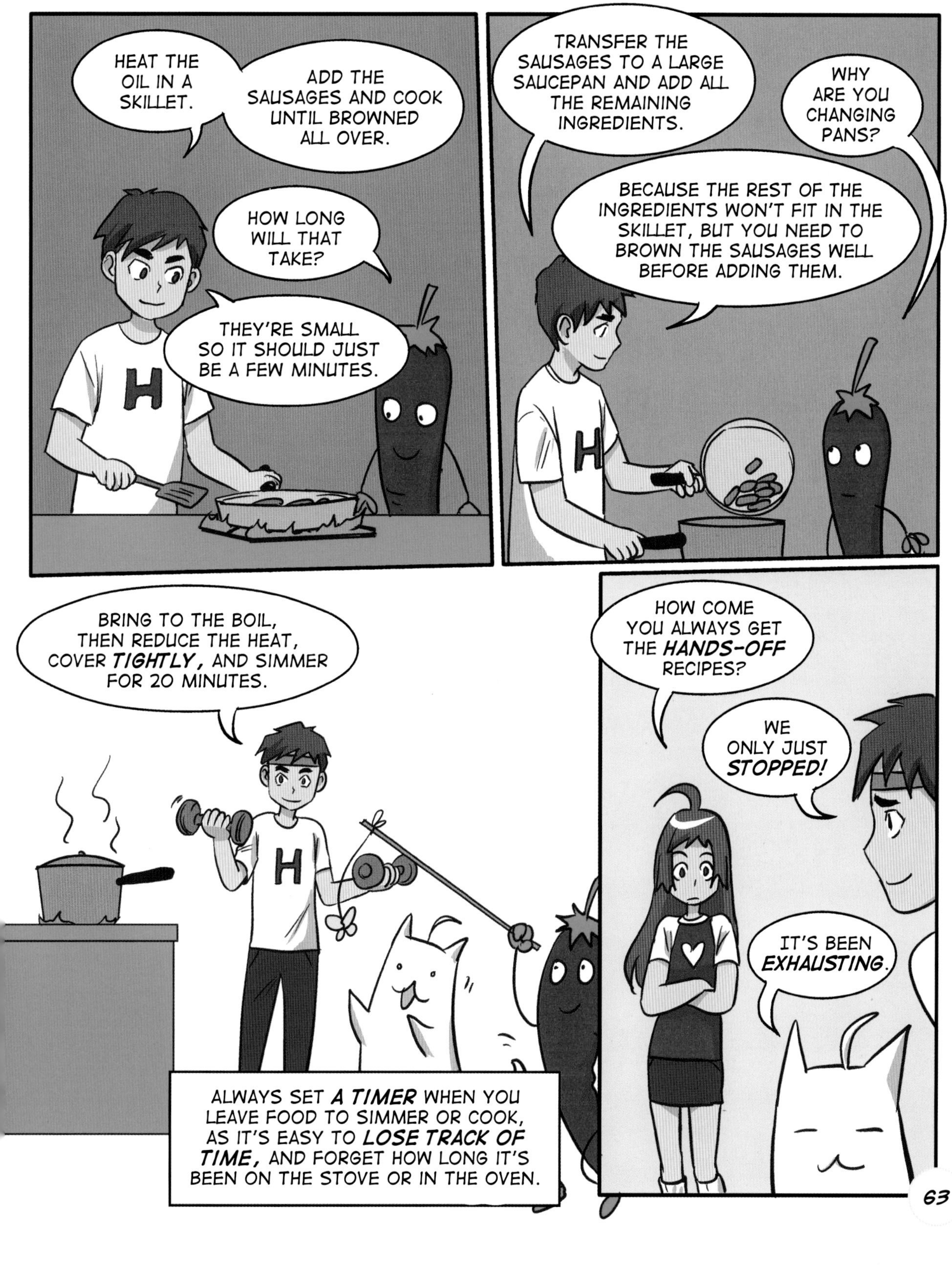
HEAT THE OIL IN A SKILLET.
ADD THE SAUSAGES AND COOK UNTIL BROWNED ALL OVER.
HOW LONG WILL THAT TAKE?
THEY'RE SMALL SO IT SHOULD JUST BE A FEW MINUTES.
TRANSFER THE SAUSAGES TO A LARGE SAUCEPAN AND ADD ALL THE REMAINING INGREDIENTS.
WHY ARE YOU CHANGING PANS?
BECAUSE THE REST OF THE INGREDIENTS WON'T FIT IN THE SKILLET, BUT YOU NEED TO BROWN THE SAUSAGES WELL BEFORE ADDING THEM.
BRING TO THE BOIL, THEN REDUCE THE HEAT, COVER ***TIGHTLY,*** AND SIMMER FOR 20 MINUTES.
ALWAYS SET ***A TIMER*** WHEN YOU LEAVE FOOD TO SIMMER OR COOK, AS IT'S EASY TO ***LOSE TRACK OF TIME,*** AND FORGET HOW LONG IT'S BEEN ON THE STOVE OR IN THE OVEN.
HOW COME YOU ALWAYS GET THE ***HANDS-OFF*** RECIPES?
WE ONLY JUST ***STOPPED!***
IT'S BEEN ***EXHAUSTING***.

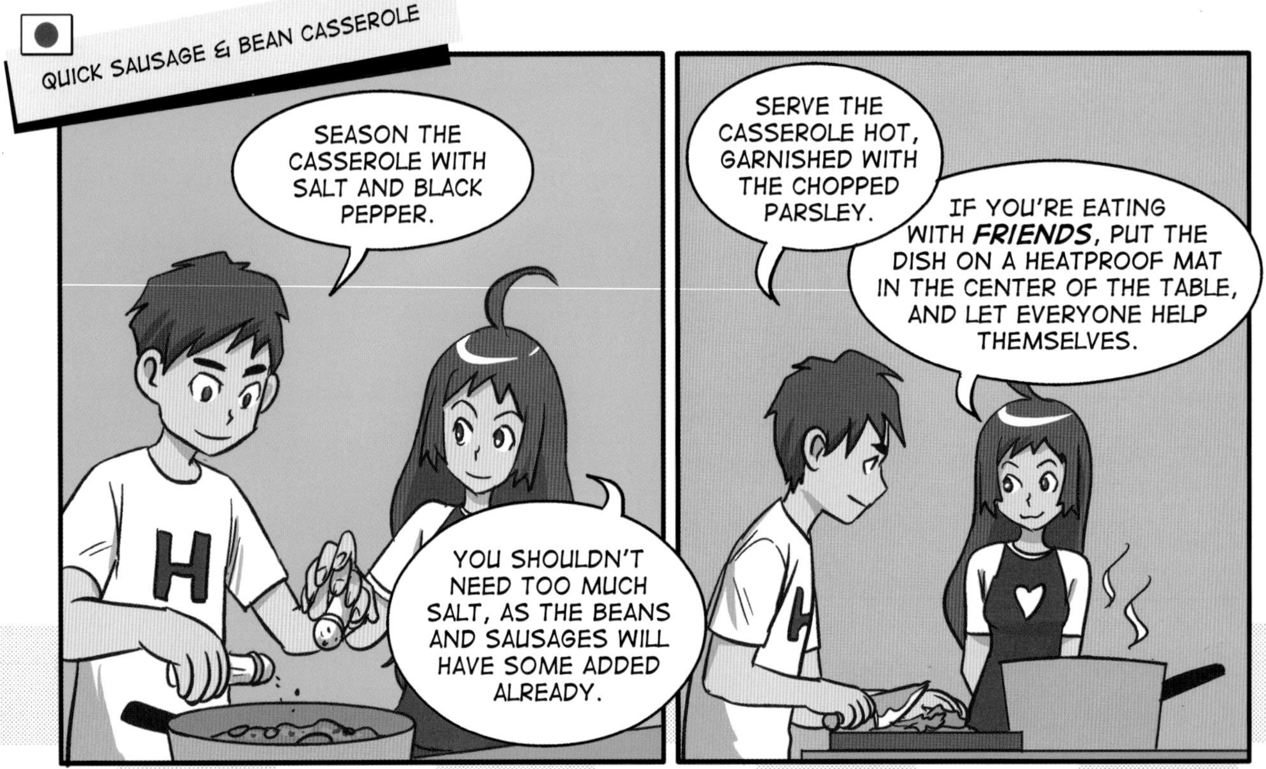
QUICK SAUSAGE & BEAN CASSEROLE
SEASON THE CASSEROLE WITH SALT AND BLACK PEPPER.
YOU SHOULDN'T NEED TOO MUCH SALT, AS THE BEANS AND SAUSAGES WILL HAVE SOME ADDED ALREADY.
SERVE THE CASSEROLE HOT, GARNISHED WITH THE CHOPPED PARSLEY.
IF YOU'RE EATING WITH ***FRIENDS***, PUT THE DISH ON A HEATPROOF MAT IN THE CENTER OF THE TABLE, AND LET EVERYONE HELP THEMSELVES.

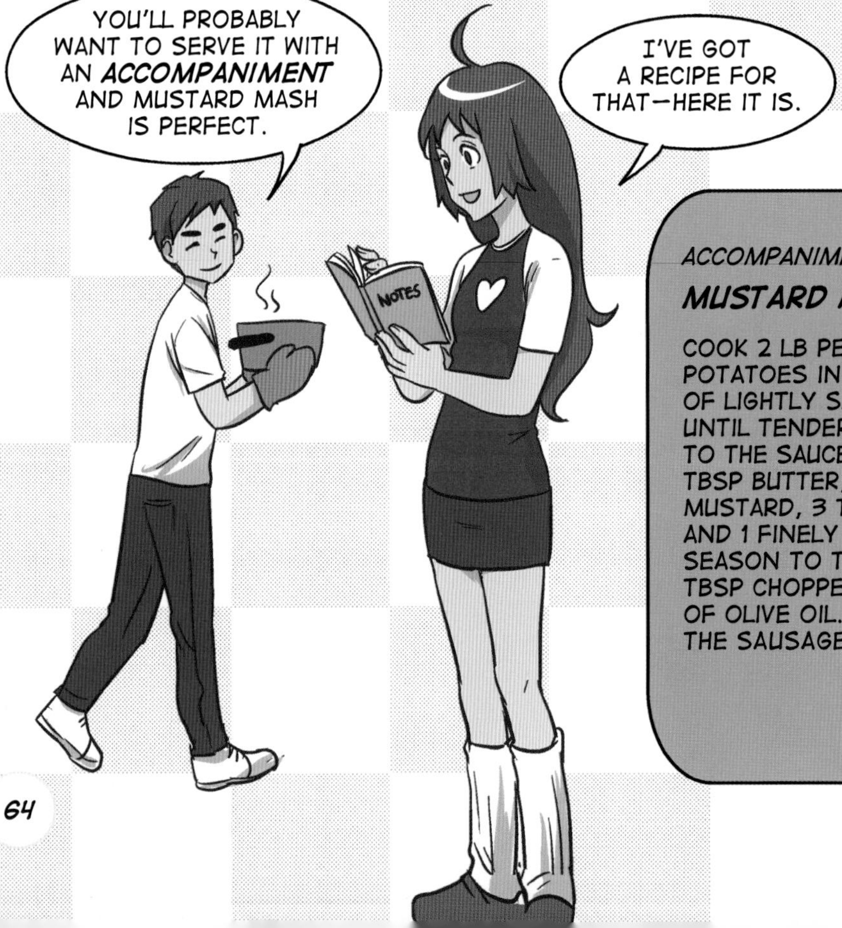
YOU'LL PROBABLY WANT TO SERVE IT WITH AN ***ACCOMPANIMENT*** AND MUSTARD MASH IS PERFECT.
I'VE GOT A RECIPE FOR THAT—HERE IT IS.
NOTES

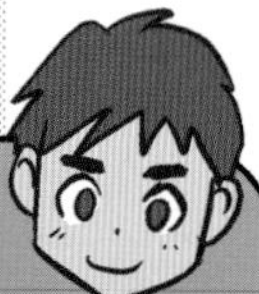

ACCOMPANIMENT

MUSTARD MASH

COOK 2 LB PEELED AND CHOPPED POTATOES IN A LARGE SAUCEPAN OF LIGHTLY SALTED BOILING WATER UNTIL TENDER. DRAIN AND RETURN TO THE SAUCEPAN. MASH WITH 5 TBSP BUTTER, 1 TBSP WHOLEGRAIN MUSTARD, 3 TSP ENGLISH MUSTARD, AND 1 FINELY CHOPPED GARLIC CLOVE. SEASON TO TASTE, THEN BEAT IN 2 TBSP CHOPPED PARSLEY, AND A DASH OF OLIVE OIL. SERVE HOT WITH THE SAUSAGE CASSEROLE.

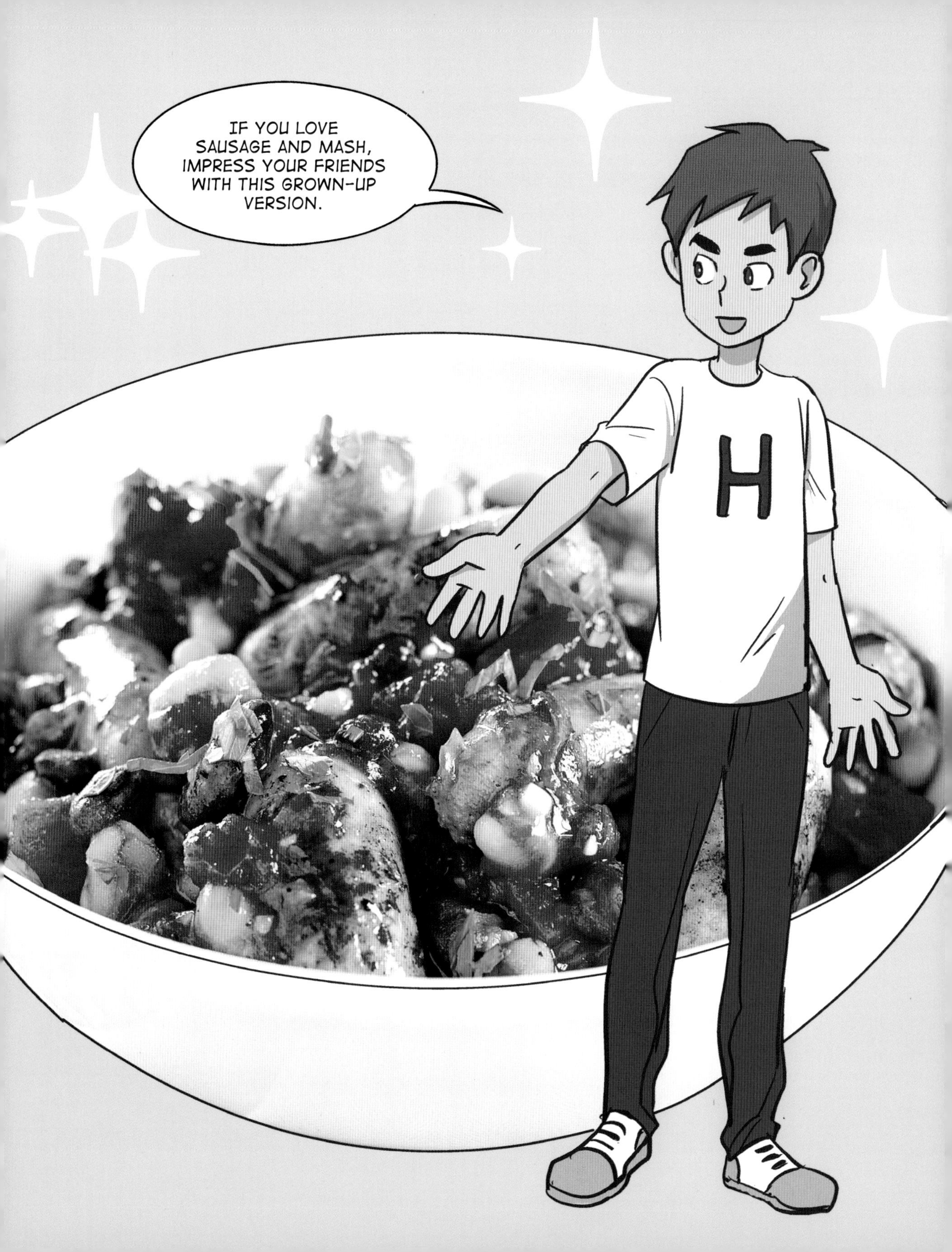
IF YOU LOVE SAUSAGE AND MASH, IMPRESS YOUR FRIENDS WITH THIS GROWN-UP VERSION.

FISH PIE

THIS FISH PIE IS NUTRITIOUS, FILLING, AND DELICIOUS.

10 OZ COOKED PEELED SHRIMP
2 TSP CORNFLOUR
10 OZ WHITE FISH FILLETS SUCH AS HADDOCK, SKINNED, AND CUT INTO CHUNKS
2 TSP GREEN PEPPERCORNS IN BRINE, RINSED, AND DRAINED
1 SMALL FENNEL BULB, COARSELY CHOPPED
1 SMALL LEEK, TRIMMED, AND COARSELY CHOPPED
1/5 OZ DILL
1/5 OZ PARSLEY
3 1/2 OZ FRESH OR FROZEN PEAS
12 OZ READY-MADE CHEESE SAUCE
1 1/2 LB LARGE POTATOES, PEELED, AND THINLY SLICED
3 OZ CHEDDAR CHEESE, GRATED
SALT AND BLACK PEPPER
STEAMED VEGETABLES OR MIXED SALAD, TO SERVE

SERVES 4 WARRIORS
PREP TIME: 15 MINUTES
COOKING TIME: 1 HOUR 10 MINUTES

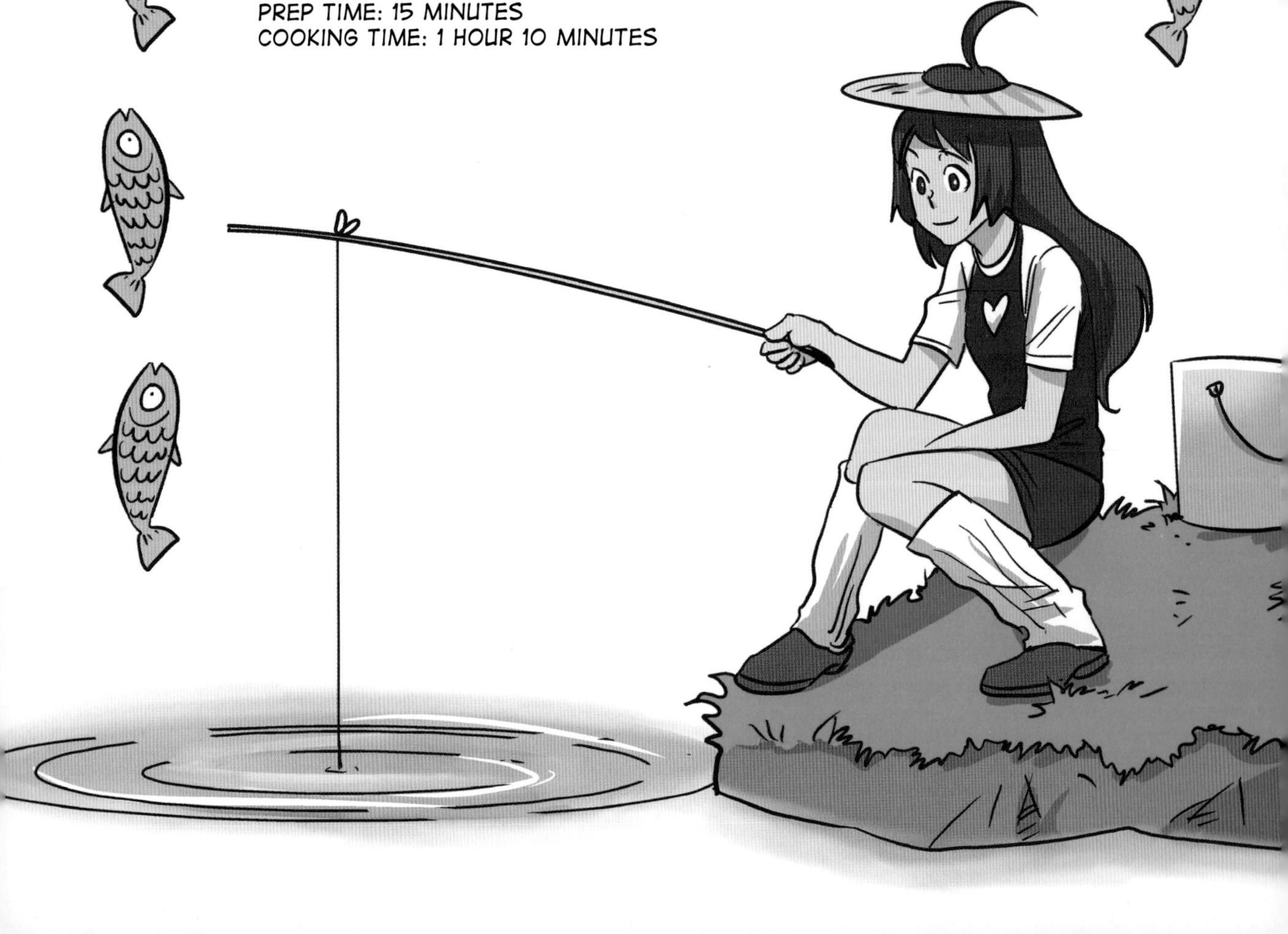

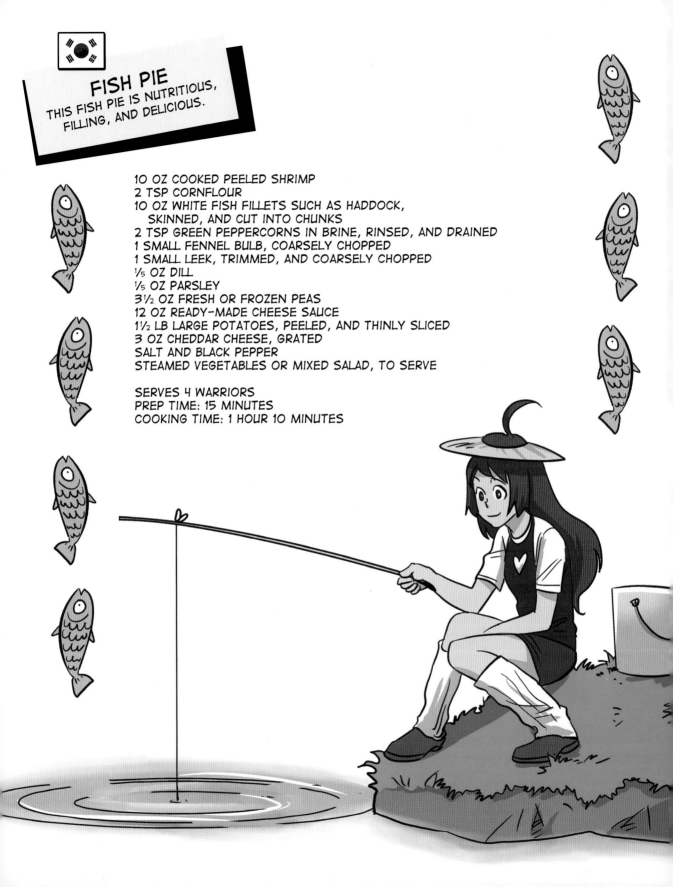

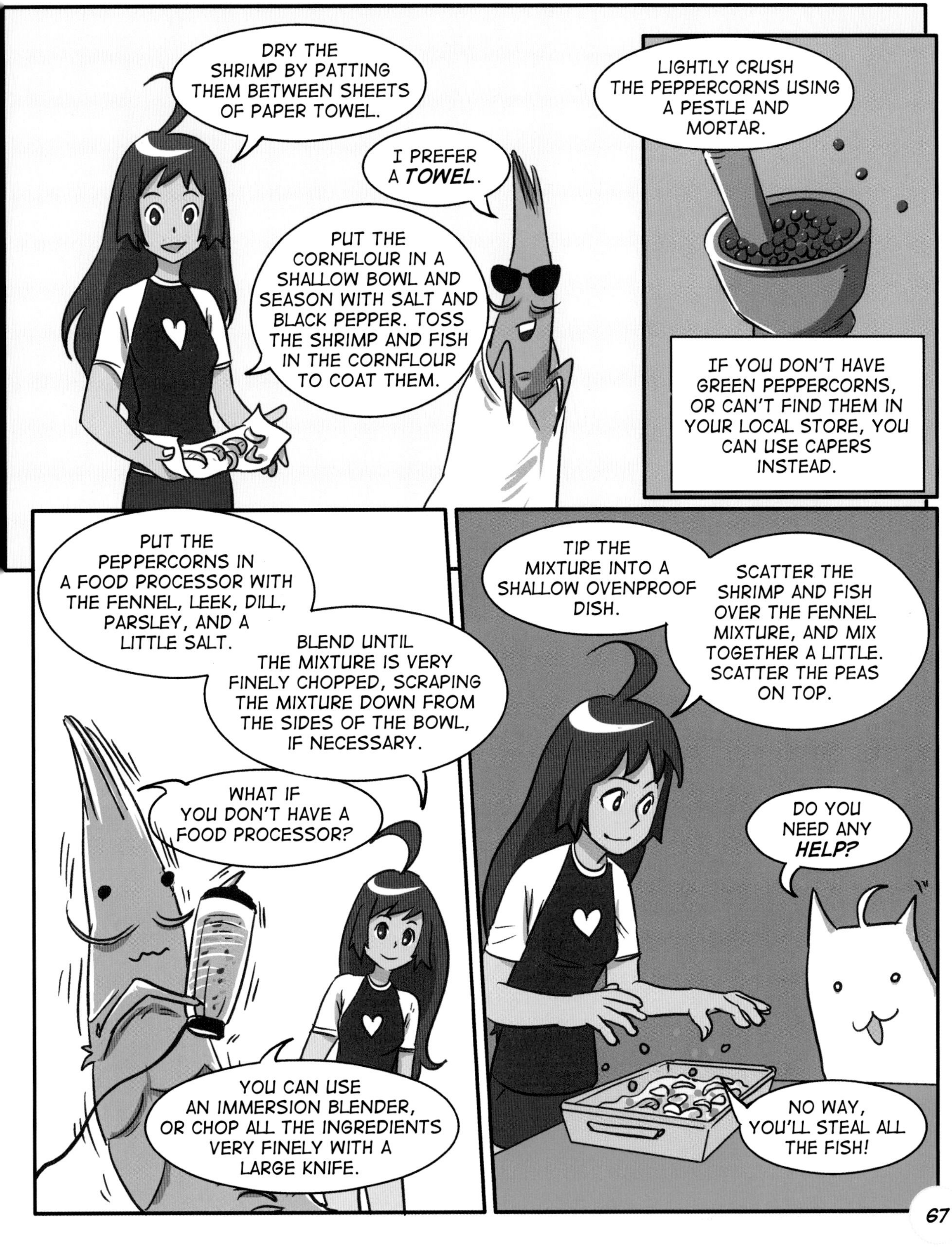
DRY THE SHRIMP BY PATTING THEM BETWEEN SHEETS OF PAPER TOWEL.
I PREFER A TOWEL.
PUT THE CORNFLOUR IN A SHALLOW BOWL AND SEASON WITH SALT AND BLACK PEPPER. TOSS THE SHRIMP AND FISH IN THE CORNFLOUR TO COAT THEM.
LIGHTLY CRUSH THE PEPPERCORNS USING A PESTLE AND MORTAR.
IF YOU DON'T HAVE GREEN PEPPERCORNS, OR CAN'T FIND THEM IN YOUR LOCAL STORE, YOU CAN USE CAPERS INSTEAD.
PUT THE PEPPERCORNS IN A FOOD PROCESSOR WITH THE FENNEL, LEEK, DILL, PARSLEY, AND A LITTLE SALT.
BLEND UNTIL THE MIXTURE IS VERY FINELY CHOPPED, SCRAPING THE MIXTURE DOWN FROM THE SIDES OF THE BOWL, IF NECESSARY.
WHAT IF YOU DON'T HAVE A FOOD PROCESSOR?
YOU CAN USE AN IMMERSION BLENDER, OR CHOP ALL THE INGREDIENTS VERY FINELY WITH A LARGE KNIFE.
TIP THE MIXTURE INTO A SHALLOW OVENPROOF DISH.
SCATTER THE SHRIMP AND FISH OVER THE FENNEL MIXTURE, AND MIX TOGETHER A LITTLE. SCATTER THE PEAS ON TOP.
DO YOU NEED ANY HELP?
NO WAY, YOU'LL STEAL ALL THE FISH!

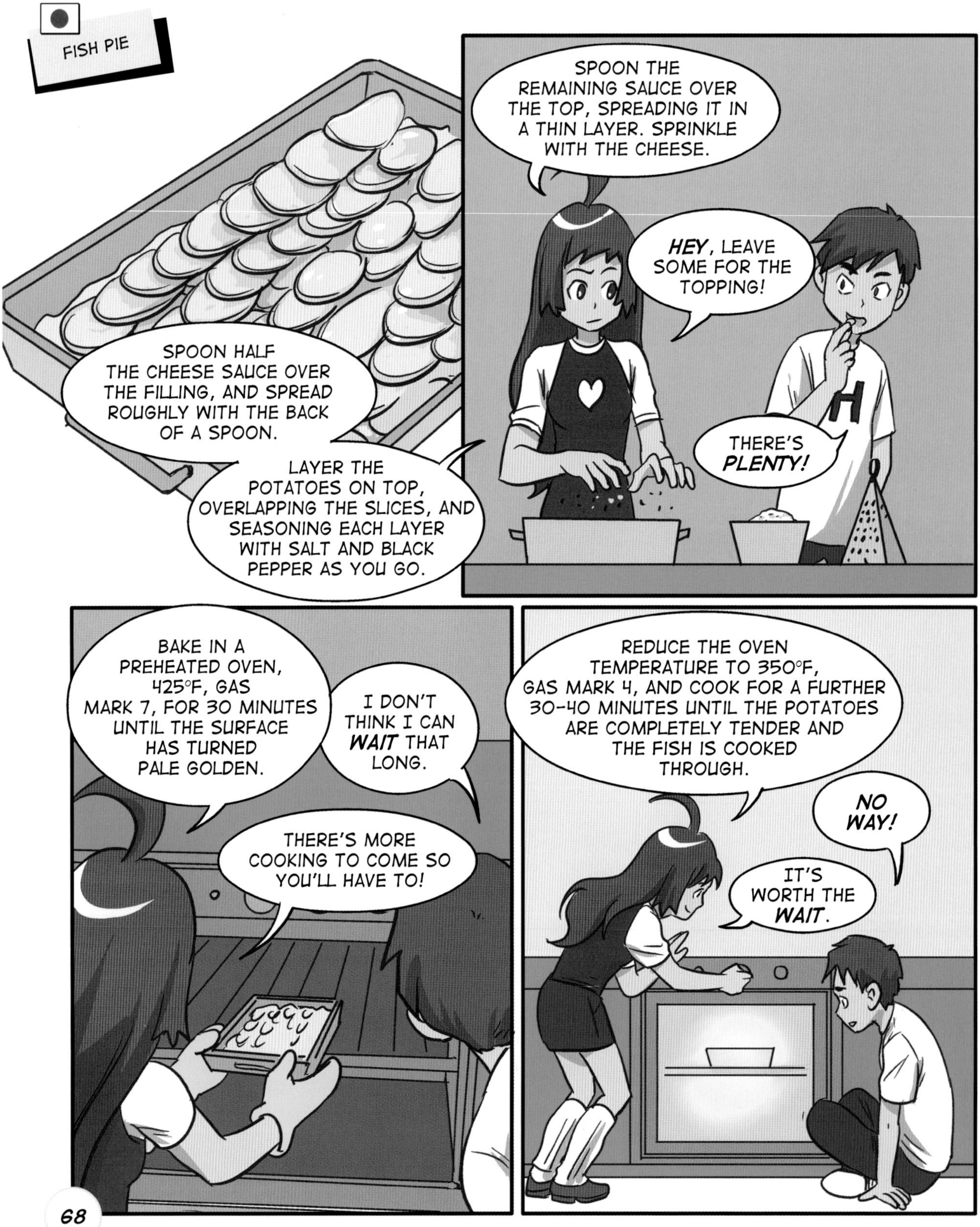
SPOON HALF THE CHEESE SAUCE OVER THE FILLING, AND SPREAD ROUGHLY WITH THE BACK OF A SPOON.
LAYER THE POTATOES ON TOP, OVERLAPPING THE SLICES, AND SEASONING EACH LAYER WITH SALT AND BLACK PEPPER AS YOU GO.
SPOON THE REMAINING SAUCE OVER THE TOP, SPREADING IT IN A THIN LAYER. SPRINKLE WITH THE CHEESE.
HEY, LEAVE SOME FOR THE TOPPING!
THERE'S PLENTY!
BAKE IN A PREHEATED OVEN, 425°F, GAS MARK 7, FOR 30 MINUTES UNTIL THE SURFACE HAS TURNED PALE GOLDEN.
I DON'T THINK I CAN WAIT THAT LONG.
THERE'S MORE COOKING TO COME SO YOU'LL HAVE TO!
REDUCE THE OVEN TEMPERATURE TO 350°F, GAS MARK 4, AND COOK FOR A FURTHER 30–40 MINUTES UNTIL THE POTATOES ARE COMPLETELY TENDER AND THE FISH IS COOKED THROUGH.
NO WAY!
IT'S WORTH THE WAIT.

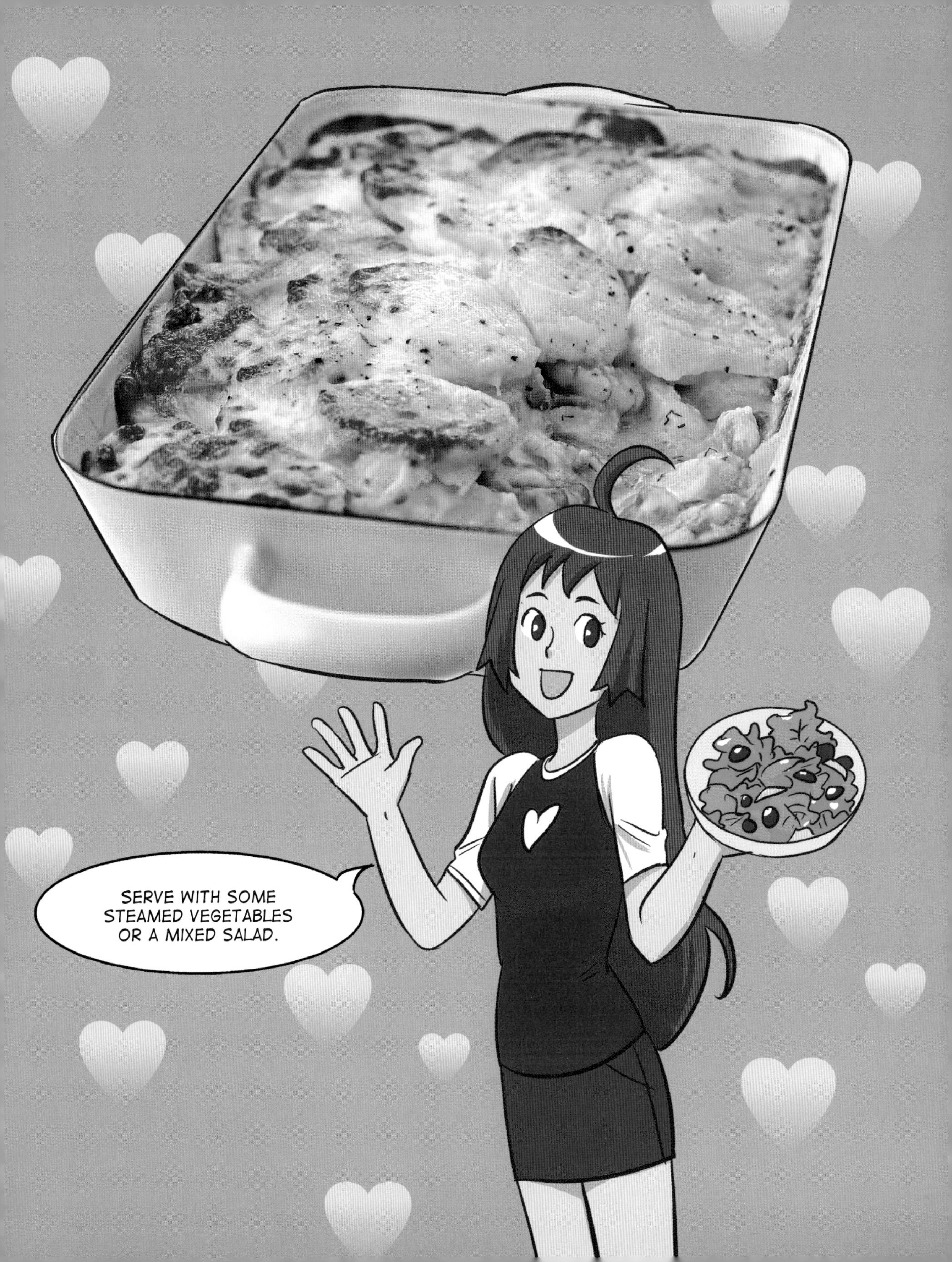
SERVE WITH SOME STEAMED VEGETABLES OR A MIXED SALAD.

SPICY FISH SKEWERS

IF YOU USUALLY CHOOSE LAMB OR CHICKEN FOR SPICY DISHES, WHY NOT TRY FISH FOR A CHANGE?

1 GARLIC CLOVE, PEELED
2 RED SHALLOTS, CHOPPED
1 LEMON GRASS STALK
½ TSP GROUND TURMERIC
½ TSP GROUND GINGER
1 MILD RED CHILE, DESEEDED,
    AND COARSELY CHOPPED
1 TBSP GROUNDNUT OIL
2 TSP THAI FISH SAUCE
10 OZ WHITE FISH FILLETS,
    CUT INTO BITE-SIZED PIECES
SALT AND BLACK PEPPER
1 TBSP CHOPPED FRESH CORIANDER, TO GARNISH
CHINESE GREENS, TO SERVE

YOU'LL ALSO NEED 4 WOODEN SKEWERS

SERVES 2 WARRIORS
PREP TIME: 10 MINUTES, PLUS MARINATING
COOKING TIME: 5 MINUTES

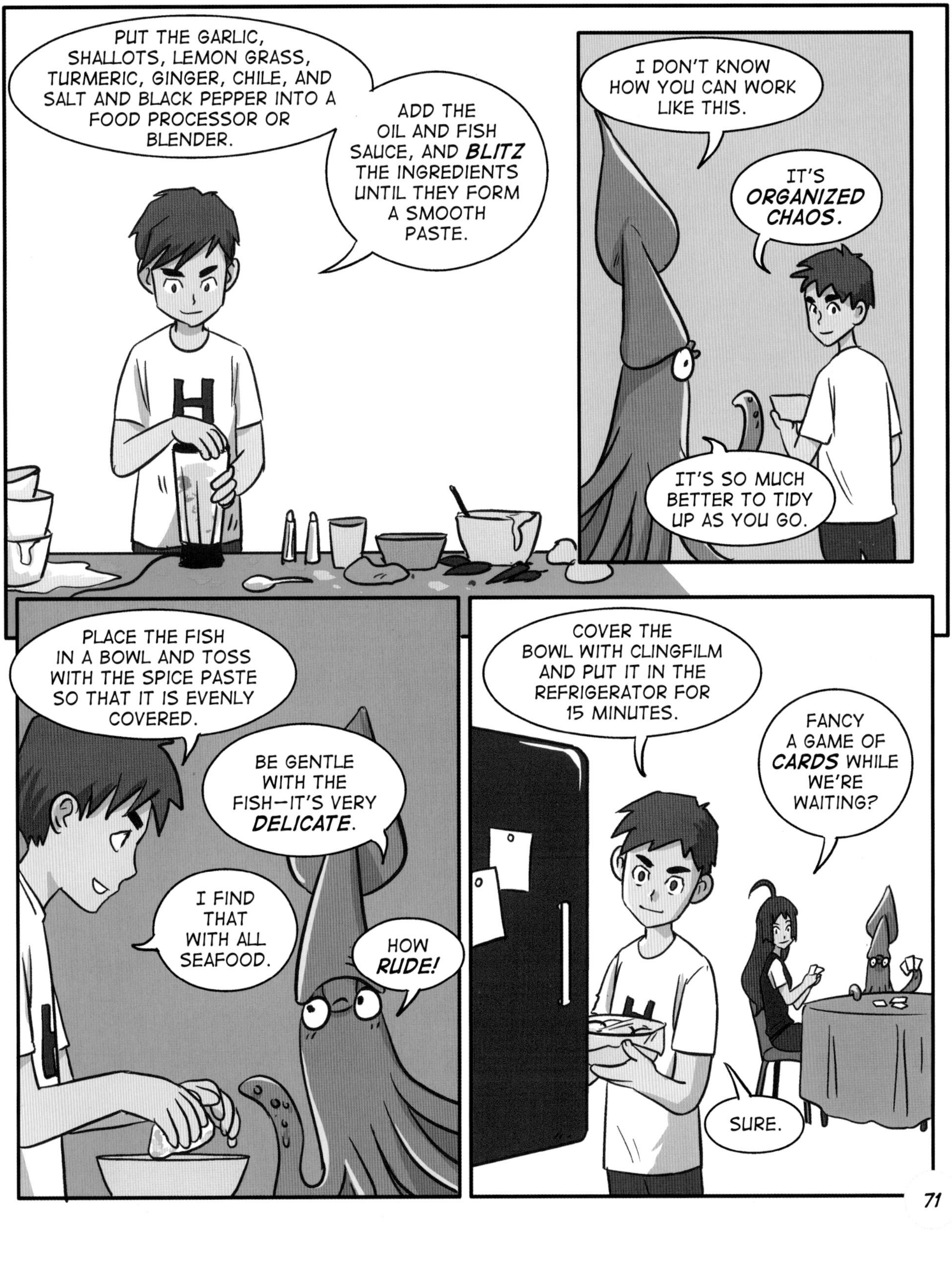
PUT THE GARLIC, SHALLOTS, LEMON GRASS, TURMERIC, GINGER, CHILE, AND SALT AND BLACK PEPPER INTO A FOOD PROCESSOR OR BLENDER.
ADD THE OIL AND FISH SAUCE, AND **BLITZ** THE INGREDIENTS UNTIL THEY FORM A SMOOTH PASTE.
I DON'T KNOW HOW YOU CAN WORK LIKE THIS.
IT'S **ORGANIZED CHAOS.**
IT'S SO MUCH BETTER TO TIDY UP AS YOU GO.
PLACE THE FISH IN A BOWL AND TOSS WITH THE SPICE PASTE SO THAT IT IS EVENLY COVERED.
BE GENTLE WITH THE FISH—IT'S VERY **DELICATE**.
I FIND THAT WITH ALL SEAFOOD.
HOW **RUDE!**
COVER THE BOWL WITH CLINGFILM AND PUT IT IN THE REFRIGERATOR FOR 15 MINUTES.
FANCY A GAME OF **CARDS** WHILE WE'RE WAITING?
SURE.

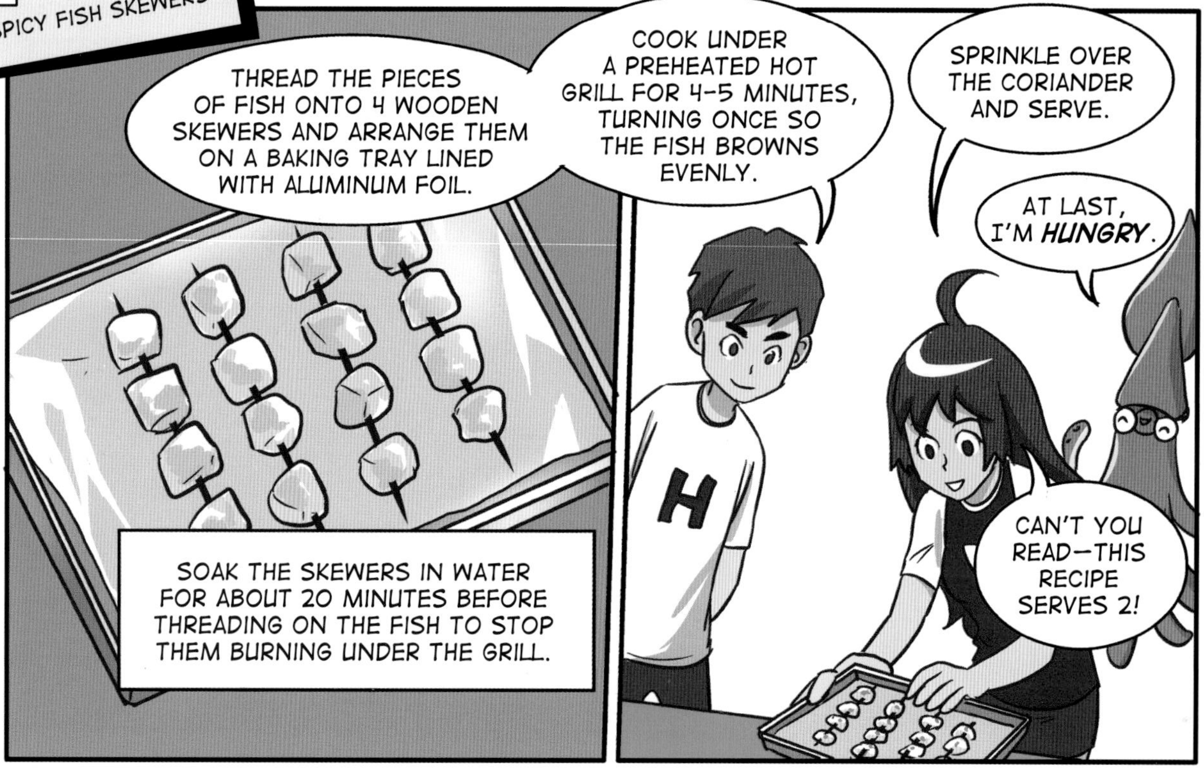
THREAD THE PIECES OF FISH ONTO 4 WOODEN SKEWERS AND ARRANGE THEM ON A BAKING TRAY LINED WITH ALUMINUM FOIL.
SOAK THE SKEWERS IN WATER FOR ABOUT 20 MINUTES BEFORE THREADING ON THE FISH TO STOP THEM BURNING UNDER THE GRILL.
COOK UNDER A PREHEATED HOT GRILL FOR 4–5 MINUTES, TURNING ONCE SO THE FISH BROWNS EVENLY.
SPRINKLE OVER THE CORIANDER AND SERVE.
AT LAST, I'M ***HUNGRY***.
CAN'T YOU READ—THIS RECIPE SERVES 2!

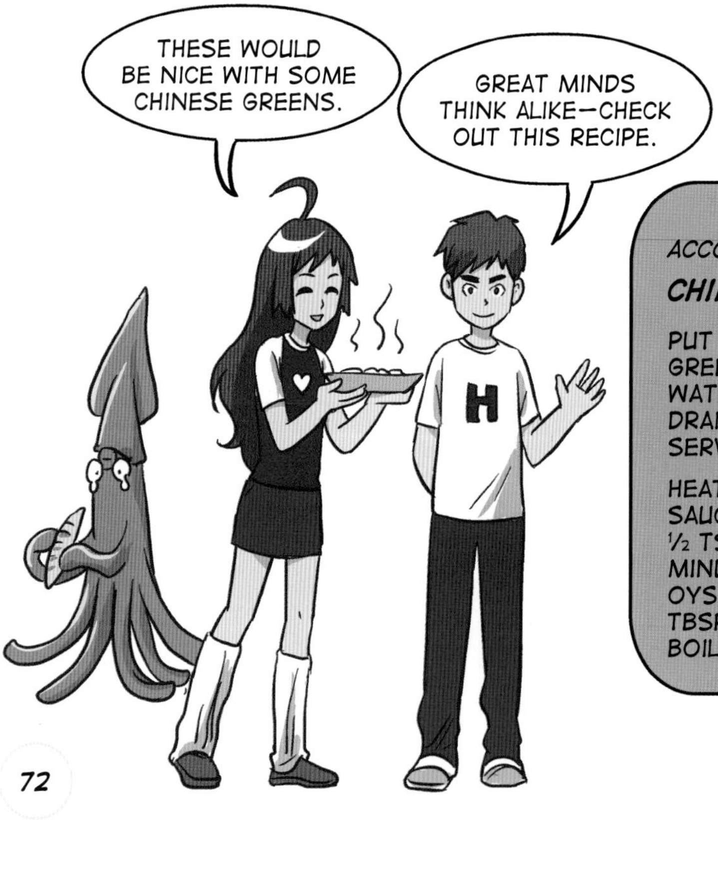
THESE WOULD BE NICE WITH SOME CHINESE GREENS.
GREAT MINDS THINK ALIKE—CHECK OUT THIS RECIPE.

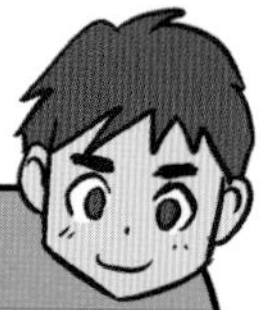

ACCOMPANIMENT

CHINESE GREENS

PUT 10 OZ SHREDDED CHINESE GREENS IN A SAUCEPAN OF BOILING WATER AND COOK FOR 1–2 MINUTES. DRAIN WELL AND PLACE ON WARMED SERVING PLATES.

HEAT 1 TSP GROUNDNUT OIL IN A SMALL SAUCEPAN OVER A LOW HEAT AND COOK ½ TSP FINELY CHOPPED GARLIC FOR 1 MINUTE UNTIL SOFTENED. STIR IN 1 TSP OYSTER SAUCE, 1 TBSP WATER, AND ½ TBSP SESAME OIL, THEN BRING TO THE BOIL. POUR OVER THE GREENS.

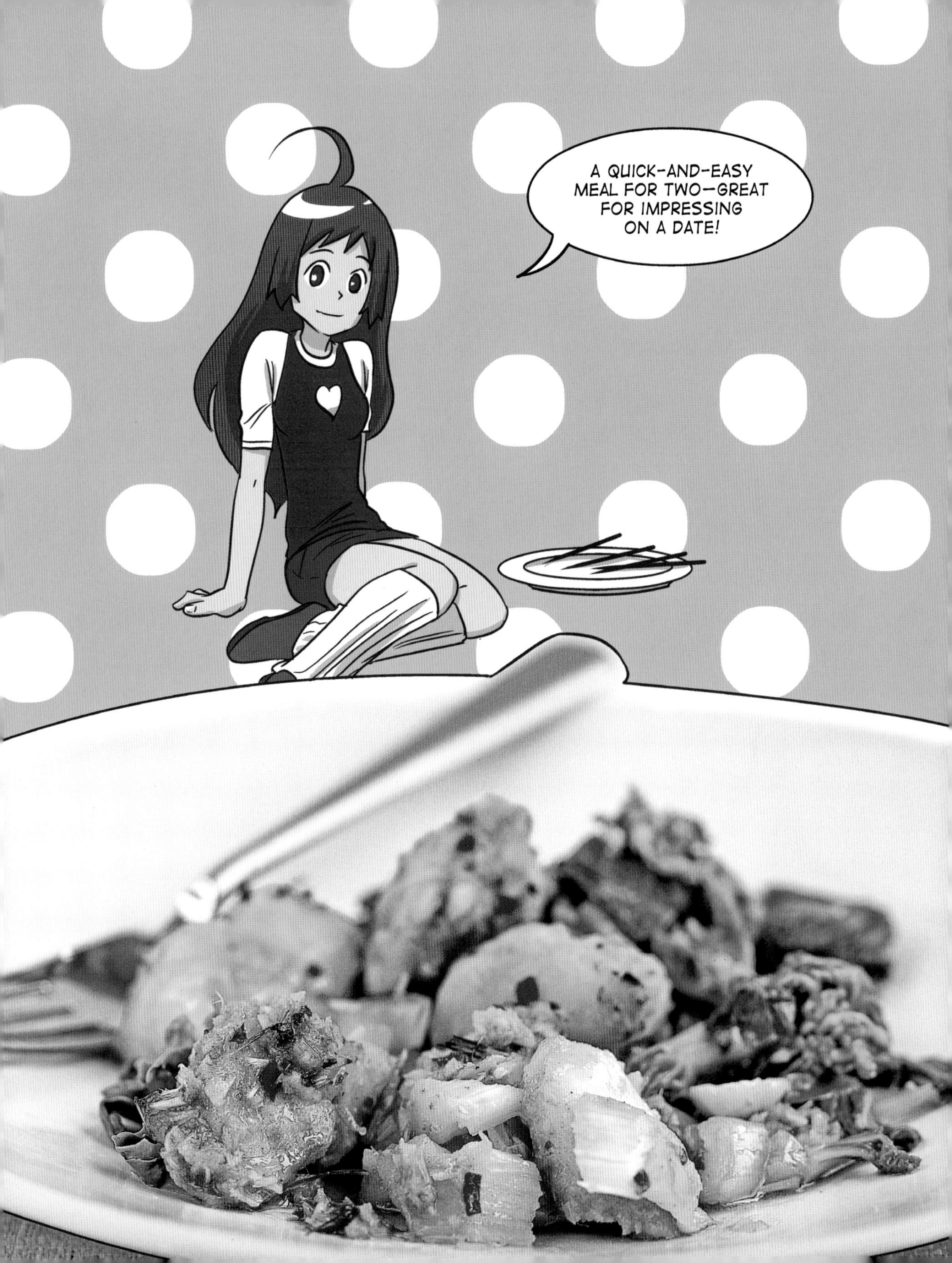
A QUICK-AND-EASY MEAL FOR TWO—GREAT FOR IMPRESSING ON A DATE!

CREAMY GARLIC MUSSELS
MUSSELS ARE REALLY QUICK AND EASY TO
PREPARE BUT LOOK VERY IMPRESSIVE!

3 LB FRESH, LIVE MUSSELS
1 TBSP BUTTER
1 ONION, FINELY CHOPPED
6 GARLIC CLOVES, FINELY CHOPPED
3½ FL OZ WHITE WINE
¼ PINT SINGLE CREAM
LARGE HANDFUL OF PARSLEY,
  COARSELY CHOPPED
SALT AND BLACK PEPPER
CRUSTY BREAD, TO SERVE

SERVES 4 WARRIORS
PREP TIME: 15 MINUTES
COOKING TIME: ABOUT 10 MINUTES

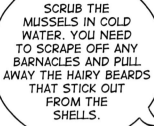

SCRUB THE MUSSELS IN COLD WATER. YOU NEED TO SCRAPE OFF ANY BARNACLES AND PULL AWAY THE HAIRY BEARDS THAT STICK OUT FROM THE SHELLS.

DISCARD ANY MUSSELS WITH **BROKEN SHELLS** OR ANY OPEN MUSSELS THAT DO NOT CLOSE WHEN TAPPED SHARPLY.

MELT THE BUTTER IN A LARGE SAUCEPAN.

ADD THE ONION AND GARLIC, AND COOK GENTLY FOR 7 MINUTES UNTIL THE ONION IS TRANSPARENT AND SOFTENED.

ONION NEEDS TO BE REALLY SOFT IF IT'S GOING TO BE PART OF A SAUCE.

INCREASE THE HEAT AND TIP THE MUSSELS, AND THE WINE INTO THE SAUCEPAN.

COVER THE SAUCEPAN AND COOK FOR 3 MINUTES OR UNTIL THE MUSSEL SHELLS HAVE OPENED.

MAKE SURE YOU THROW OUT ANY THAT STAY CLOSED—THAT MEANS THEY'RE NO GOOD.

I KNOW THAT.

JUST REMINDING YOU.

IT'S EASY BEING AN **ARMCHAIR CHEF**.

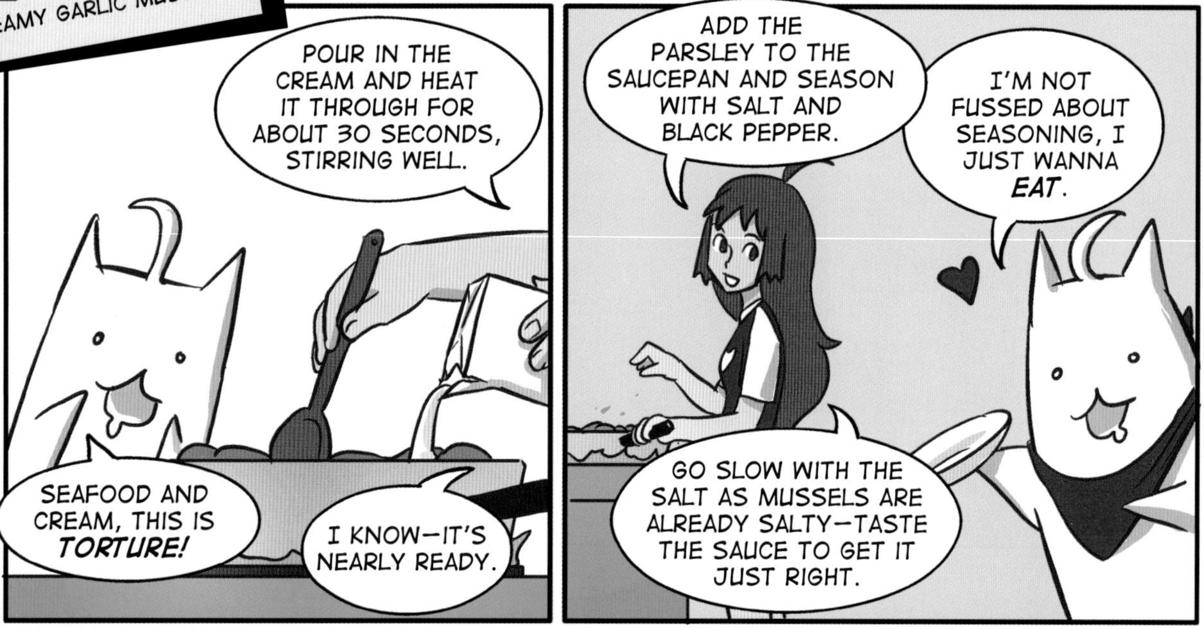
POUR IN THE CREAM AND HEAT IT THROUGH FOR ABOUT 30 SECONDS, STIRRING WELL.
SEAFOOD AND CREAM, THIS IS *TORTURE!*
I KNOW—IT'S NEARLY READY.
ADD THE PARSLEY TO THE SAUCEPAN AND SEASON WITH SALT AND BLACK PEPPER.
I'M NOT FUSSED ABOUT SEASONING, I JUST WANNA *EAT*.
GO SLOW WITH THE SALT AS MUSSELS ARE ALREADY SALTY—TASTE THE SAUCE TO GET IT JUST RIGHT.

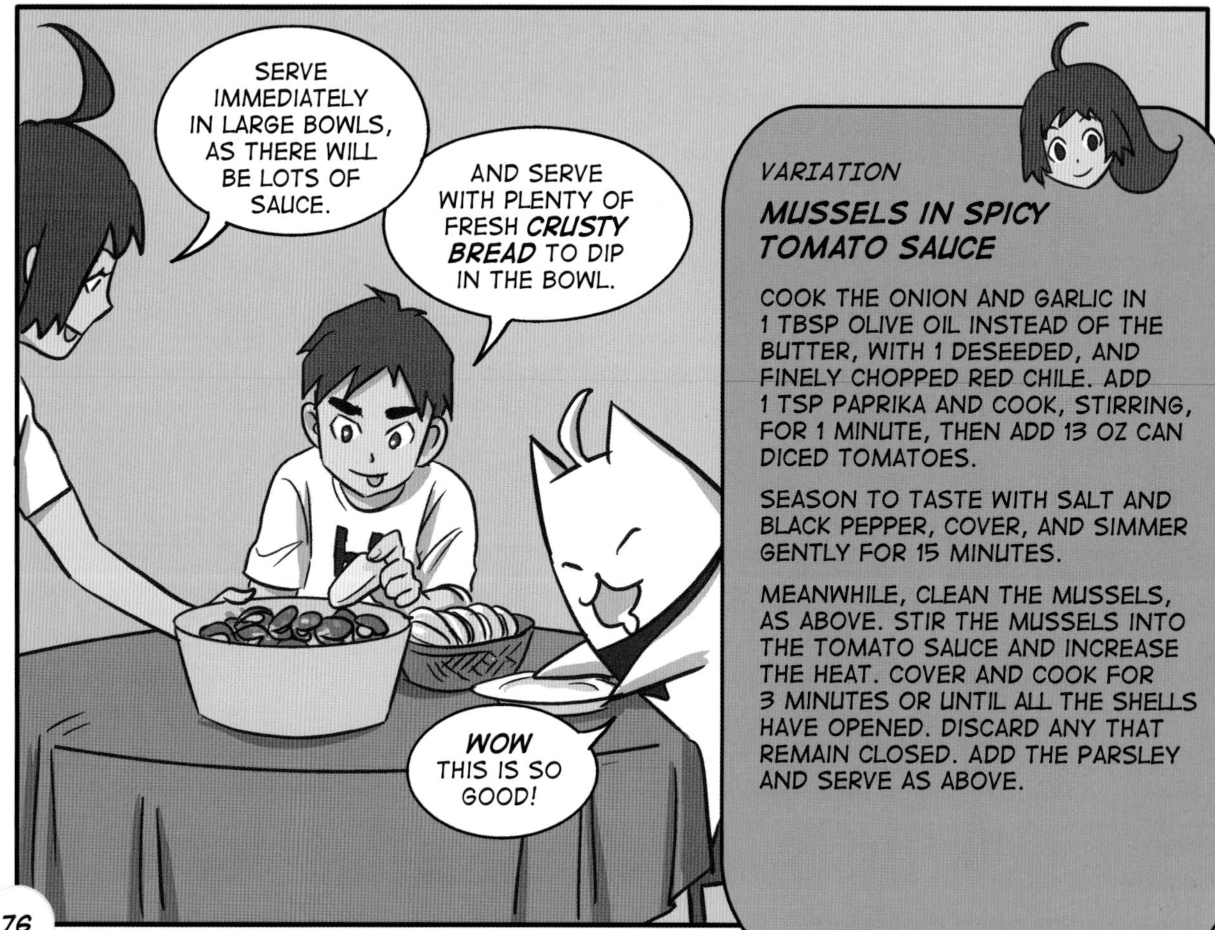
SERVE IMMEDIATELY IN LARGE BOWLS, AS THERE WILL BE LOTS OF SAUCE.
AND SERVE WITH PLENTY OF FRESH ***CRUSTY BREAD*** TO DIP IN THE BOWL.
WOW THIS IS SO GOOD!

VARIATION

MUSSELS IN SPICY TOMATO SAUCE

COOK THE ONION AND GARLIC IN 1 TBSP OLIVE OIL INSTEAD OF THE BUTTER, WITH 1 DESEEDED, AND FINELY CHOPPED RED CHILE. ADD 1 TSP PAPRIKA AND COOK, STIRRING, FOR 1 MINUTE, THEN ADD 13 OZ CAN DICED TOMATOES.

SEASON TO TASTE WITH SALT AND BLACK PEPPER, COVER, AND SIMMER GENTLY FOR 15 MINUTES.

MEANWHILE, CLEAN THE MUSSELS, AS ABOVE. STIR THE MUSSELS INTO THE TOMATO SAUCE AND INCREASE THE HEAT. COVER AND COOK FOR 3 MINUTES OR UNTIL ALL THE SHELLS HAVE OPENED. DISCARD ANY THAT REMAIN CLOSED. ADD THE PARSLEY AND SERVE AS ABOVE.

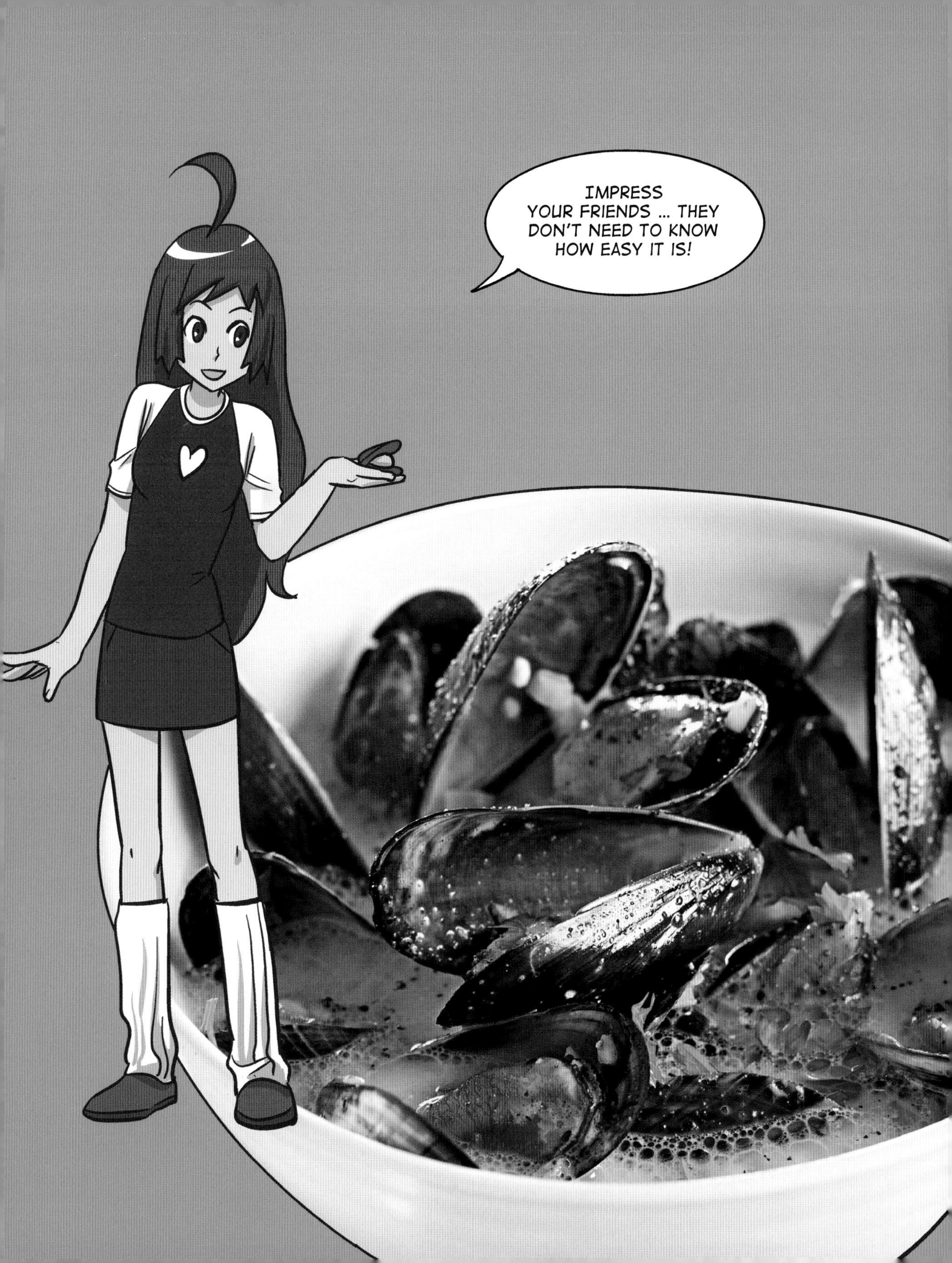
IMPRESS YOUR FRIENDS ... THEY DON'T NEED TO KNOW HOW EASY IT IS!

VEGETARIAN

BLACK-EYED BEAN & RED BELL PEPPER STEW
A HEARTY STEW THAT WILL IMPRESS MEAT EATERS TOO.

2 TBSP OLIVE OIL
4 SHALLOTS, FINELY CHOPPED
2 GARLIC CLOVES, FINELY CHOPPED
2 CELERY STICKS, DICED
1 LARGE CARROT, PEELED, AND CUT INTO 1/2 INCH PIECES
1 RED BELL PEPPER, CORED, DESEEDED, AND CUT
   INTO ½ INCH PIECES
1 TSP DRIED MIXED HERBS
2 TSP GROUND CUMIN
1 TSP GROUND CINNAMON
2 X 13 OZ CANS TOMATOES
2 TBSP SUN-DRIED TOMATO PASTE
3 FL OZ VEGETABLE STOCK
2 X 13 OZ CANS BLACK-EYED BEANS
   IN WATER, RINSED, AND DRAINED
SALT AND BLACK PEPPER
4 TBSP FINELY CHOPPED CORIANDER LEAVES,
   TO GARNISH
BOILED BASMATI RICE, TO SERVE

SERVES 4 WARRIORS
PREP TIME: 20 MINUTES
COOKING TIME: 15-20 MINUTES

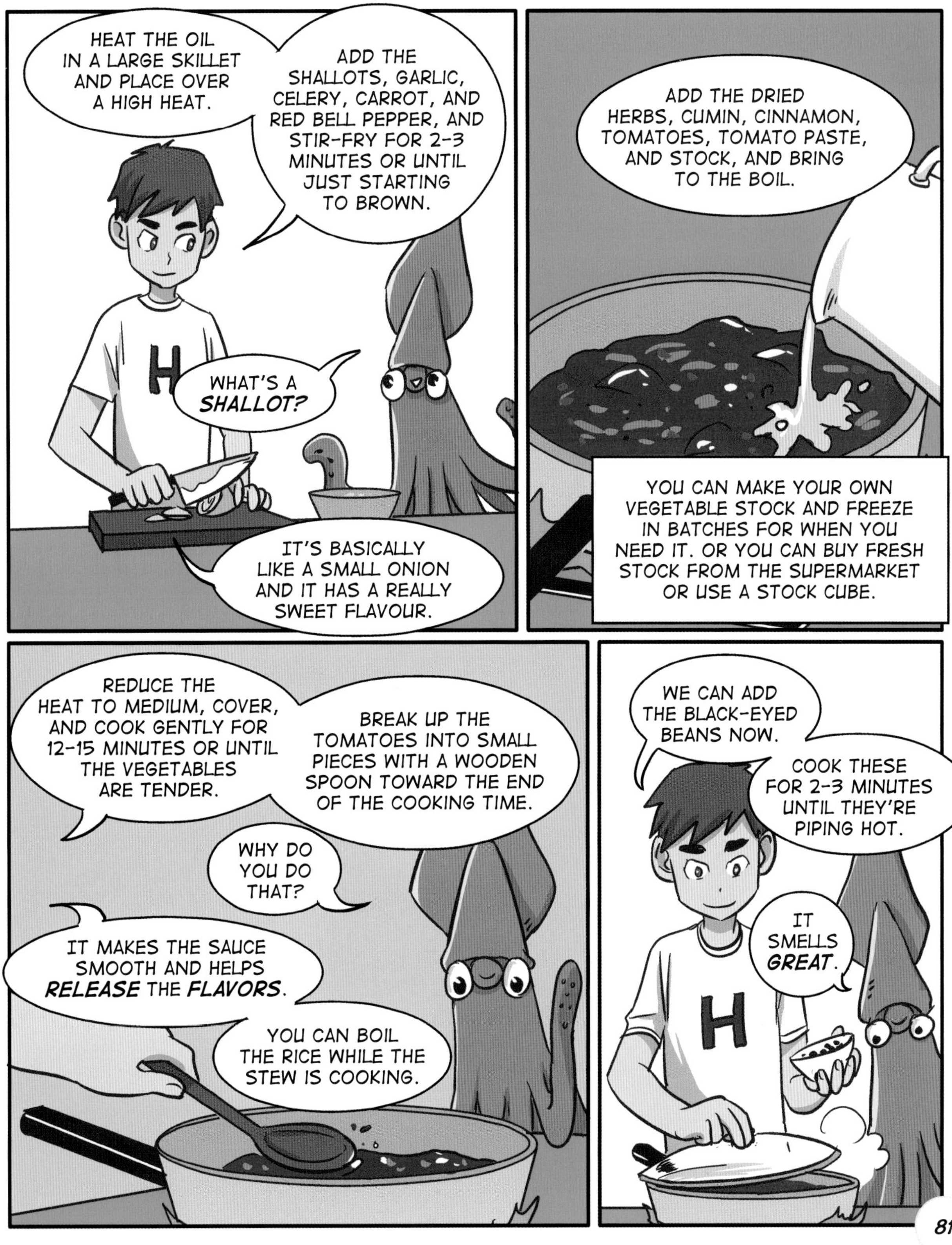
HEAT THE OIL IN A LARGE SKILLET AND PLACE OVER A HIGH HEAT.
ADD THE SHALLOTS, GARLIC, CELERY, CARROT, AND RED BELL PEPPER, AND STIR-FRY FOR 2-3 MINUTES OR UNTIL JUST STARTING TO BROWN.
WHAT'S A *SHALLOT?*
IT'S BASICALLY LIKE A SMALL ONION AND IT HAS A REALLY SWEET FLAVOUR.
ADD THE DRIED HERBS, CUMIN, CINNAMON, TOMATOES, TOMATO PASTE, AND STOCK, AND BRING TO THE BOIL.
YOU CAN MAKE YOUR OWN VEGETABLE STOCK AND FREEZE IN BATCHES FOR WHEN YOU NEED IT. OR YOU CAN BUY FRESH STOCK FROM THE SUPERMARKET OR USE A STOCK CUBE.
REDUCE THE HEAT TO MEDIUM, COVER, AND COOK GENTLY FOR 12-15 MINUTES OR UNTIL THE VEGETABLES ARE TENDER.
BREAK UP THE TOMATOES INTO SMALL PIECES WITH A WOODEN SPOON TOWARD THE END OF THE COOKING TIME.
WHY DO YOU DO THAT?
IT MAKES THE SAUCE SMOOTH AND HELPS ***RELEASE*** THE ***FLAVORS***.
YOU CAN BOIL THE RICE WHILE THE STEW IS COOKING.
WE CAN ADD THE BLACK-EYED BEANS NOW.
COOK THESE FOR 2-3 MINUTES UNTIL THEY'RE PIPING HOT.
IT SMELLS ***GREAT***.

BLACK-EYED BEAN & RED BELL PEPPER STEW

SEASON WELL WITH SALT AND BLACK PEPPER THEN REMOVE THE SKILLET FROM THE HEAT AND SPRINKLE OVER THE CHOPPED CORIANDER.

CORIANDER ADDS *COLOR* AS WELL AS FLAVOR.

I LOVE THIS MEAL.

PUT THE POT OF STEW AND THE RICE ON THE TABLE AND DINNER IS SERVED.

LET'S EAT!

VARIATION

COLORFUL BLACK-EYED BEAN & VEGETABLE SALAD

FINELY CHOP 2 CARROTS, 2 CELERY STICKS, 1 RED BELL PEPPER, 2 TOMATOES, AND 2 SHALLOTS, AND PLACE IN A BOWL WITH 4 TBSP OLIVE OIL AND THE JUICE OF 2 LIMES. SEASON AND ADD A 13 OZ CAN BLACK-EYED BEANS, RINSED AND DRAINED, AND A LARGE HANDFUL OF CHOPPED CORIANDER AND MINT LEAVES. TOSS TO MIX WELL AND SERVE WITH WARM FLATBREADS.

VARIATION

HEARTY BEAN & VEGETABLE BROTH

PLACE 1 FINELY DICED CARROT, 2 FINELY DICED CELERY STICKS, 2 FINELY DICED SHALLOTS, 2 FINELY CHOPPED GARLIC CLOVES, 2 TBSP SUN-DRIED TOMATO PASTE, AND 2 TSP DRIED MIXED HERBS IN A HEAVY-BASED SAUCEPAN WITH 1¾ PINTS HOT VEGETABLE STOCK AND BRING TO THE BOIL.

COOK, UNCOVERED, OVER A MEDIUM HEAT FOR 10-12 MINUTES. STIR IN 2 X 13 OZ CANS BLACK-EYED BEANS, RINSED, AND DRAINED, AND BRING BACK TO THE BOIL. SEASON, REMOVE FROM THE HEAT, AND SERVE WITH CRUSTY BREAD.

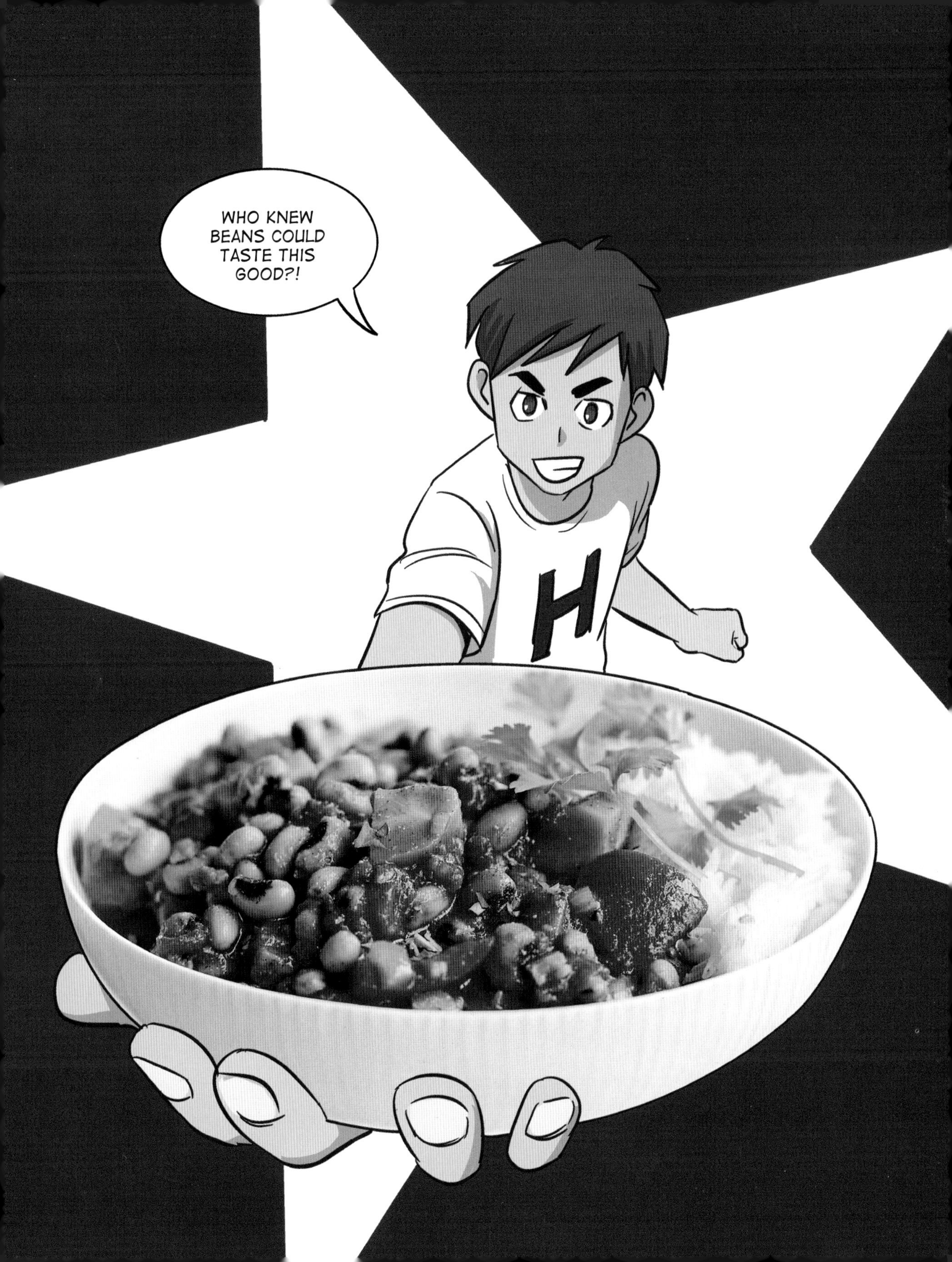
WHO KNEW BEANS COULD TASTE THIS GOOD?!

HEARTY MINESTRONE

THIS IS NO ORDINARY SOUP—IT'S A MEAL IN A BOWL!

- 3 CARROTS, COARSELY CHOPPED
- 1 RED ONION, COARSELY CHOPPED
- 6 CELERY STICKS, COARSELY CHOPPED
- 2 TBSP OLIVE OIL
- 2 GARLIC CLOVES, FINELY CHOPPED
- 7 OZ POTATOES, PEELED, AND CUT INTO ½-INCH DICE
- 4 TBSP TOMATO PASTE
- 2½ PINTS VEGETABLE STOCK
- 13 OZ CAN DICED TOMATOES
- 5 OZ SMALL SOUP PASTA
- 13 OZ CAN CANNELLINI BEANS, RINSED, AND DRAINED
- 3½ OZ BABY SPINACH
- SALT AND BLACK PEPPER
- CRUSTY BREAD, TO SERVE

SERVES 4 WARRIORS
PREP TIME: 15 MINUTES
COOKING TIME: 15–20 MINUTES

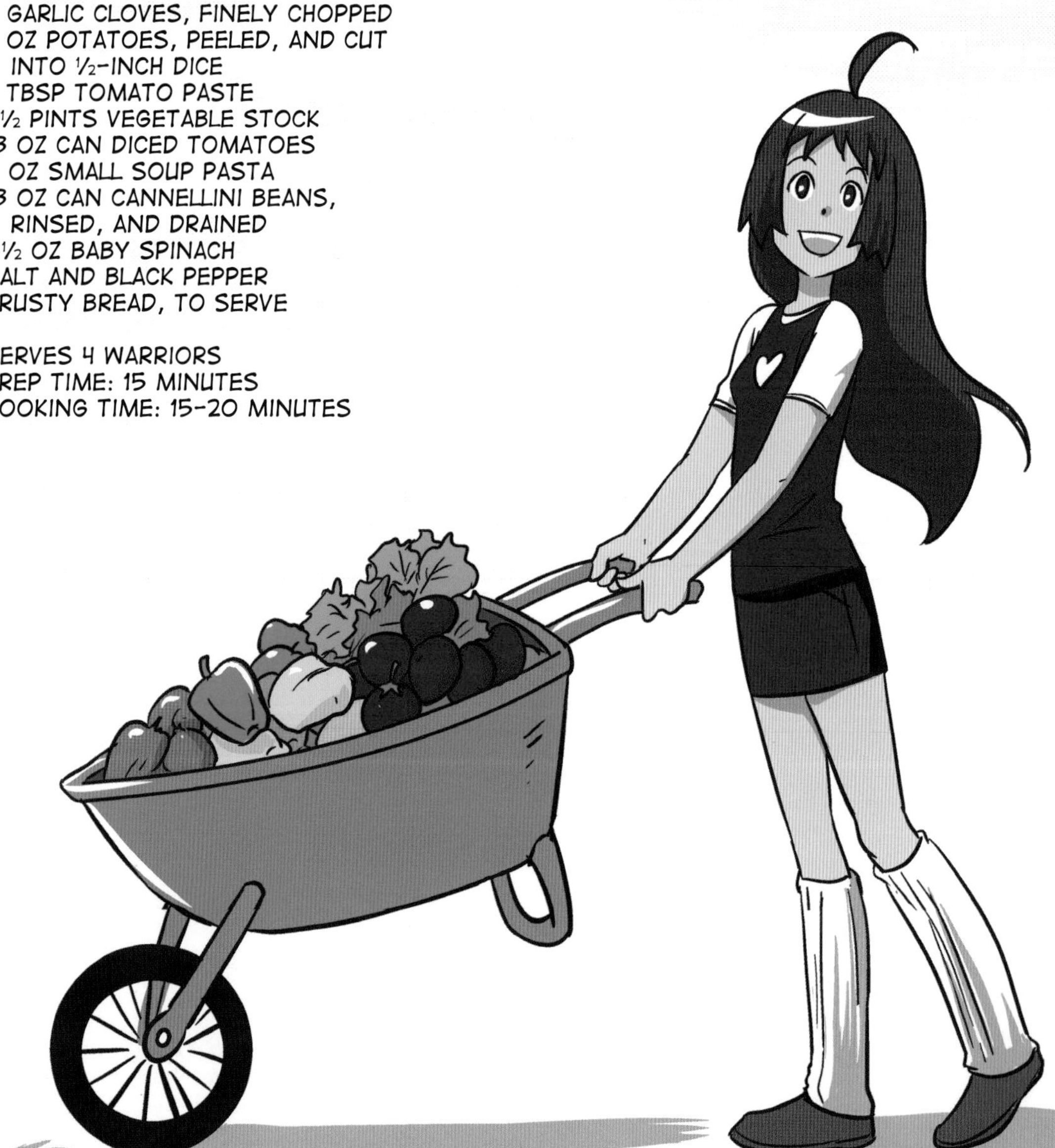

WHIZZ THE CARROTS, ONION, AND CELERY IN A FOOD PROCESSOR UNTIL FINELY CHOPPED.

AS WITH OTHER RECIPES, IF YOU DON'T HAVE A FOOD PROCESSOR YOU CAN VERY FINELY CHOP ALL THE VEGETABLES WITH A SHARP KNIFE.

EXACTLY—IT'S A CHUNKY SOUP SO THAT'S FINE.

HEAT THE OIL IN A LARGE SAUCEPAN, ADD THE CHOPPED VEGETABLES, GARLIC, POTATOES, TOMATO PASTE, STOCK, TOMATOES, AND PASTA TO THE SAUCEPAN.

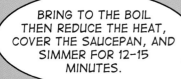

BRING TO THE BOIL THEN REDUCE THE HEAT, COVER THE SAUCEPAN, AND SIMMER FOR 12–15 MINUTES.

WHEN YOU COOK ALL THE VEGETABLES TOGETHER LIKE THIS IT PRESERVES THE NUTRIENTS SO THIS IS A HEALTHY MEAL.

ADD THE CANNELLINI BEANS AND THE SPINACH FOR THE FINAL 2 MINUTES OF COOKING TIME.

LOOKS LIKE I WOKE UP JUST IN TIME.

YOU'RE VERY GOOD AT DOING THAT!

SEASON TO TASTE WITH SALT AND BLACK PEPPER.

ADD A LITTLE AT A TIME AND TASTE AS YOU GO UNTIL YOU GET IT JUST HOW YOU WANT IT.

YOU TOOK YOUR TIME, WE'RE READY TO EAT.

SORRY, THERE WAS A QUEUE.

AND YOU HAVE TO HAVE **BREAD** WITH SOUP.

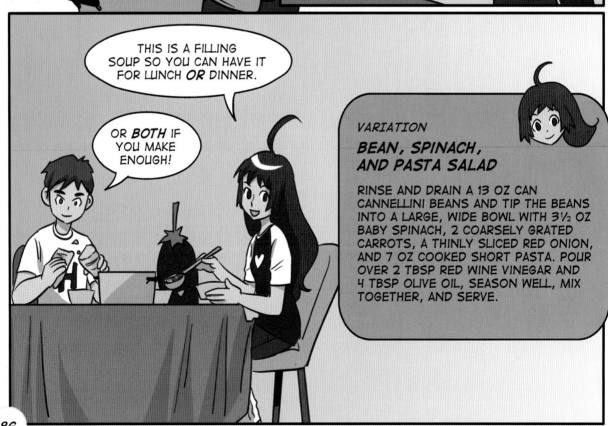

THIS IS A FILLING SOUP SO YOU CAN HAVE IT FOR LUNCH *OR* DINNER.

OR *BOTH* IF YOU MAKE ENOUGH!

VARIATION

BEAN, SPINACH, AND PASTA SALAD

RINSE AND DRAIN A 13 OZ CAN CANNELLINI BEANS AND TIP THE BEANS INTO A LARGE, WIDE BOWL WITH 3½ OZ BABY SPINACH, 2 COARSELY GRATED CARROTS, A THINLY SLICED RED ONION, AND 7 OZ COOKED SHORT PASTA. POUR OVER 2 TBSP RED WINE VINEGAR AND 4 TBSP OLIVE OIL, SEASON WELL, MIX TOGETHER, AND SERVE.

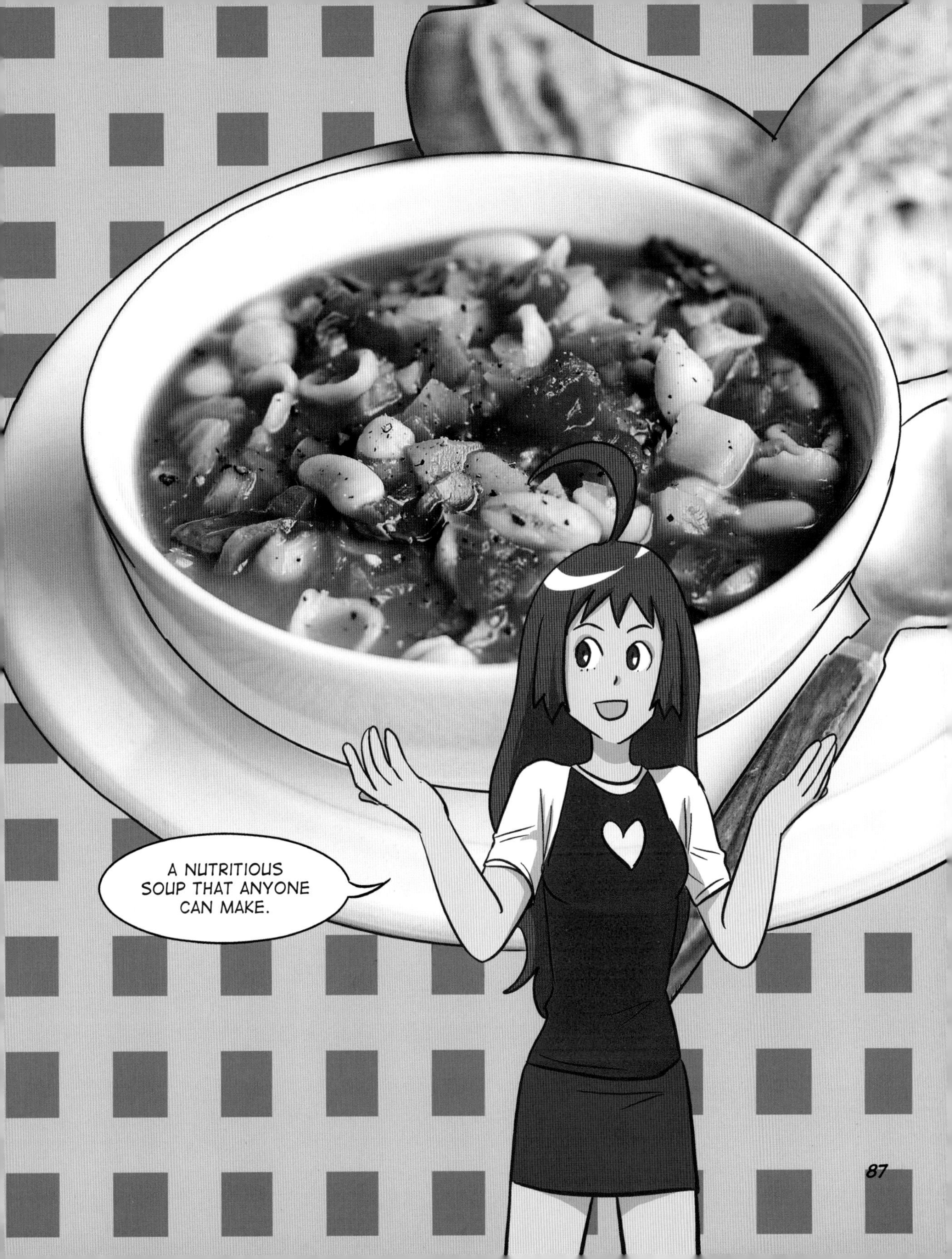
A NUTRITIOUS SOUP THAT ANYONE CAN MAKE.

CHUNKY PASTA SAUCE

THIS IS A CLASSIC SAUCE THAT YOU CAN ADAPT
TO USE WITH LOTS OF DIFFERENT DISHES.

2 TBSP OLIVE OIL
2 GARLIC CLOVES, CHOPPED
1 RED ONION, CHOPPED
2 CELERY STICKS, CHOPPED
1 CARROT, CHOPPED
13 OZ CAN DICED TOMATOES
12 OZ DRIED PENNE PASTA
3½ OZ BABY SPINACH
7 OZ DRAINED CANNED BORLOTTI
   OR KIDNEY BEANS
GRATED PARMESAN CHEESE, TO SERVE

SERVES 4 WARRIORS
PREP TIME: 15 MINUTES
COOKING TIME: 15-20 MINUTES

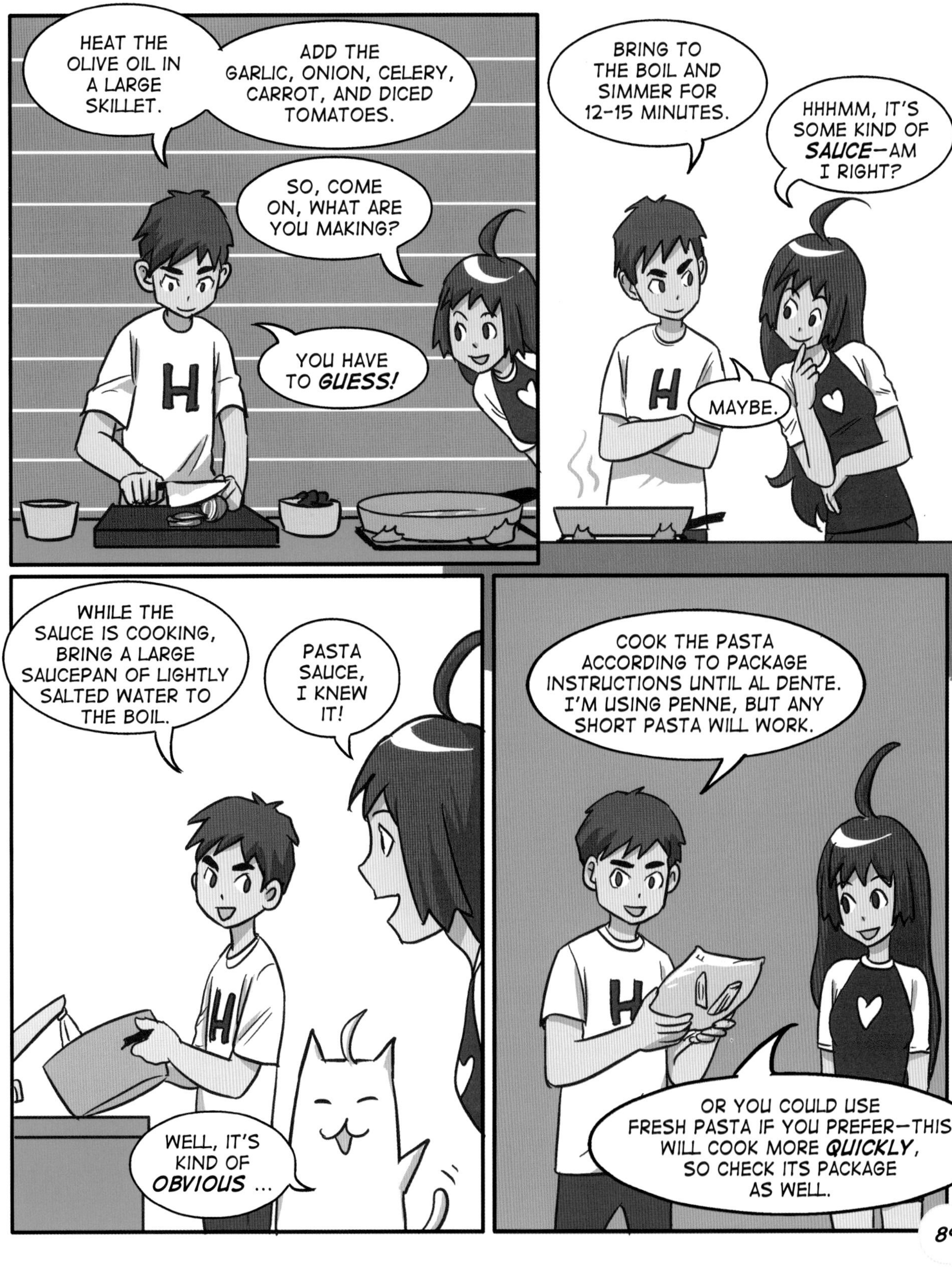
HEAT THE OLIVE OIL IN A LARGE SKILLET.
ADD THE GARLIC, ONION, CELERY, CARROT, AND DICED TOMATOES.
SO, COME ON, WHAT ARE YOU MAKING?
YOU HAVE TO **GUESS!**
BRING TO THE BOIL AND SIMMER FOR 12–15 MINUTES.
HHHMM, IT'S SOME KIND OF **SAUCE**—AM I RIGHT?
MAYBE.
WHILE THE SAUCE IS COOKING, BRING A LARGE SAUCEPAN OF LIGHTLY SALTED WATER TO THE BOIL.
PASTA SAUCE, I KNEW IT!
WELL, IT'S KIND OF **OBVIOUS** ...
COOK THE PASTA ACCORDING TO PACKAGE INSTRUCTIONS UNTIL AL DENTE. I'M USING PENNE, BUT ANY SHORT PASTA WILL WORK.
OR YOU COULD USE FRESH PASTA IF YOU PREFER—THIS WILL COOK MORE **QUICKLY**, SO CHECK ITS PACKAGE AS WELL.

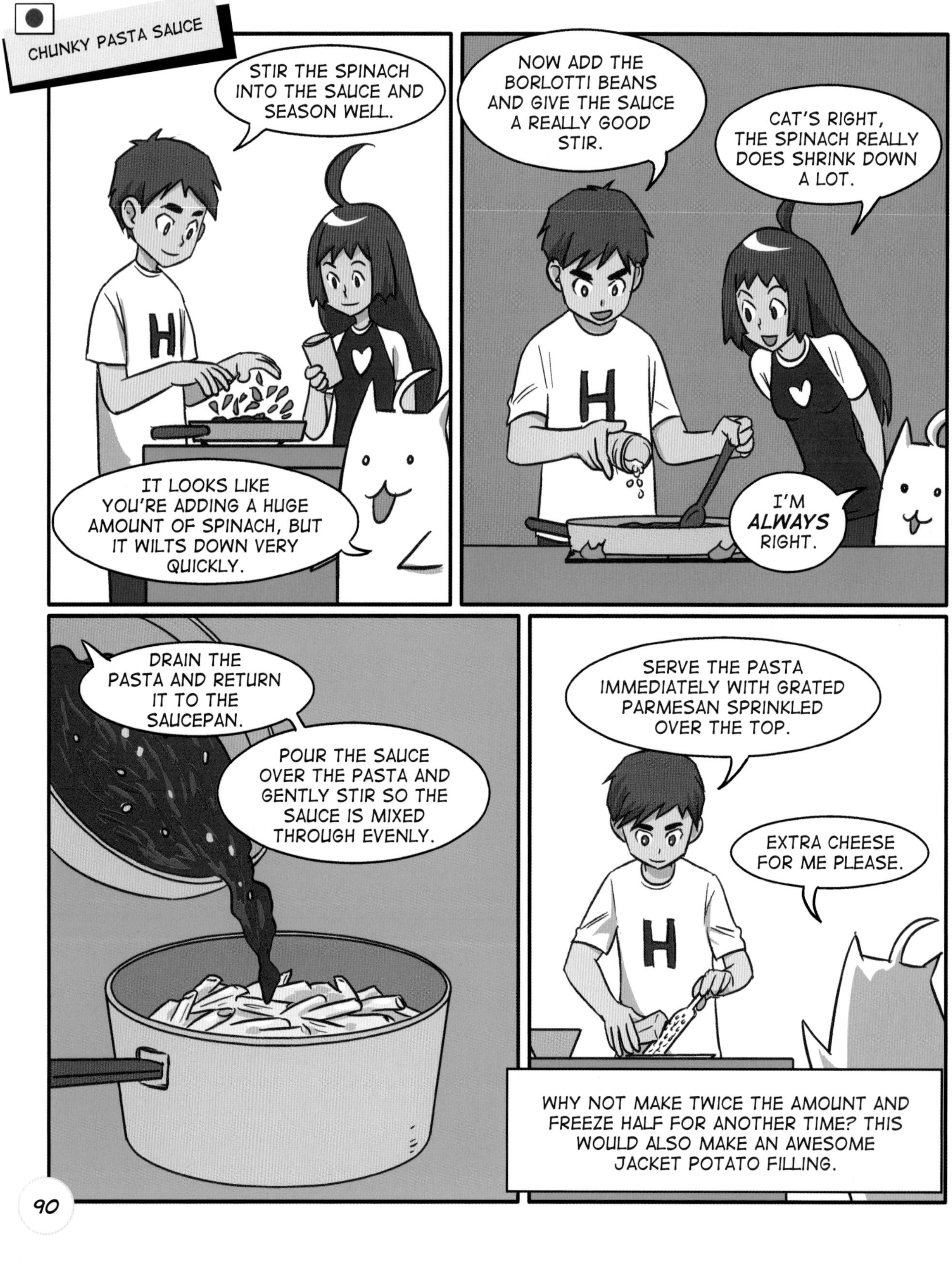
CHUNKY PASTA SAUCE
STIR THE SPINACH INTO THE SAUCE AND SEASON WELL.
IT LOOKS LIKE YOU'RE ADDING A HUGE AMOUNT OF SPINACH, BUT IT WILTS DOWN VERY QUICKLY.
NOW ADD THE BORLOTTI BEANS AND GIVE THE SAUCE A REALLY GOOD STIR.
CAT'S RIGHT, THE SPINACH REALLY DOES SHRINK DOWN A LOT.
I'M *ALWAYS* RIGHT.
DRAIN THE PASTA AND RETURN IT TO THE SAUCEPAN.
POUR THE SAUCE OVER THE PASTA AND GENTLY STIR SO THE SAUCE IS MIXED THROUGH EVENLY.
SERVE THE PASTA IMMEDIATELY WITH GRATED PARMESAN SPRINKLED OVER THE TOP.
EXTRA CHEESE FOR ME PLEASE.
WHY NOT MAKE TWICE THE AMOUNT AND FREEZE HALF FOR ANOTHER TIME? THIS WOULD ALSO MAKE AN AWESOME JACKET POTATO FILLING.

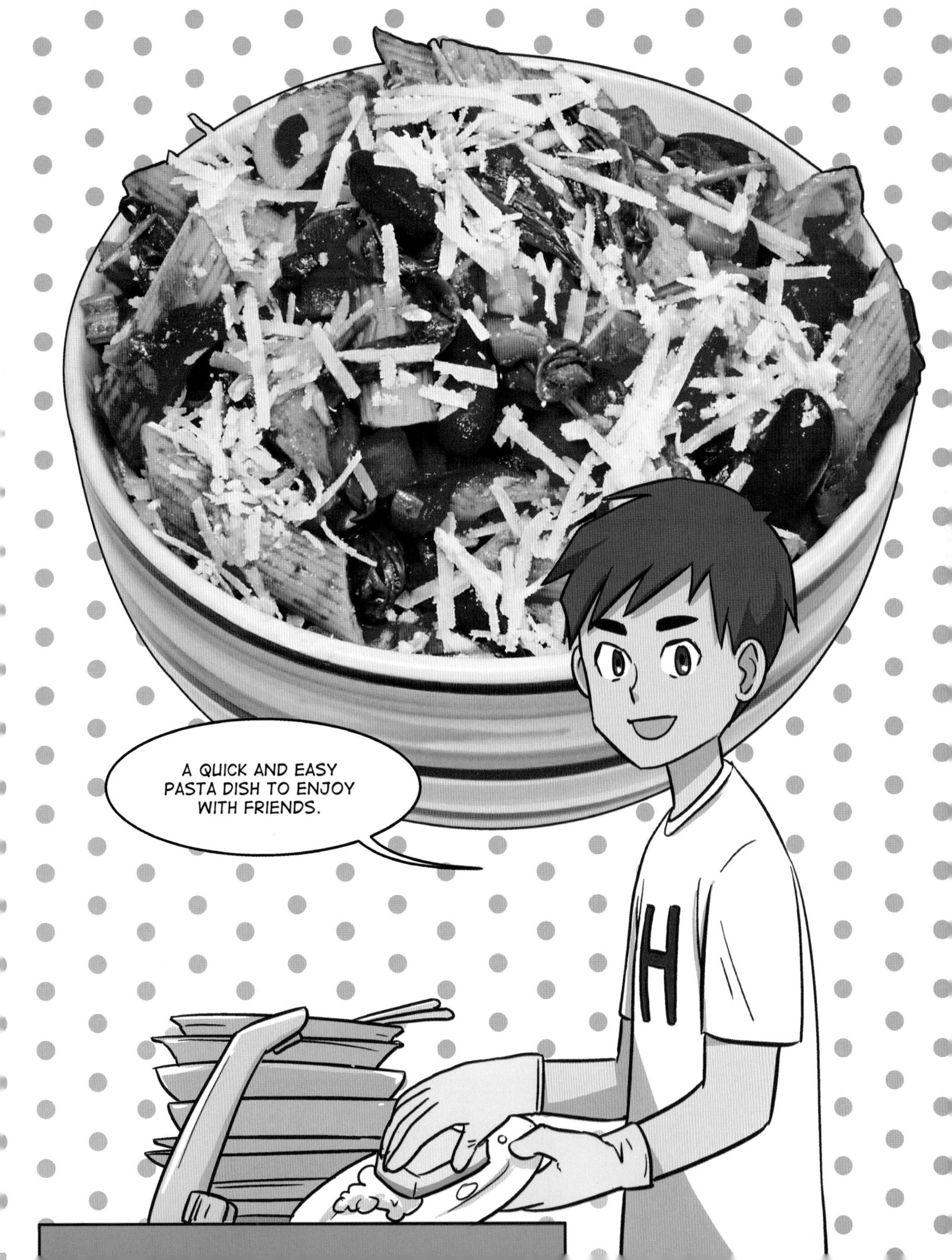
A QUICK AND EASY PASTA DISH TO ENJOY WITH FRIENDS.

QUICK ONE-POT RATATOUILLE

ENJOY THIS MEDLEY OF MEDITERRANEAN VEGETABLES.

3½ FL OZ OLIVE OIL
2 ONIONS, CHOPPED
1 EGG PLANT, CUT INTO BITE-SIZED PIECES
2 LARGE ZUCCHINI, CUT INTO BITE-SIZED PIECES
1 RED BELL PEPPER, CORED, DESEEDED, AND CUT INTO BITE-SIZED PIECES
1 YELLOW BELL PEPPER, CORED, DESEEDED, AND CUT INTO BITE-SIZED PIECES
2 GARLIC CLOVES, FINELY CHOPPED
13 OZ CAN DICED TOMATOES
4 TBSP CHOPPED BASIL
SALT AND BLACK PEPPER

TO SERVE:
CRUSTY BREAD
SALAD

SERVES 4 WARRIORS
PREP TIME: 10 MINUTES
COOKING TIME: 25 MINUTES

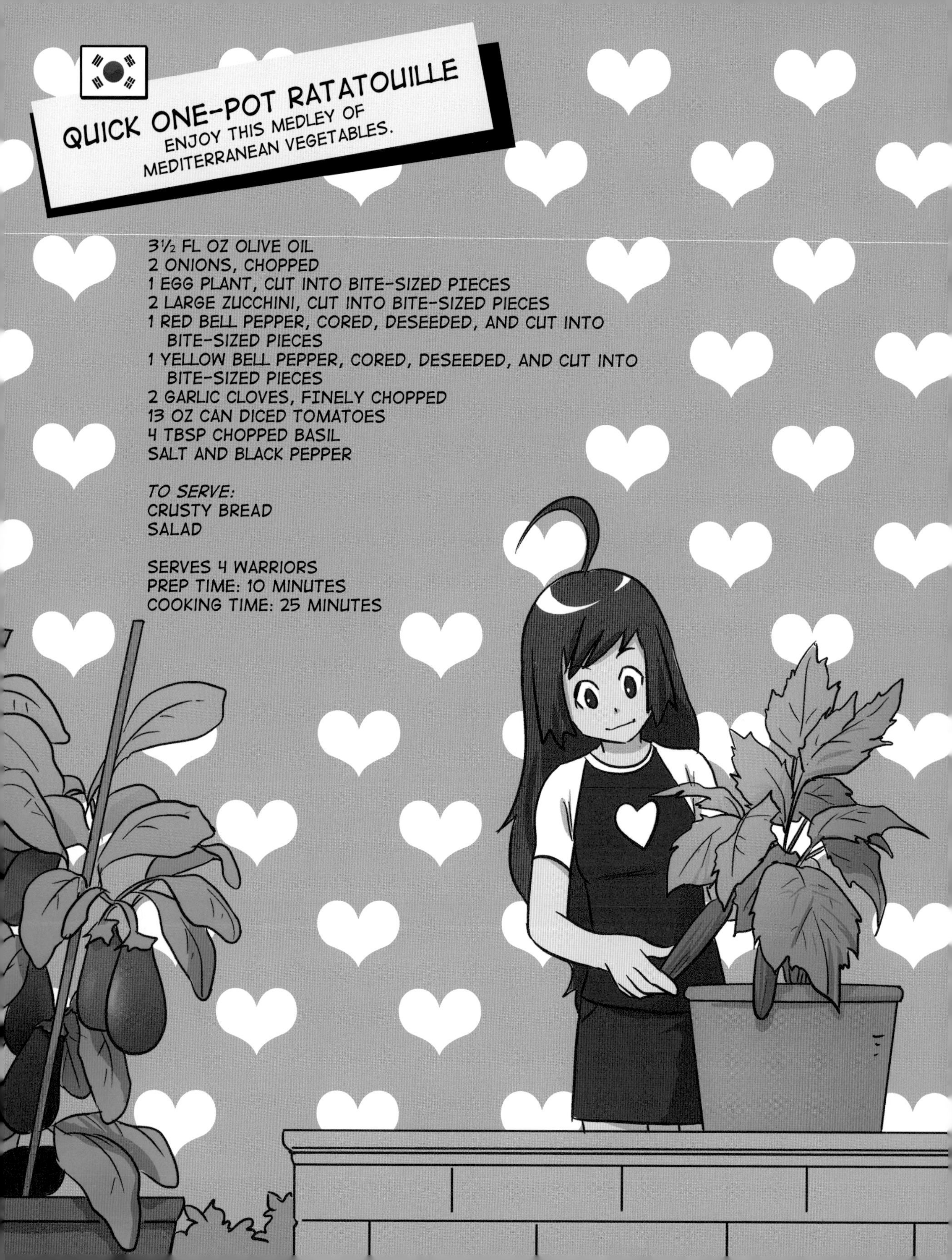

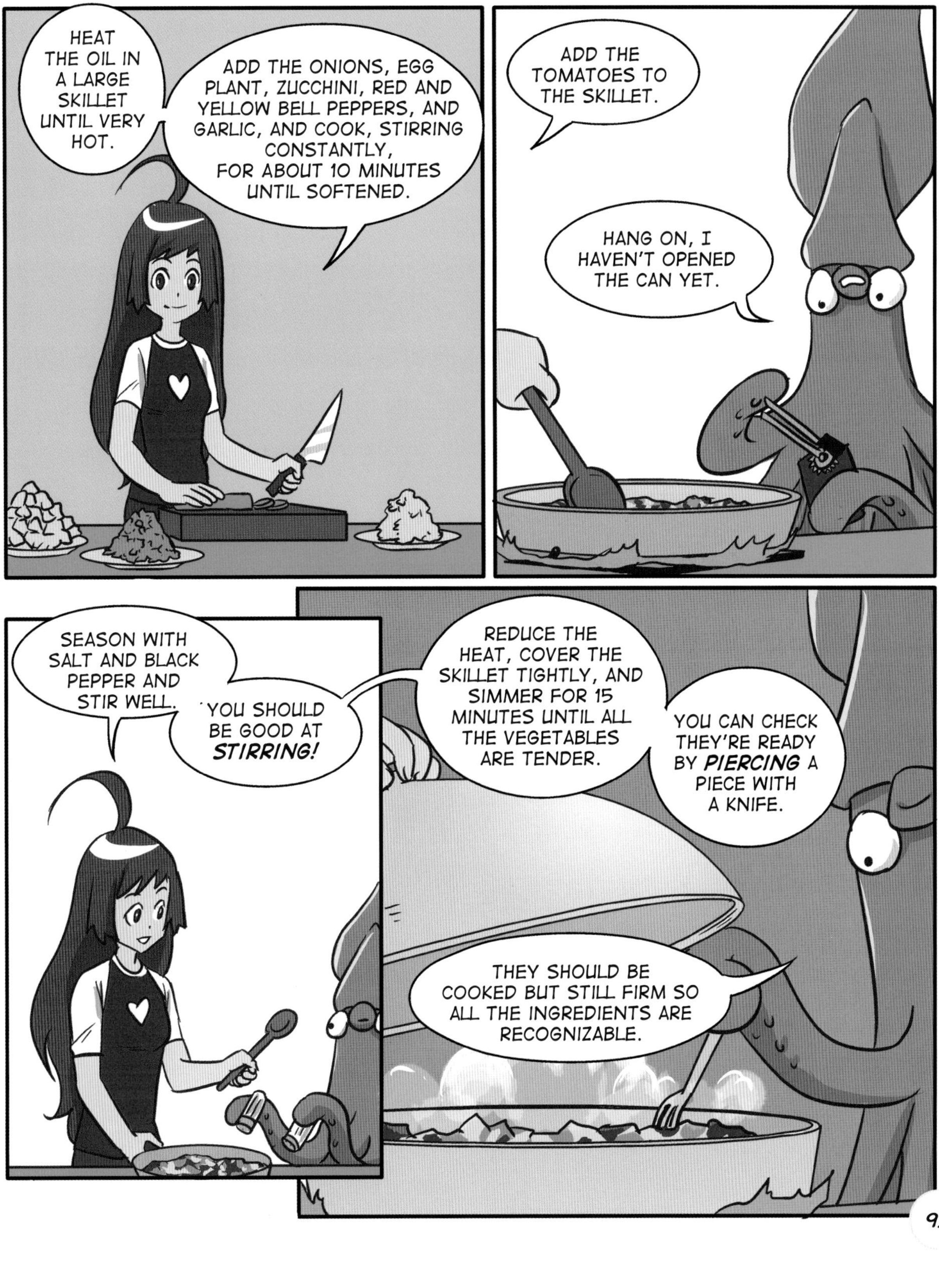
HEAT THE OIL IN A LARGE SKILLET UNTIL VERY HOT.
ADD THE ONIONS, EGG PLANT, ZUCCHINI, RED AND YELLOW BELL PEPPERS, AND GARLIC, AND COOK, STIRRING CONSTANTLY, FOR ABOUT 10 MINUTES UNTIL SOFTENED.
ADD THE TOMATOES TO THE SKILLET.
HANG ON, I HAVEN'T OPENED THE CAN YET.
SEASON WITH SALT AND BLACK PEPPER AND STIR WELL.
YOU SHOULD BE GOOD AT *STIRRING!*
REDUCE THE HEAT, COVER THE SKILLET TIGHTLY, AND SIMMER FOR 15 MINUTES UNTIL ALL THE VEGETABLES ARE TENDER.
YOU CAN CHECK THEY'RE READY BY *PIERCING* A PIECE WITH A KNIFE.
THEY SHOULD BE COOKED BUT STILL FIRM SO ALL THE INGREDIENTS ARE RECOGNIZABLE.

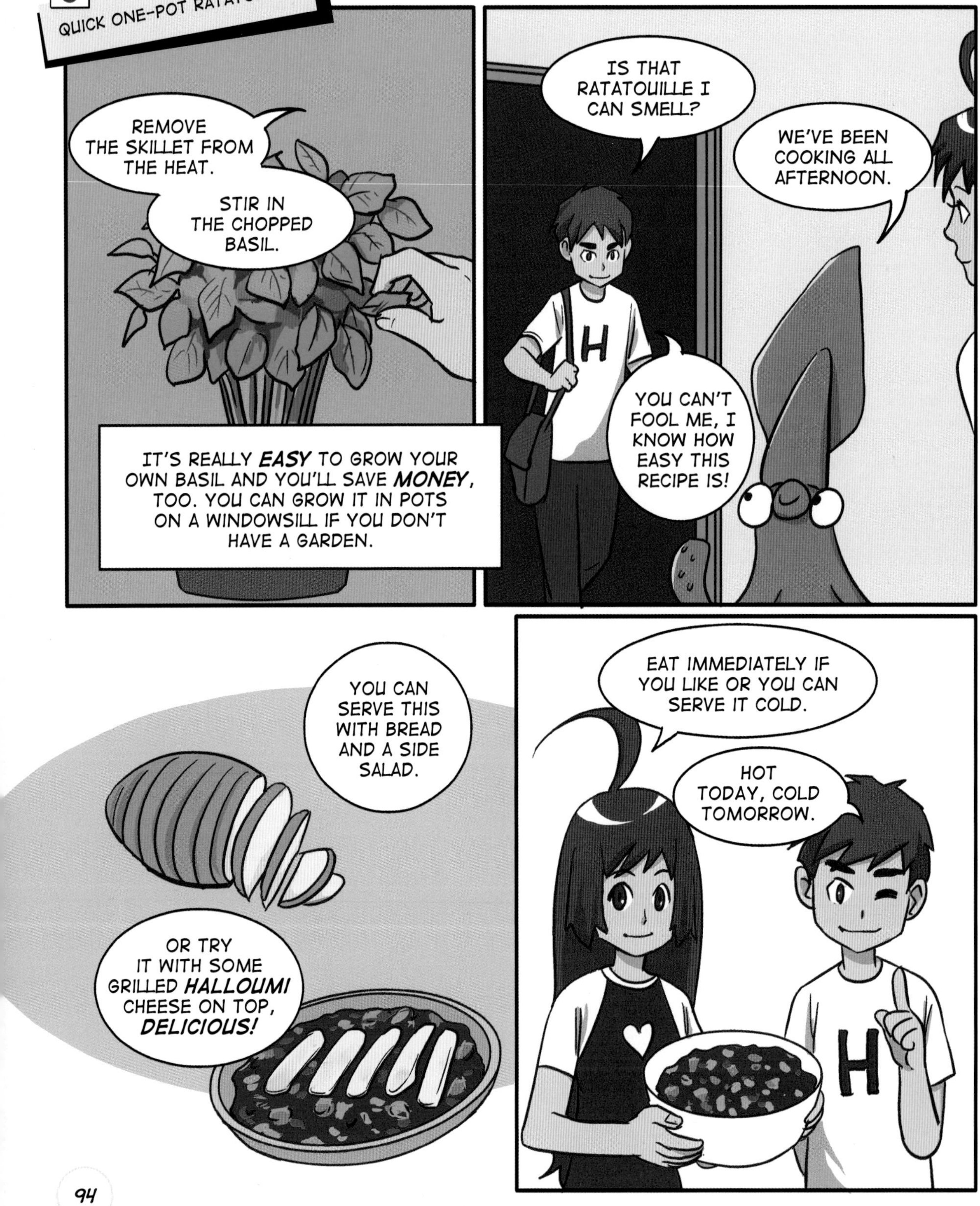
REMOVE THE SKILLET FROM THE HEAT.
STIR IN THE CHOPPED BASIL.
IT'S REALLY **EASY** TO GROW YOUR OWN BASIL AND YOU'LL SAVE **MONEY**, TOO. YOU CAN GROW IT IN POTS ON A WINDOWSILL IF YOU DON'T HAVE A GARDEN.
IS THAT RATATOUILLE I CAN SMELL?
WE'VE BEEN COOKING ALL AFTERNOON.
YOU CAN'T FOOL ME, I KNOW HOW EASY THIS RECIPE IS!
YOU CAN SERVE THIS WITH BREAD AND A SIDE SALAD.
OR TRY IT WITH SOME GRILLED **HALLOUMI** CHEESE ON TOP, **DELICIOUS!**
EAT IMMEDIATELY IF YOU LIKE OR YOU CAN SERVE IT COLD.
HOT TODAY, COLD TOMORROW.

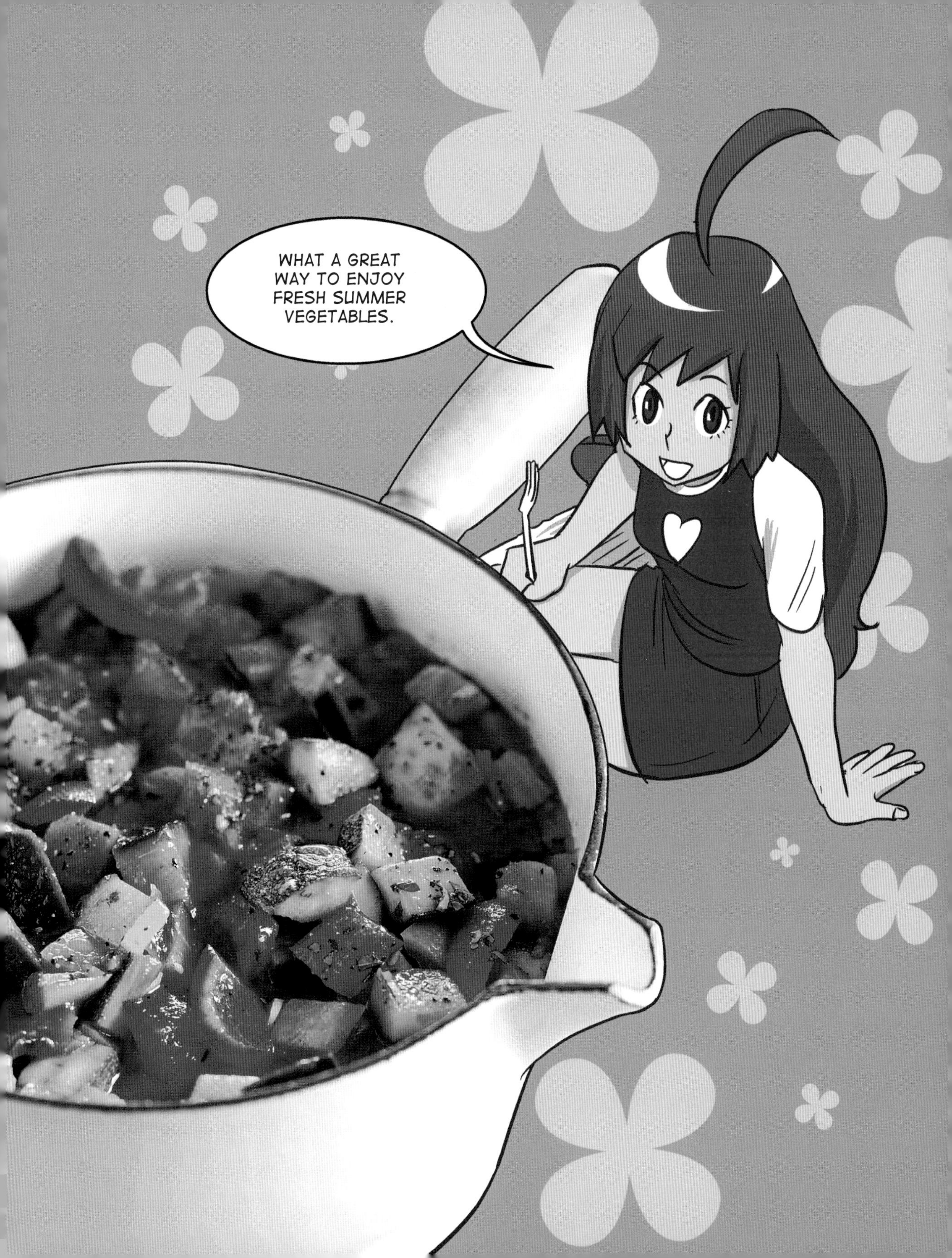
WHAT A GREAT WAY TO ENJOY FRESH SUMMER VEGETABLES.

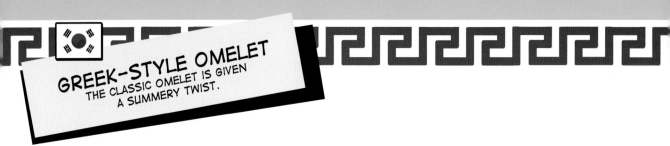

GREEK-STYLE OMELET

THE CLASSIC OMELET IS GIVEN A SUMMERY TWIST.

8 EXTRA-LARGE EGGS
1 TSP DRIED OREGANO
1 TBSP FINELY CHOPPED MINT
4 TBSP FINELY CHOPPED PARSLEY
2 TBSP OLIVE OIL
2 SMALL RED ONIONS, COARSELY CHOPPED
2 LARGE RIPE TOMATOES, COARSELY CHOPPED
½ ZUCCHINI, COARSELY CHOPPED
3½ OZ BLACK OLIVES, PITTED
3½ OZ FETA CHEESE
SALT AND BLACK PEPPER
BREAD OR GREEN SALAD, TO SERVE

SERVES 4 WARRIORS
PREP TIME: 15 MINUTES
COOKING TIME: 15–20 MINUTES

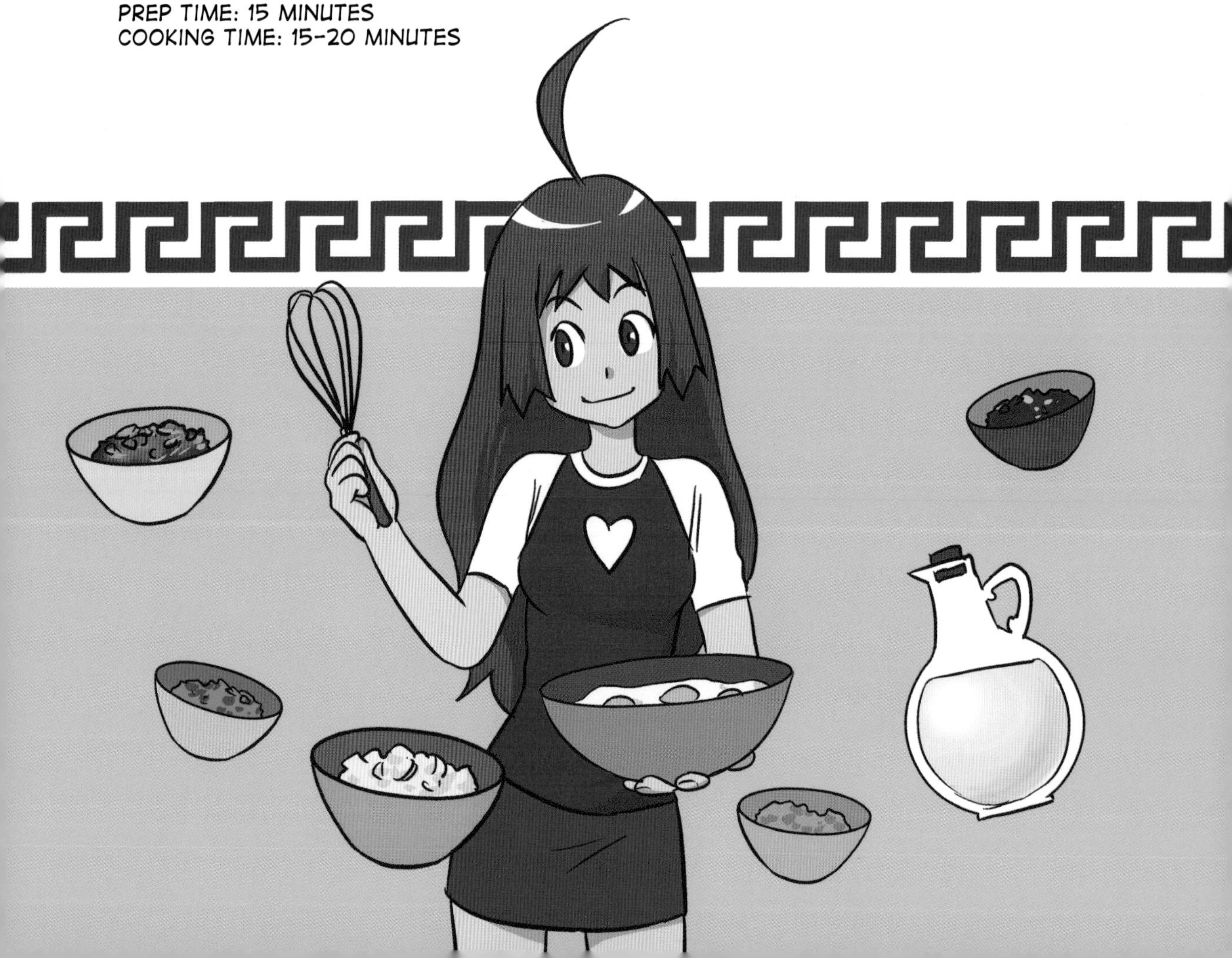

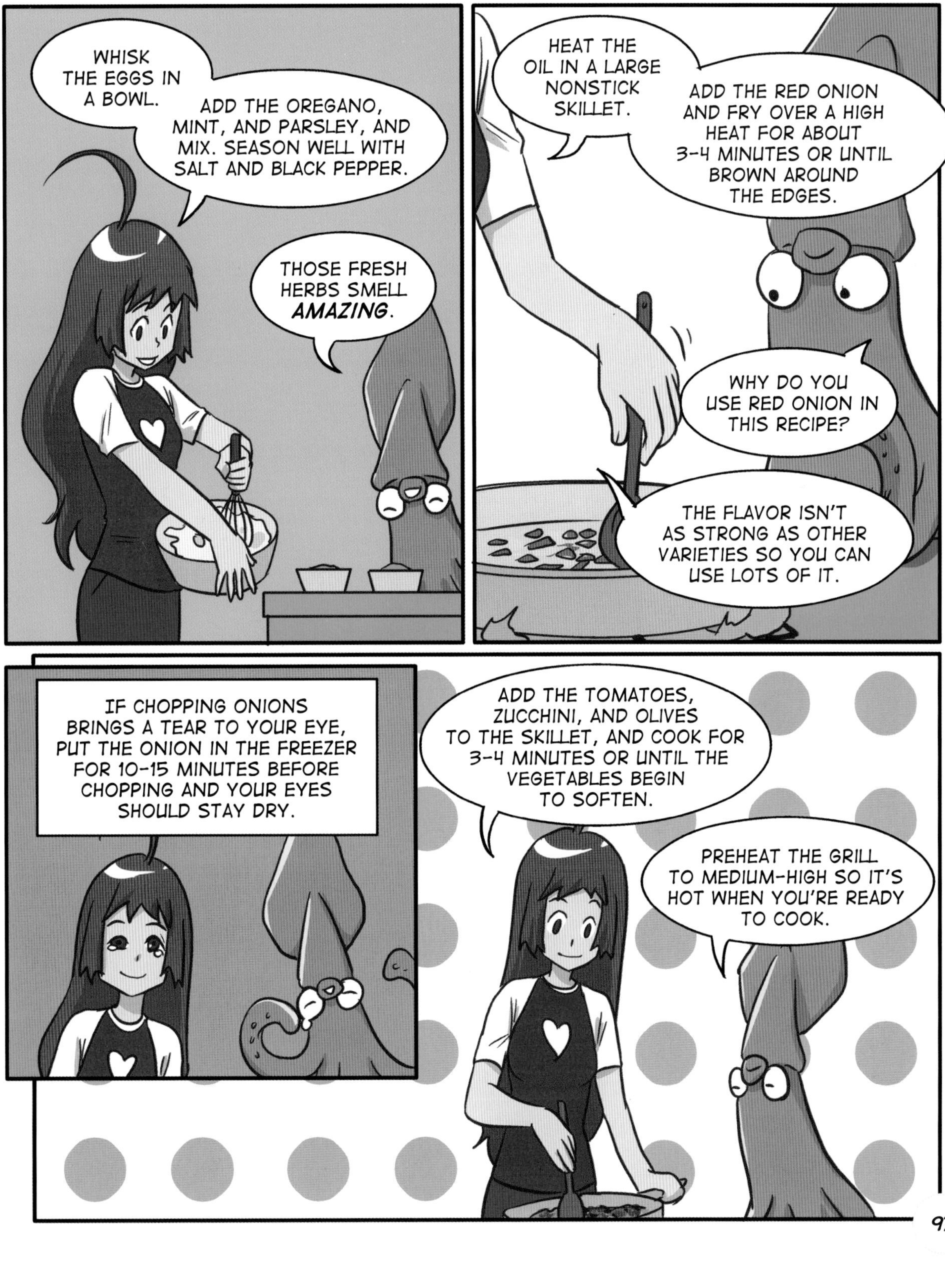
WHISK THE EGGS IN A BOWL.
ADD THE OREGANO, MINT, AND PARSLEY, AND MIX. SEASON WELL WITH SALT AND BLACK PEPPER.
THOSE FRESH HERBS SMELL ***AMAZING***.
HEAT THE OIL IN A LARGE NONSTICK SKILLET.
ADD THE RED ONION AND FRY OVER A HIGH HEAT FOR ABOUT 3-4 MINUTES OR UNTIL BROWN AROUND THE EDGES.
WHY DO YOU USE RED ONION IN THIS RECIPE?
THE FLAVOR ISN'T AS STRONG AS OTHER VARIETIES SO YOU CAN USE LOTS OF IT.
IF CHOPPING ONIONS BRINGS A TEAR TO YOUR EYE, PUT THE ONION IN THE FREEZER FOR 10-15 MINUTES BEFORE CHOPPING AND YOUR EYES SHOULD STAY DRY.
ADD THE TOMATOES, ZUCCHINI, AND OLIVES TO THE SKILLET, AND COOK FOR 3-4 MINUTES OR UNTIL THE VEGETABLES BEGIN TO SOFTEN.
PREHEAT THE GRILL TO MEDIUM-HIGH SO IT'S HOT WHEN YOU'RE READY TO COOK.

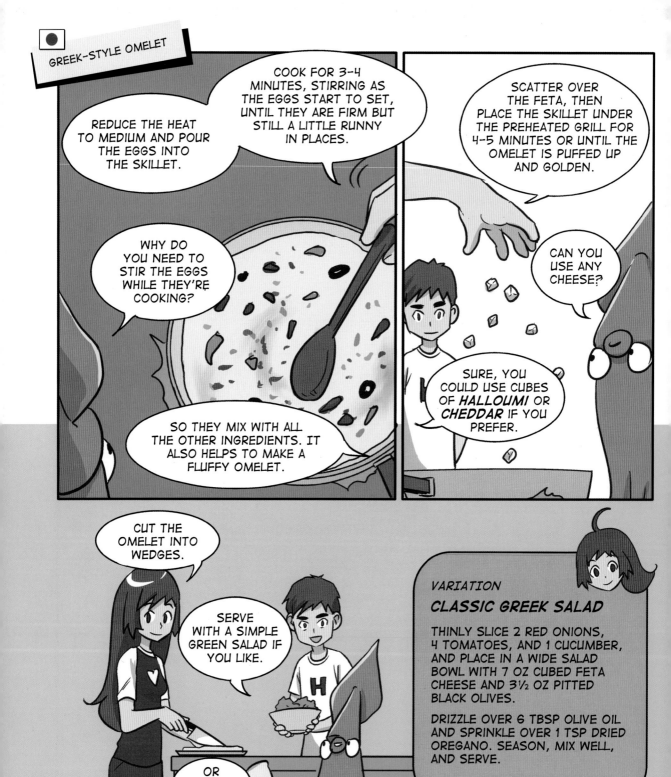

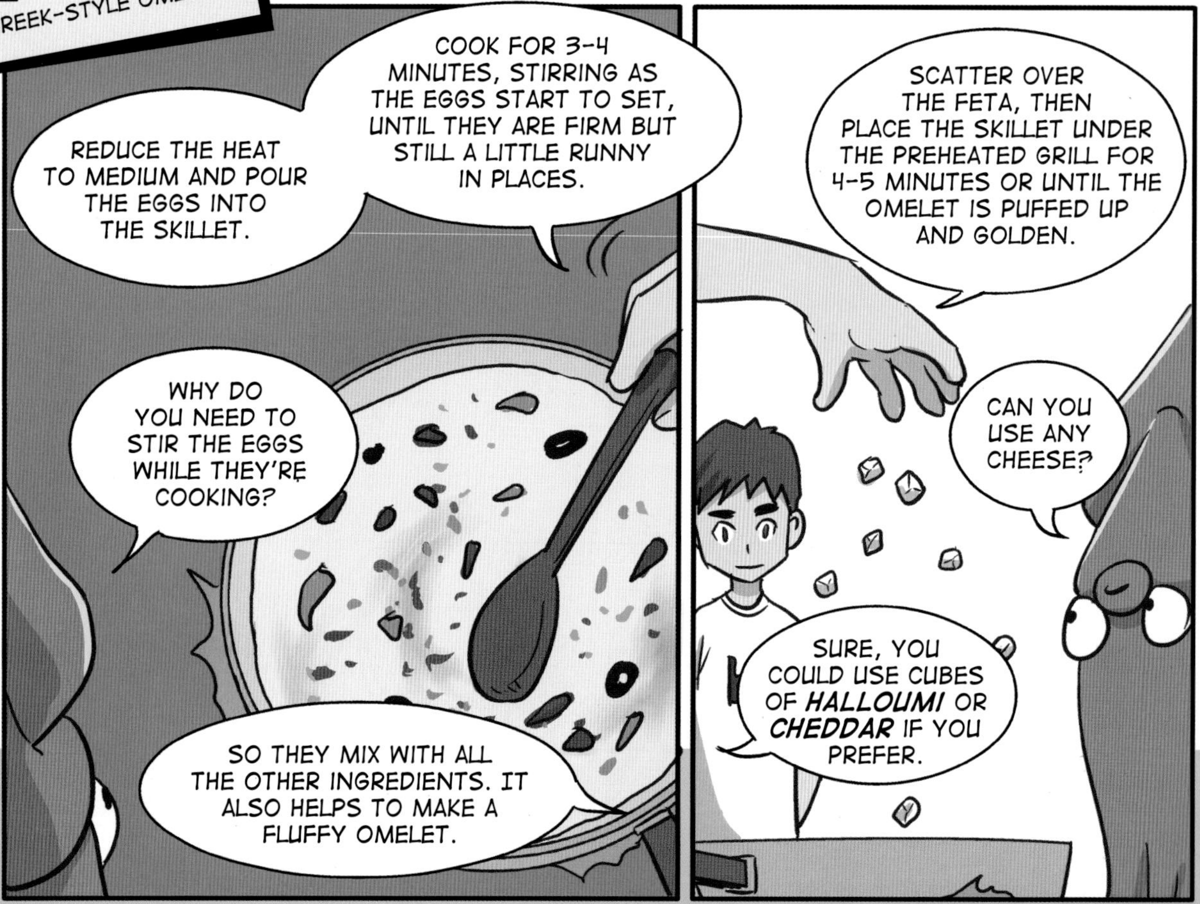
REDUCE THE HEAT TO MEDIUM AND POUR THE EGGS INTO THE SKILLET.
COOK FOR 3-4 MINUTES, STIRRING AS THE EGGS START TO SET, UNTIL THEY ARE FIRM BUT STILL A LITTLE RUNNY IN PLACES.
WHY DO YOU NEED TO STIR THE EGGS WHILE THEY'RE COOKING?
SO THEY MIX WITH ALL THE OTHER INGREDIENTS. IT ALSO HELPS TO MAKE A FLUFFY OMELET.
SCATTER OVER THE FETA, THEN PLACE THE SKILLET UNDER THE PREHEATED GRILL FOR 4-5 MINUTES OR UNTIL THE OMELET IS PUFFED UP AND GOLDEN.
CAN YOU USE ANY CHEESE?
SURE, YOU COULD USE CUBES OF **HALLOUMI** OR **CHEDDAR** IF YOU PREFER.

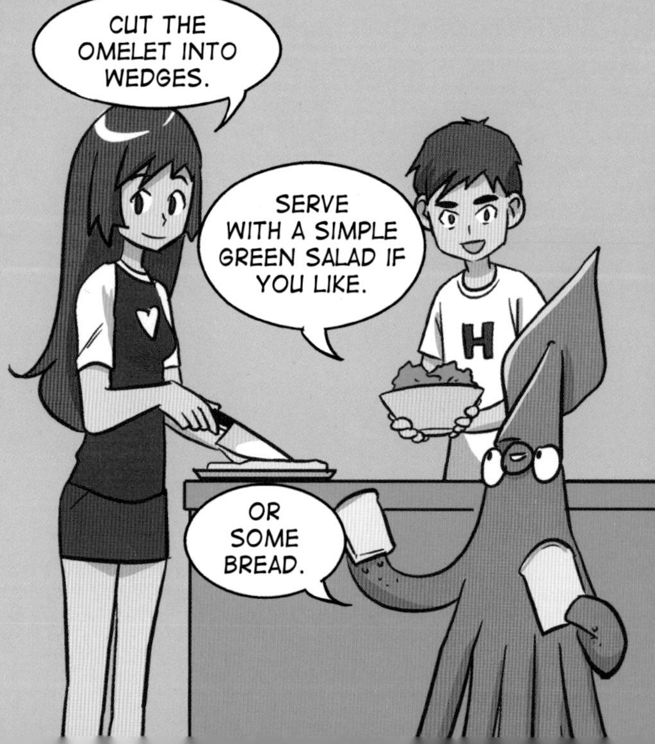
CUT THE OMELET INTO WEDGES.
SERVE WITH A SIMPLE GREEN SALAD IF YOU LIKE.
OR SOME BREAD.

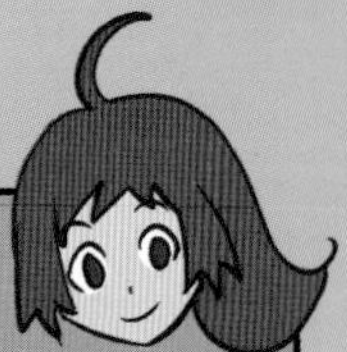

VARIATION

CLASSIC GREEK SALAD

THINLY SLICE 2 RED ONIONS, 4 TOMATOES, AND 1 CUCUMBER, AND PLACE IN A WIDE SALAD BOWL WITH 7 OZ CUBED FETA CHEESE AND 3½ OZ PITTED BLACK OLIVES.

DRIZZLE OVER 6 TBSP OLIVE OIL AND SPRINKLE OVER 1 TSP DRIED OREGANO. SEASON, MIX WELL, AND SERVE.

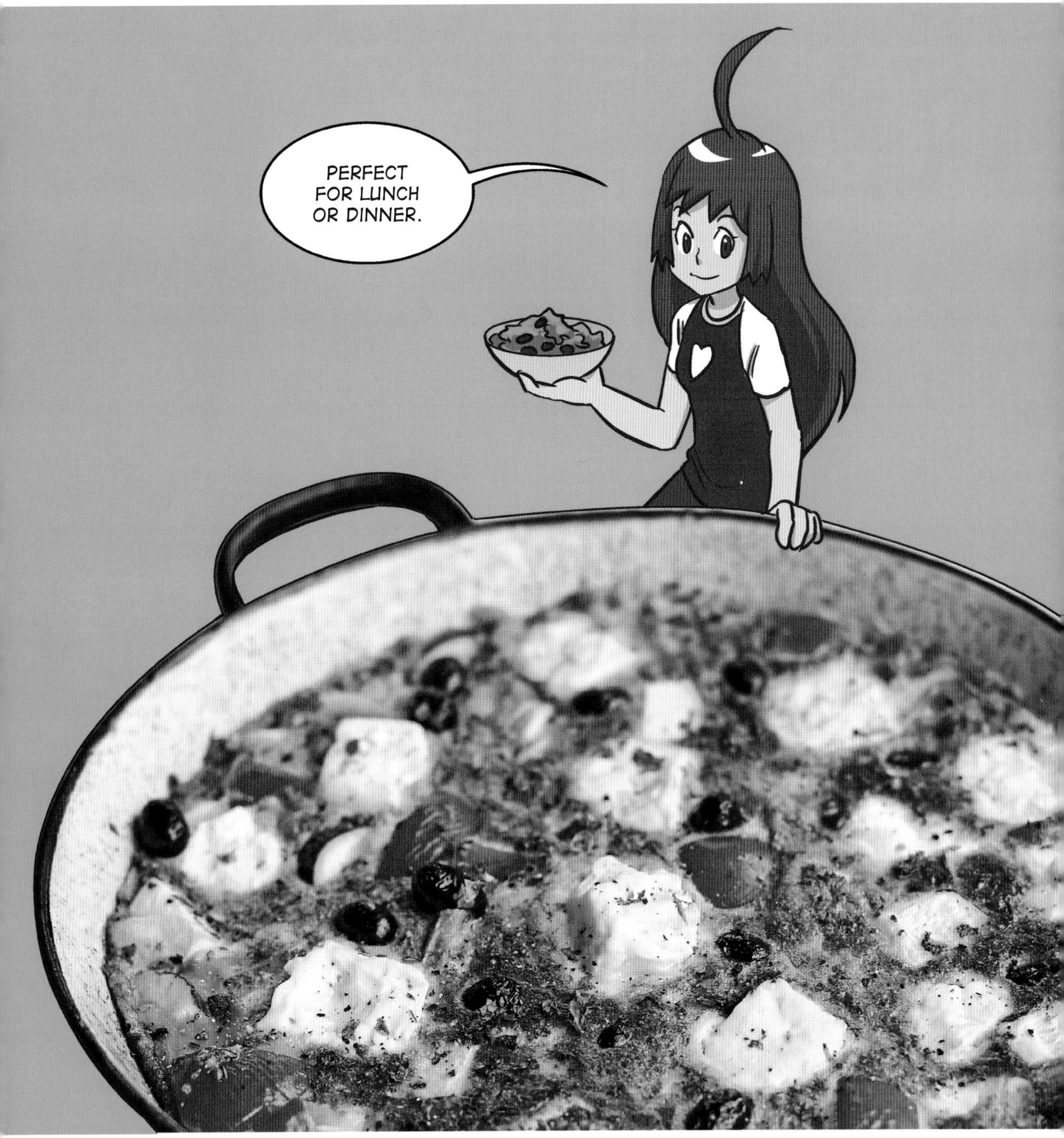
PERFECT FOR LUNCH OR DINNER.

SPINACH & MUSHROOM LASAGNE
A CLASSIC FLAVOR COMBINATION TO IMPRESS VEGETARIANS AND MEAT-EATERS ALIKE.

3 TBSP EXTRA VIRGIN OLIVE OIL, PLUS
  EXTRA FOR GREASING
1 LB MIXED MUSHROOMS, SLICED
7 OZ MASCARPONE CHEESE
12 SHEETS OF FRESH LASAGNE
5 OZ TALEGGIO CHEESE, DERINDED,
  AND CUT INTO CUBES
4 OZ BABY SPINACH LEAVES
SALT AND BLACK PEPPER
TOMATO AND ONION SALAD, TO SERVE (OPTIONAL)

SERVES 4 WARRIORS
PREP TIME: 15 MINUTES
COOKING TIME: 10 MINUTES

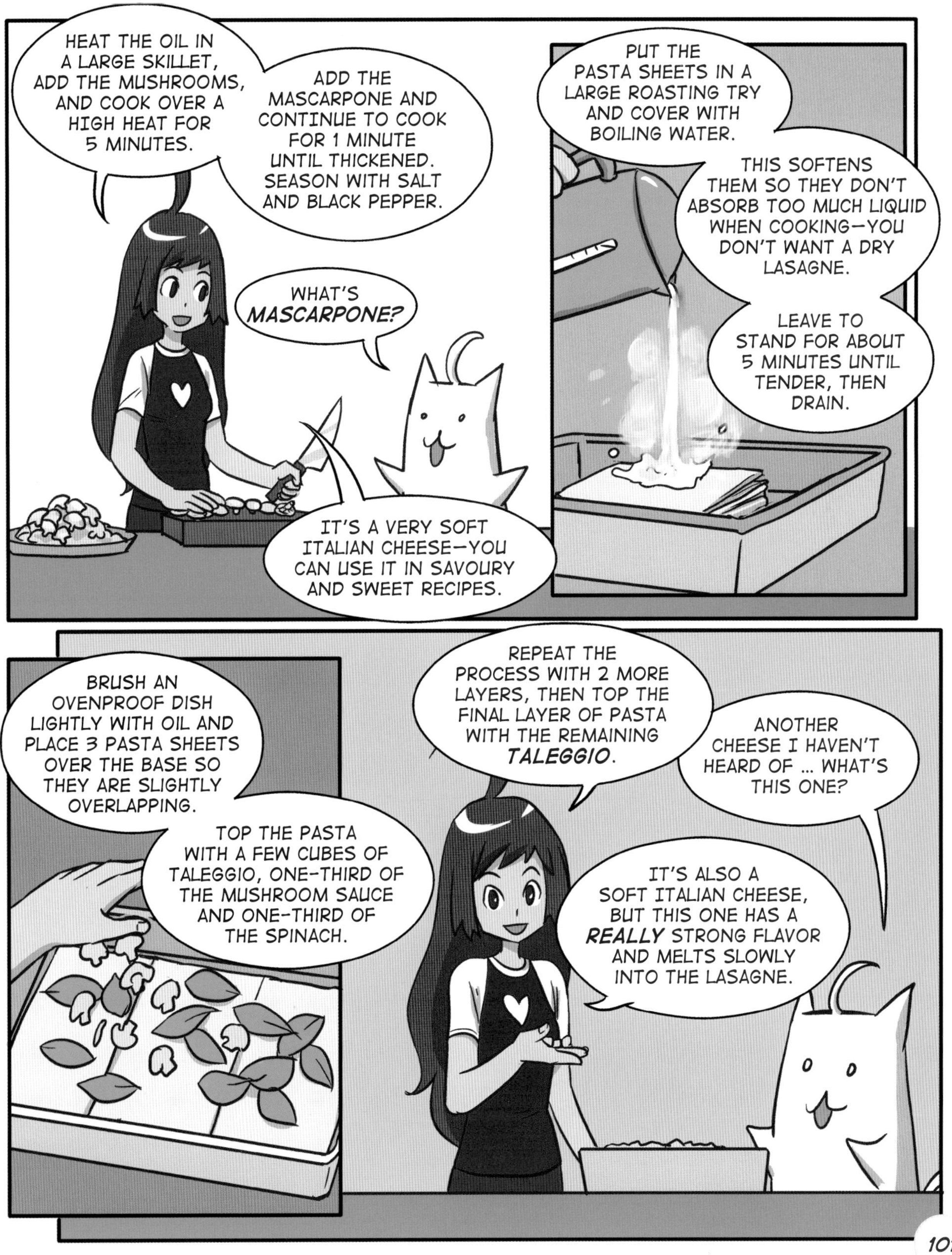

HEAT THE OIL IN A LARGE SKILLET, ADD THE MUSHROOMS, AND COOK OVER A HIGH HEAT FOR 5 MINUTES.
ADD THE MASCARPONE AND CONTINUE TO COOK FOR 1 MINUTE UNTIL THICKENED. SEASON WITH SALT AND BLACK PEPPER.
WHAT'S *MASCARPONE?*
IT'S A VERY SOFT ITALIAN CHEESE—YOU CAN USE IT IN SAVOURY AND SWEET RECIPES.
PUT THE PASTA SHEETS IN A LARGE ROASTING TRY AND COVER WITH BOILING WATER.
THIS SOFTENS THEM SO THEY DON'T ABSORB TOO MUCH LIQUID WHEN COOKING—YOU DON'T WANT A DRY LASAGNE.
LEAVE TO STAND FOR ABOUT 5 MINUTES UNTIL TENDER, THEN DRAIN.
BRUSH AN OVENPROOF DISH LIGHTLY WITH OIL AND PLACE 3 PASTA SHEETS OVER THE BASE SO THEY ARE SLIGHTLY OVERLAPPING.
TOP THE PASTA WITH A FEW CUBES OF TALEGGIO, ONE-THIRD OF THE MUSHROOM SAUCE AND ONE-THIRD OF THE SPINACH.
REPEAT THE PROCESS WITH 2 MORE LAYERS, THEN TOP THE FINAL LAYER OF PASTA WITH THE REMAINING **TALEGGIO**.
ANOTHER CHEESE I HAVEN'T HEARD OF ... WHAT'S THIS ONE?
IT'S ALSO A SOFT ITALIAN CHEESE, BUT THIS ONE HAS A ***REALLY*** STRONG FLAVOR AND MELTS SLOWLY INTO THE LASAGNE.

SPINACH & MUSHROOM LASAGNE

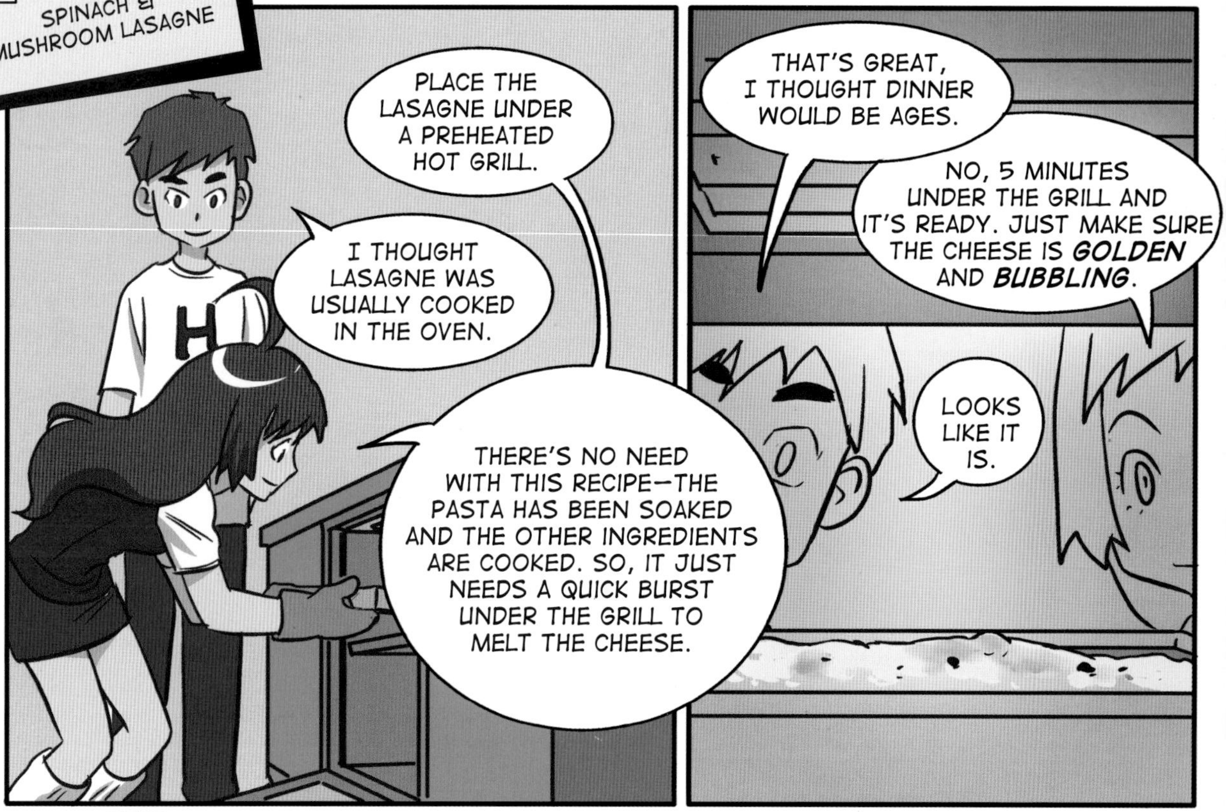
PLACE THE LASAGNE UNDER A PREHEATED HOT GRILL.
I THOUGHT LASAGNE WAS USUALLY COOKED IN THE OVEN.
THERE'S NO NEED WITH THIS RECIPE—THE PASTA HAS BEEN SOAKED AND THE OTHER INGREDIENTS ARE COOKED. SO, IT JUST NEEDS A QUICK BURST UNDER THE GRILL TO MELT THE CHEESE.
THAT'S GREAT, I THOUGHT DINNER WOULD BE AGES.
NO, 5 MINUTES UNDER THE GRILL AND IT'S READY. JUST MAKE SURE THE CHEESE IS ***GOLDEN*** AND ***BUBBLING***.
LOOKS LIKE IT IS.

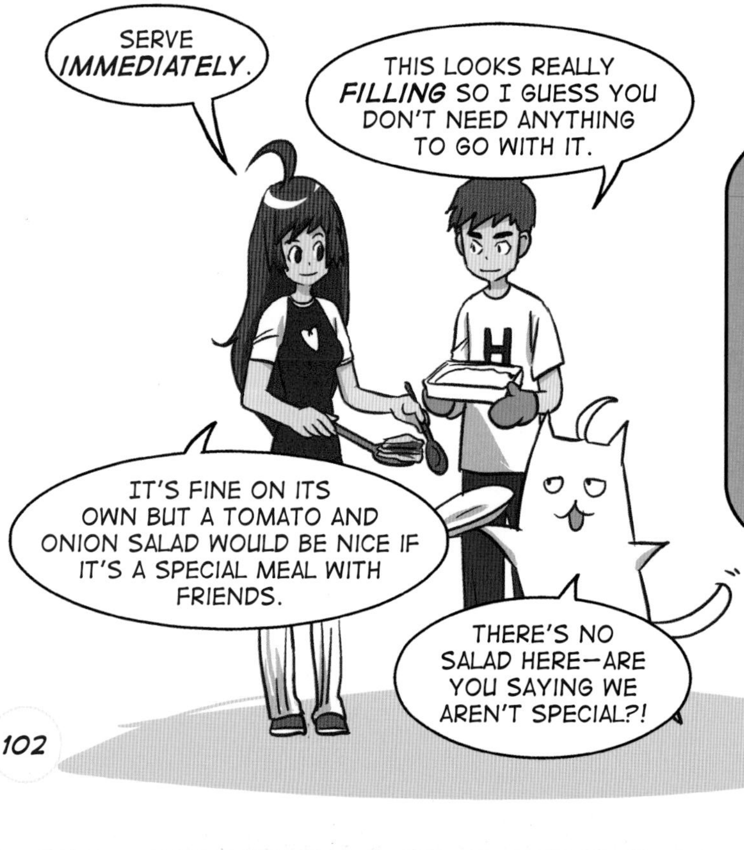
SERVE ***IMMEDIATELY***.
THIS LOOKS REALLY ***FILLING*** SO I GUESS YOU DON'T NEED ANYTHING TO GO WITH IT.
IT'S FINE ON ITS OWN BUT A TOMATO AND ONION SALAD WOULD BE NICE IF IT'S A SPECIAL MEAL WITH FRIENDS.
THERE'S NO SALAD HERE—ARE YOU SAYING WE AREN'T SPECIAL?!

VARIATION

MUSHROOM, TOMATO, & ZUCCHINI LASAGNE

USE 1 LB TOMATOES AND 2 ZUCCHINI INSTEAD OF THE SPINACH. DROP THE TOMATOES IN A SAUCEPAN OF BOILING WATER FOR 1 MINUTE, THEN SKIN, AND SLICE THEM. VERY THINLY SLICE THE ZUCCHINI BEFORE PROCEEDING WITH THE RECIPE.

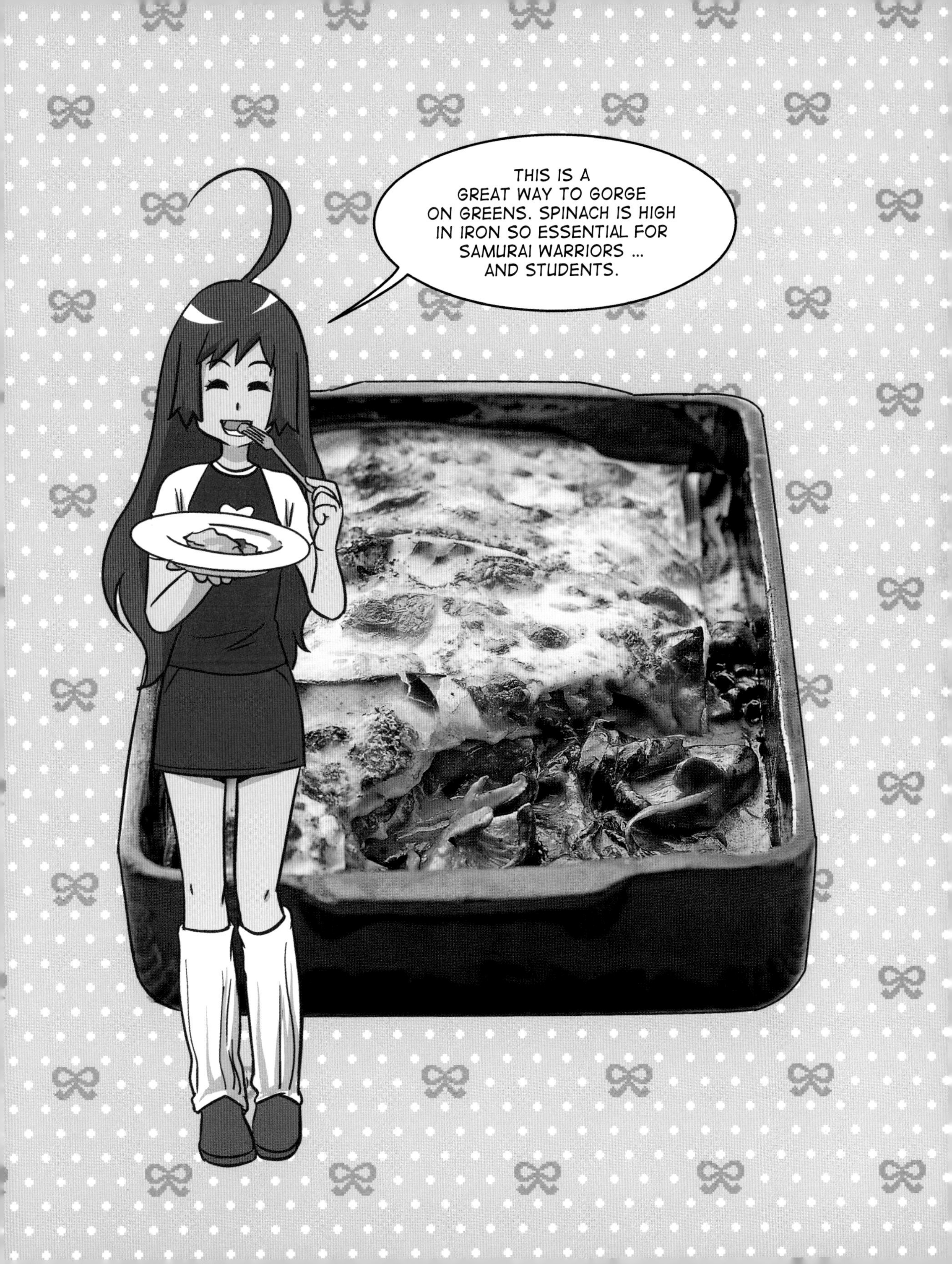
THIS IS A GREAT WAY TO GORGE ON GREENS. SPINACH IS HIGH IN IRON SO ESSENTIAL FOR SAMURAI WARRIORS ... AND STUDENTS.

QUICK CAULIFLOWER CHEESE
CAULIFLOWER CHEESE IS THE ULTIMATE COMFORT FOOD.

1 CAULIFLOWER, BROKEN INTO LARGE PIECES
2 OZ PLAIN FLOUR
2 TBSP BUTTER, PLUS EXTRA FOR GREASING
1 TSP MUSTARD POWDER (OPTIONAL)
¾ PINT MILK
7 OZ CHEESE, GRATED
   (RED LEICESTER OR CHEDDAR WORK WELL)
SALT AND BLACK PEPPER

TO SERVE:
GREEN SALAD
CRUSTY BREAD

SERVES 4 WARRIORS
PREP TIME: 10 MINUTES
COOKING TIME: 15 MINUTES

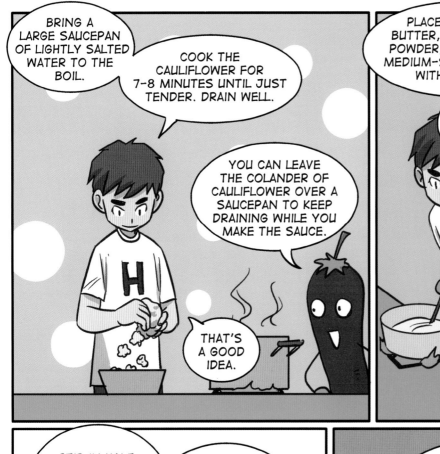

BRING A LARGE SAUCEPAN OF LIGHTLY SALTED WATER TO THE BOIL.

COOK THE CAULIFLOWER FOR 7-8 MINUTES UNTIL JUST TENDER. DRAIN WELL.

YOU CAN LEAVE THE COLANDER OF CAULIFLOWER OVER A SAUCEPAN TO KEEP DRAINING WHILE YOU MAKE THE SAUCE.

THAT'S A GOOD IDEA.

PLACE THE FLOUR, BUTTER, AND MUSTARD POWDER, IF USING, IN A MEDIUM-SIZED SAUCEPAN WITH THE MILK.

SLOWLY BRING TO THE BOIL, STIRRING CONSTANTLY, UNTIL SMOOTH AND THICKENED.

TAKE YOUR TIME WITH THIS OR YOU'LL END UP WITH A *LUMPY* SAUCE.

STIR IN HALF THE CHEESE AND, ONCE IT HAS MELTED, SEASON TO TASTE WITH SALT AND BLACK PEPPER.

THE CHEESE THICKENS UP THE SAUCE SO DON'T WORRY IF IT IS A LITTLE RUNNY AT FIRST.

TIP THE CAULIFLOWER INTO A BUTTERED OVENPROOF DISH, POUR OVER THE CHEESY SAUCE, AND SPRINKLE OVER THE REMAINING CHEESE.

USE A BRUSH TO BUTTER THE DISH OR TEAR OFF A PIECE OF THE BUTTER WRAPPER, SPOON SOME BUTTER ON IT, AND USE THE WRAPPER TO SMEAR AROUND THE INSIDE OF THE DISH.

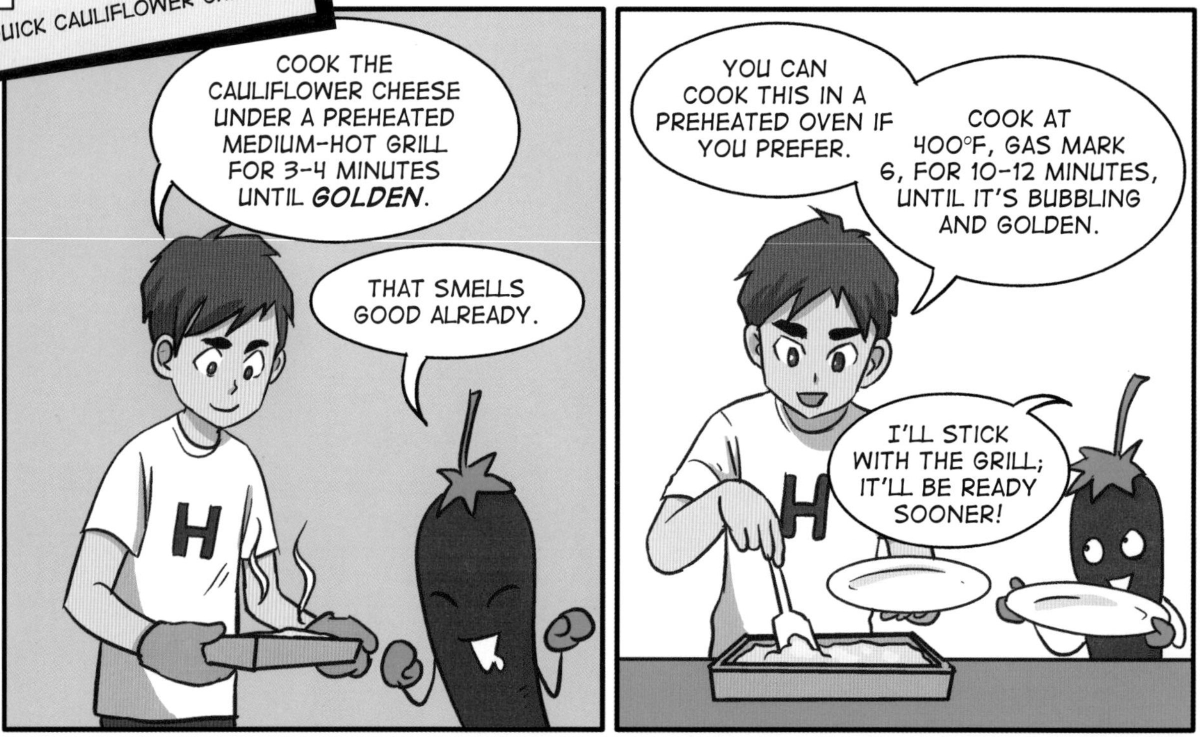
COOK THE CAULIFLOWER CHEESE UNDER A PREHEATED MEDIUM-HOT GRILL FOR 3-4 MINUTES UNTIL ***GOLDEN***.
THAT SMELLS GOOD ALREADY.
YOU CAN COOK THIS IN A PREHEATED OVEN IF YOU PREFER.
COOK AT 400°F, GAS MARK 6, FOR 10-12 MINUTES, UNTIL IT'S BUBBLING AND GOLDEN.
I'LL STICK WITH THE GRILL; IT'LL BE READY SOONER!
H
H

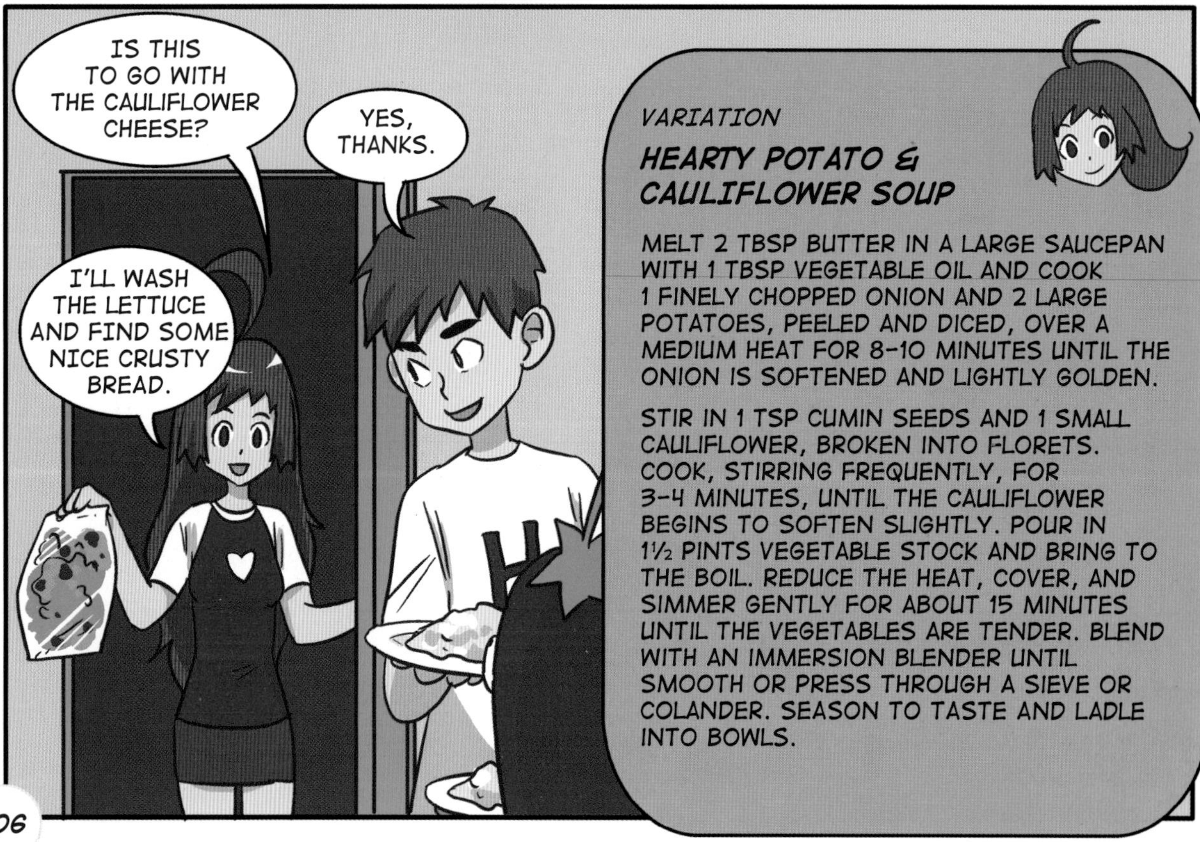
IS THIS TO GO WITH THE CAULIFLOWER CHEESE?
YES, THANKS.
I'LL WASH THE LETTUCE AND FIND SOME NICE CRUSTY BREAD.
H

VARIATION

HEARTY POTATO & CAULIFLOWER SOUP

MELT 2 TBSP BUTTER IN A LARGE SAUCEPAN WITH 1 TBSP VEGETABLE OIL AND COOK 1 FINELY CHOPPED ONION AND 2 LARGE POTATOES, PEELED AND DICED, OVER A MEDIUM HEAT FOR 8-10 MINUTES UNTIL THE ONION IS SOFTENED AND LIGHTLY GOLDEN.

STIR IN 1 TSP CUMIN SEEDS AND 1 SMALL CAULIFLOWER, BROKEN INTO FLORETS. COOK, STIRRING FREQUENTLY, FOR 3-4 MINUTES, UNTIL THE CAULIFLOWER BEGINS TO SOFTEN SLIGHTLY. POUR IN 1½ PINTS VEGETABLE STOCK AND BRING TO THE BOIL. REDUCE THE HEAT, COVER, AND SIMMER GENTLY FOR ABOUT 15 MINUTES UNTIL THE VEGETABLES ARE TENDER. BLEND WITH AN IMMERSION BLENDER UNTIL SMOOTH OR PRESS THROUGH A SIEVE OR COLANDER. SEASON TO TASTE AND LADLE INTO BOWLS.

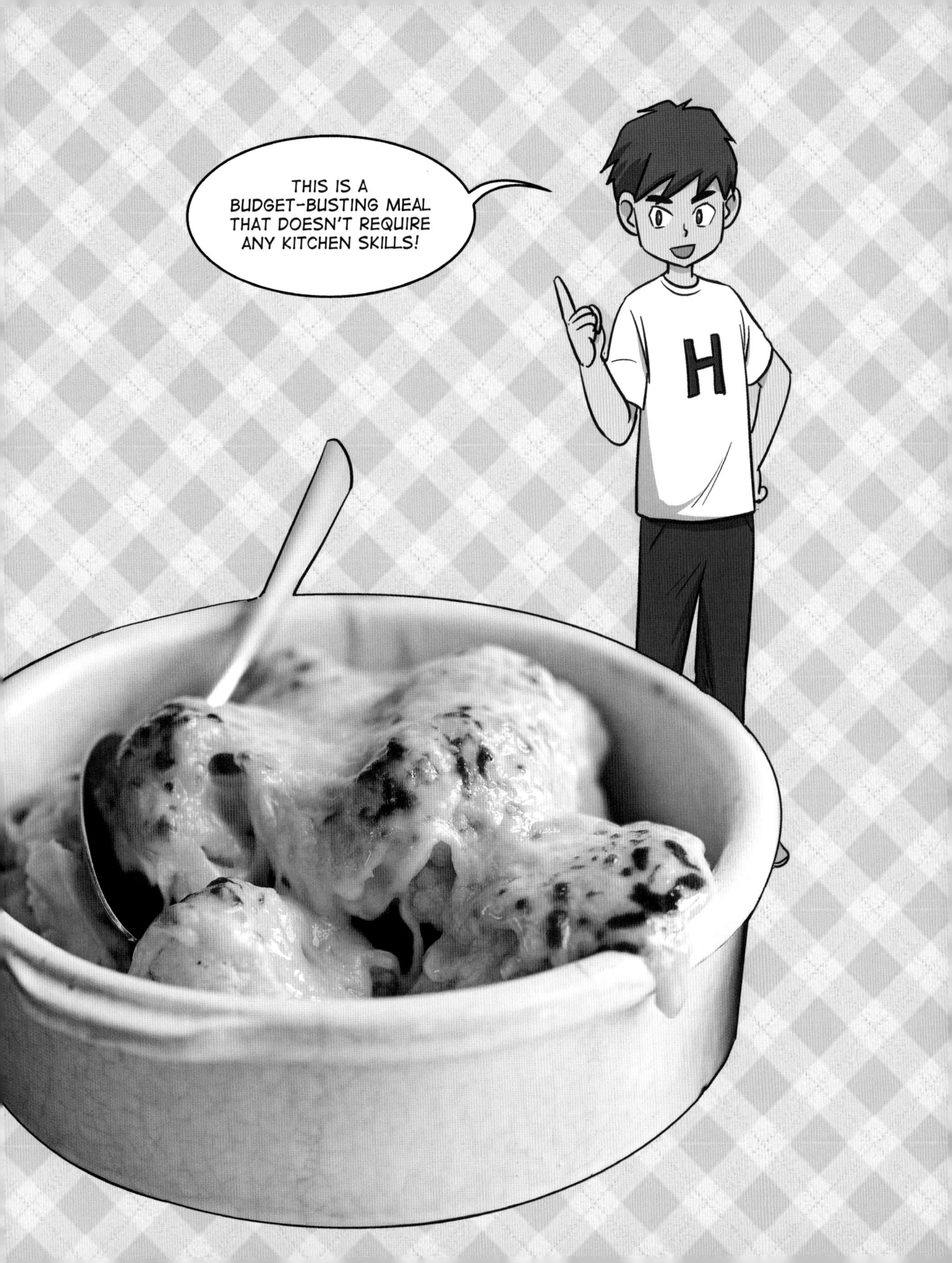
THIS IS A BUDGET-BUSTING MEAL THAT DOESN'T REQUIRE ANY KITCHEN SKILLS!

POTATO GRATIN

WITH JUST A HANDFUL OF INGREDIENTS YOU CAN CREATE A DELICIOUS DINNER.

1¼ LB POTATOES, THINLY SLICED
1 LB SPINACH LEAVES
BUTTER, FOR GREASING
7 OZ MOZZARELLA CHEESE, GRATED
4 TOMATOES, SLICED
3 EGGS, BEATEN
½ PINT WHIPPING CREAM
SALT AND BLACK PEPPER

TO SERVE:
SALAD
CRUSTY BREAD

SERVES 4 WARRIORS
PREP TIME: 10 MINUTES
COOKING TIME: 35 MINUTES

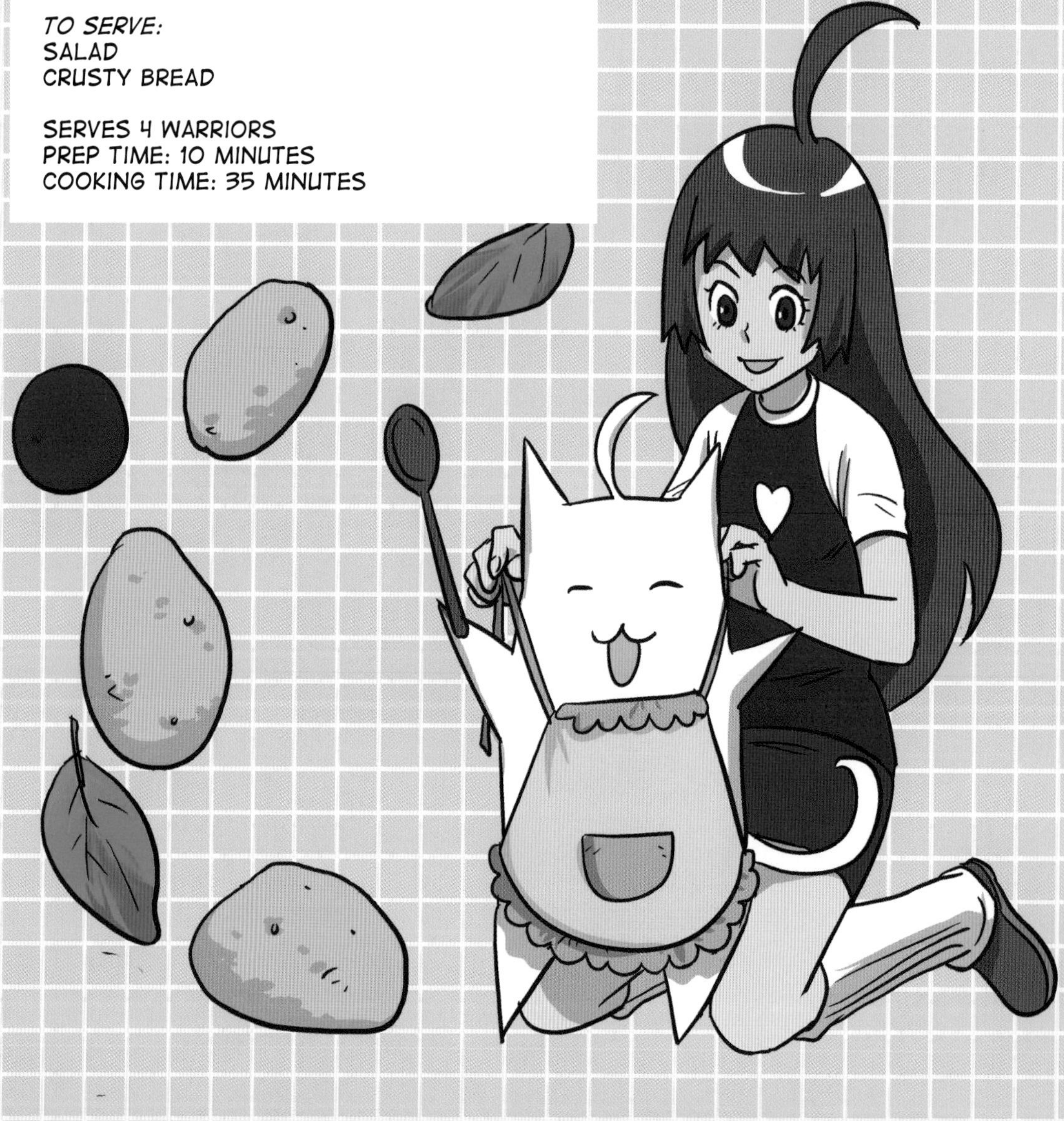

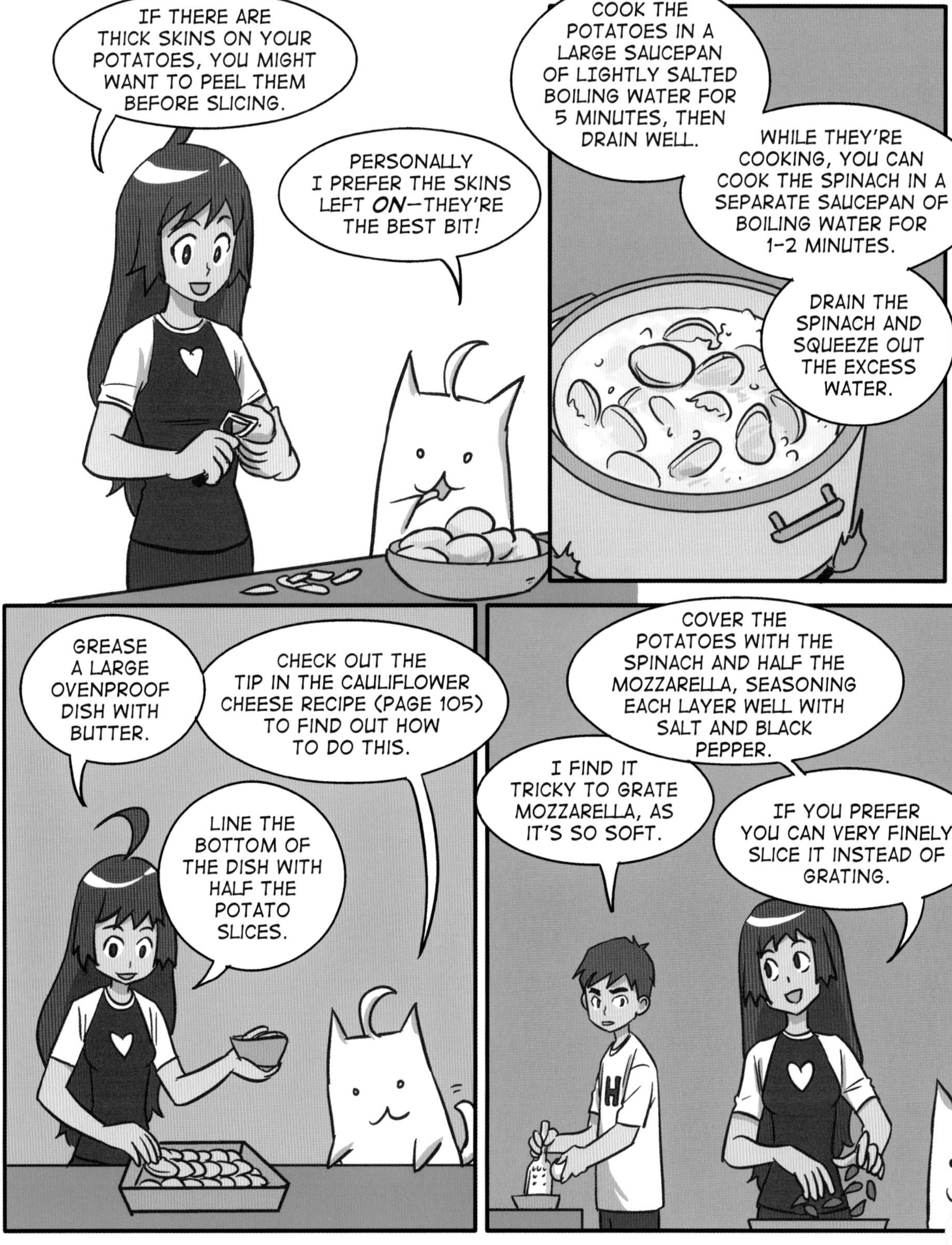
IF THERE ARE THICK SKINS ON YOUR POTATOES, YOU MIGHT WANT TO PEEL THEM BEFORE SLICING.
PERSONALLY I PREFER THE SKINS LEFT *ON*—THEY'RE THE BEST BIT!
COOK THE POTATOES IN A LARGE SAUCEPAN OF LIGHTLY SALTED BOILING WATER FOR 5 MINUTES, THEN DRAIN WELL.
WHILE THEY'RE COOKING, YOU CAN COOK THE SPINACH IN A SEPARATE SAUCEPAN OF BOILING WATER FOR 1–2 MINUTES.
DRAIN THE SPINACH AND SQUEEZE OUT THE EXCESS WATER.
GREASE A LARGE OVENPROOF DISH WITH BUTTER.
CHECK OUT THE TIP IN THE CAULIFLOWER CHEESE RECIPE (PAGE 105) TO FIND OUT HOW TO DO THIS.
LINE THE BOTTOM OF THE DISH WITH HALF THE POTATO SLICES.
COVER THE POTATOES WITH THE SPINACH AND HALF THE MOZZARELLA, SEASONING EACH LAYER WELL WITH SALT AND BLACK PEPPER.
I FIND IT TRICKY TO GRATE MOZZARELLA, AS IT'S SO SOFT.
IF YOU PREFER YOU CAN VERY FINELY SLICE IT INSTEAD OF GRATING.
H

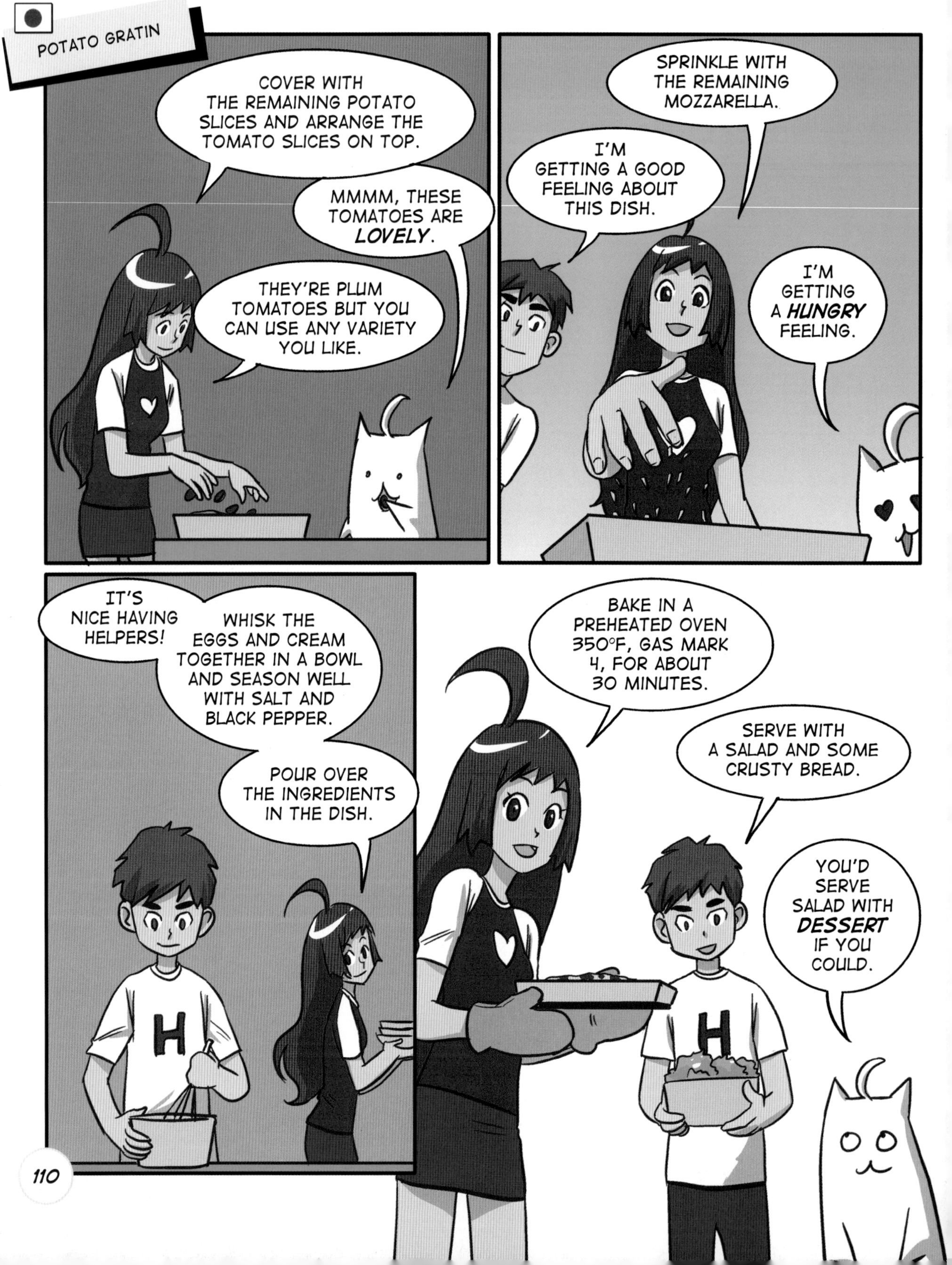

POTATO GRATIN
COVER WITH THE REMAINING POTATO SLICES AND ARRANGE THE TOMATO SLICES ON TOP.
MMMM, THESE TOMATOES ARE LOVELY.
THEY'RE PLUM TOMATOES BUT YOU CAN USE ANY VARIETY YOU LIKE.
SPRINKLE WITH THE REMAINING MOZZARELLA.
I'M GETTING A GOOD FEELING ABOUT THIS DISH.
I'M GETTING A HUNGRY FEELING.
IT'S NICE HAVING HELPERS!
WHISK THE EGGS AND CREAM TOGETHER IN A BOWL AND SEASON WELL WITH SALT AND BLACK PEPPER.
POUR OVER THE INGREDIENTS IN THE DISH.
BAKE IN A PREHEATED OVEN 350°F, GAS MARK 4, FOR ABOUT 30 MINUTES.
SERVE WITH A SALAD AND SOME CRUSTY BREAD.
YOU'D SERVE SALAD WITH DESSERT IF YOU COULD.

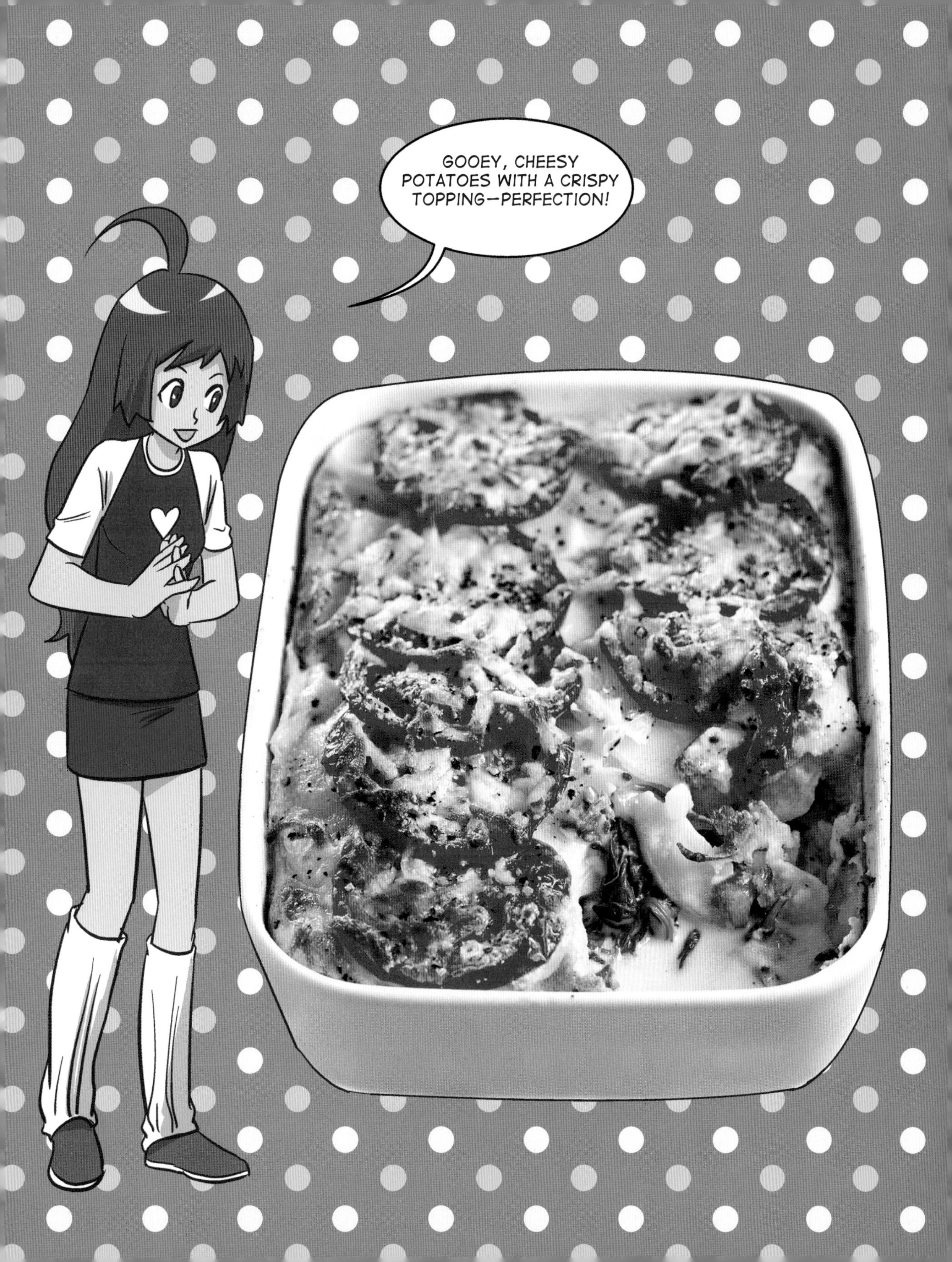
GOOEY, CHEESY POTATOES WITH A CRISPY TOPPING—PERFECTION!

MIXED BEAN KEDGEREE

THIS IS A VEGETARIAN VERSION OF THE ANGLO-INDIAN BREAKFAST DISH SO WHY NOT SWAP YOUR CORNFLAKES FOR KEDGEREE?

2 TBSP OLIVE OIL
1 ONION, CHOPPED
2 TBSP MILD CURRY POWDER
8 OZ LONG-GRAIN RICE
1¼ PINTS VEGETABLE STOCK
4 EGGS
2 X 13 OZ CANS MIXED BEANS, RINSED, AND DRAINED
¼ PINT SOUR CREAM
SALT AND BLACK PEPPER

TO GARNISH:
2 TOMATOES, FINELY CHOPPED
CHOPPED PARSLEY

SERVES 4 WARRIORS
PREP TIME: 10 MINUTES
COOKING TIME: 25 MINUTES

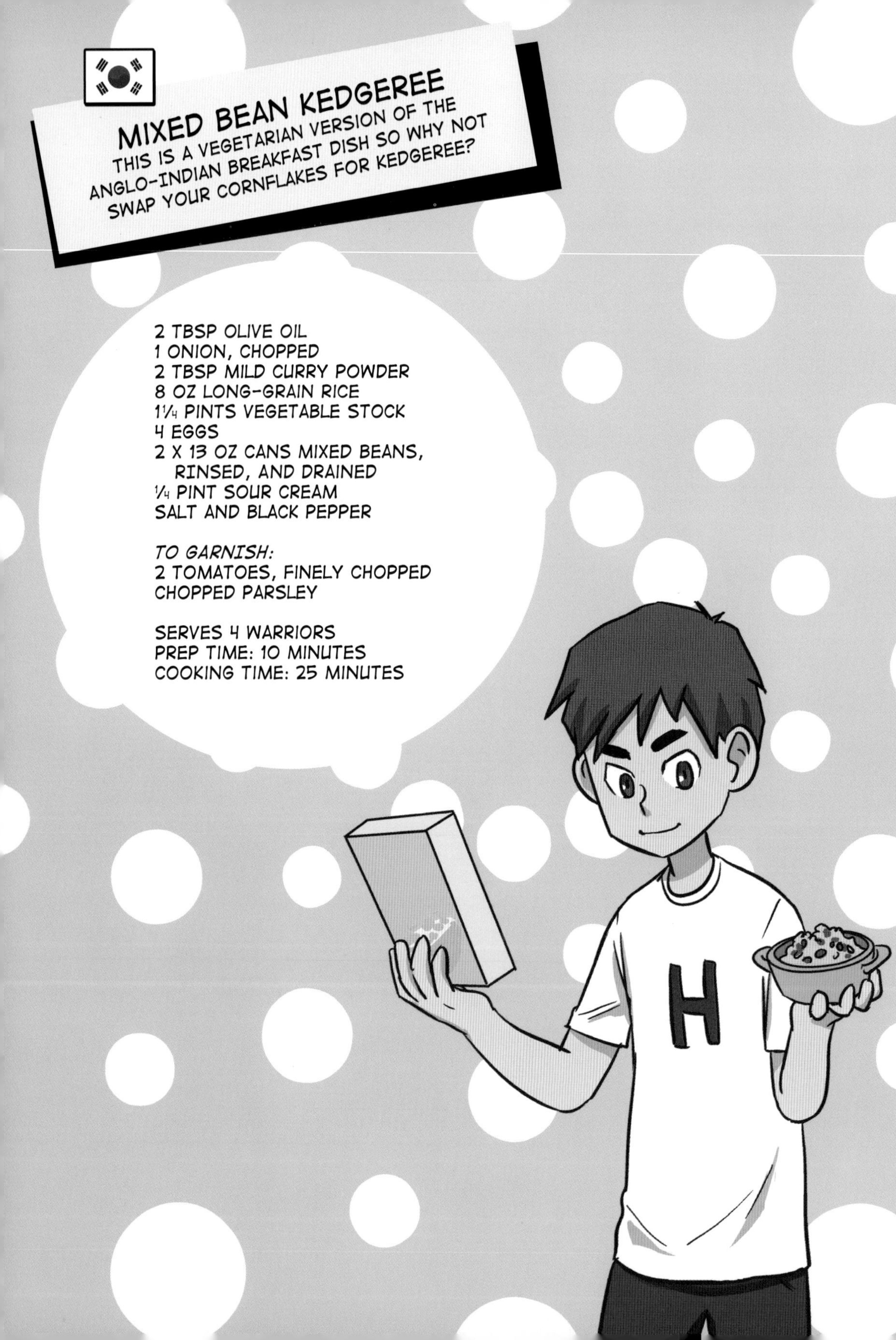
H

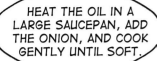

HEAT THE OIL IN A LARGE SAUCEPAN, ADD THE ONION, AND COOK GENTLY UNTIL SOFT.

STIR IN THE CURRY POWDER AND RICE.

ARE YOU *REALLY* GOING TO HAVE THIS FOR BREAKFAST?

SURE, WHY NOT? BUT IT WOULD BE GREAT FOR DINNER, TOO.

ADD THE STOCK AND SEASON WITH SALT AND BLACK PEPPER.

BRING TO THE BOIL, THEN REDUCE THE HEAT, COVER, AND SIMMER, STIRRING OCCASIONALLY, FOR 10-15 MINUTES UNTIL ALL THE STOCK HAS BEEN ABSORBED AND THE RICE IS *TENDER*.

IF THE RICE IS DRYING OUT, YOU CAN ADD A LITTLE MORE STOCK OR BOILED WATER TO THE DISH. ADD A LITTLE AT A TIME, AS YOU DON'T WANT IT TO BE TOO WET.

MEANWHILE, PUT THE EGGS IN A SAUCEPAN OF COLD WATER AND BRING TO THE BOIL.

ADD A FEW DROPS OF *VINEGAR* TO THE WATER, AS THIS HELPS TO PREVENT THE EGGS FROM LEAKING OUT IF THE SHELLS CRACK.

COOK THE EGGS FOR 10 MINUTES, THEN RINSE IN COLD WATER, REFILL THE PAN WITH COLD WATER, AND LEAVE TO COOL.

WHY DO YOU NEED TO DO THAT?

IT STOPS THE COOKING PROCESS SO THE EGGS STAY NICE AND *SOFT* IN THE MIDDLE.

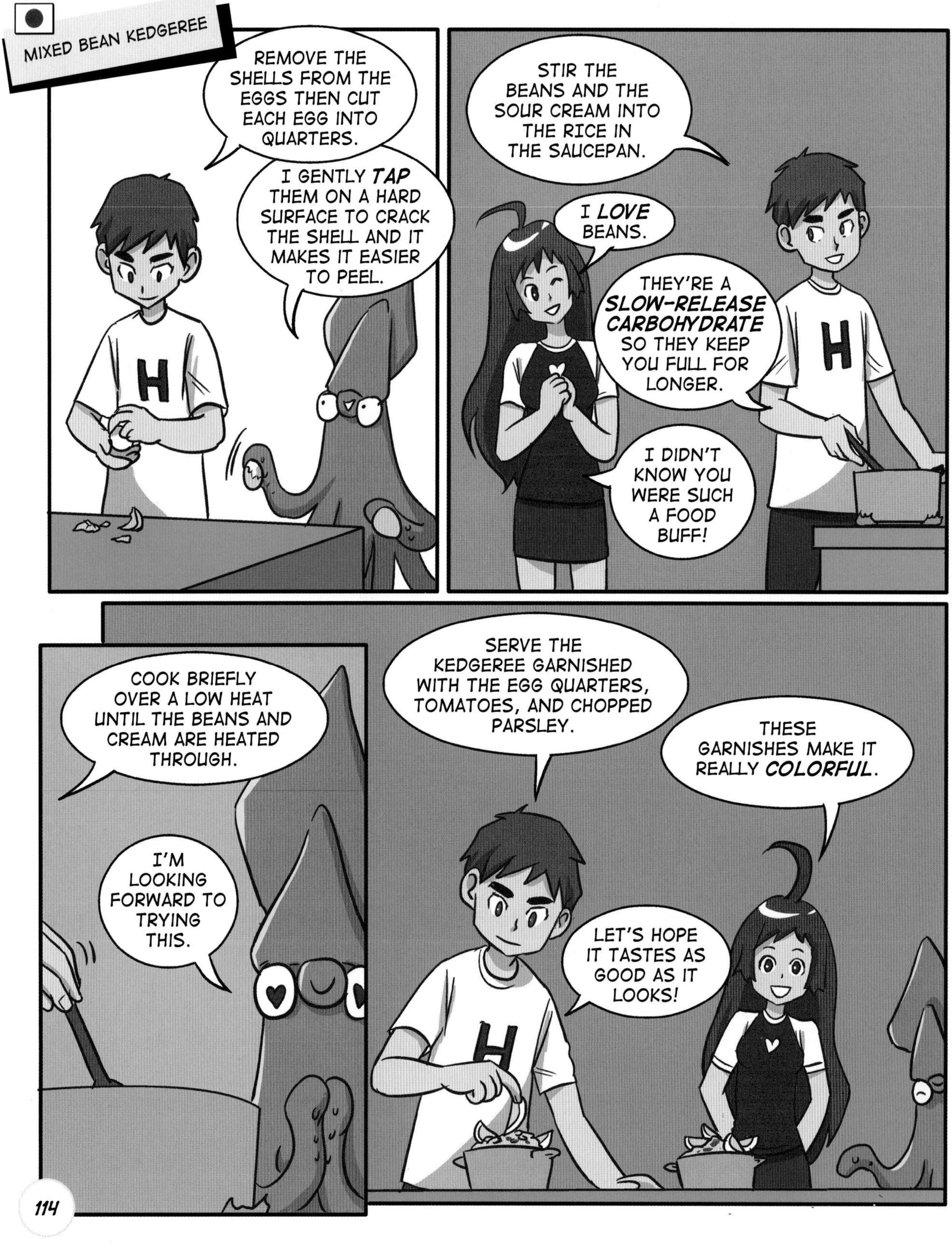
MIXED BEAN KEDGEREE
REMOVE THE SHELLS FROM THE EGGS THEN CUT EACH EGG INTO QUARTERS.
I GENTLY TAP THEM ON A HARD SURFACE TO CRACK THE SHELL AND IT MAKES IT EASIER TO PEEL.
STIR THE BEANS AND THE SOUR CREAM INTO THE RICE IN THE SAUCEPAN.
I LOVE BEANS.
THEY'RE A SLOW-RELEASE CARBOHYDRATE SO THEY KEEP YOU FULL FOR LONGER.
I DIDN'T KNOW YOU WERE SUCH A FOOD BUFF!
COOK BRIEFLY OVER A LOW HEAT UNTIL THE BEANS AND CREAM ARE HEATED THROUGH.
I'M LOOKING FORWARD TO TRYING THIS.
SERVE THE KEDGEREE GARNISHED WITH THE EGG QUARTERS, TOMATOES, AND CHOPPED PARSLEY.
THESE GARNISHES MAKE IT REALLY COLORFUL.
LET'S HOPE IT TASTES AS GOOD AS IT LOOKS!

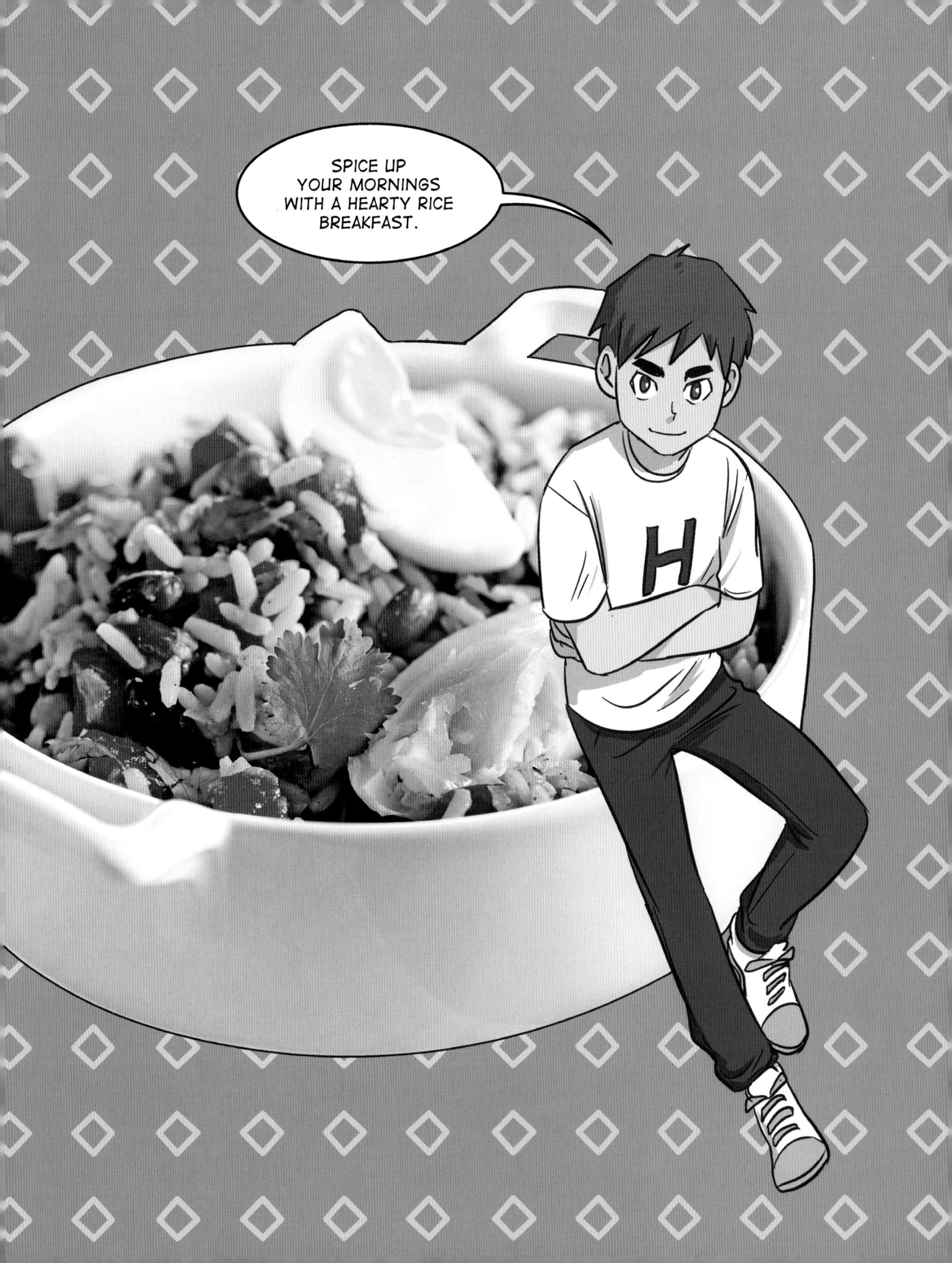
SPICE UP YOUR MORNINGS WITH A HEARTY RICE BREAKFAST.

ONION & MUSHROOM QUESADILLAS

THESE MAKE A GREAT POST-PARTY SNACK
OR AN EASY MEAL FOR FRIENDS.

3 TBSP OLIVE OIL
2 RED ONIONS, THINLY SLICED
1 TSP CASTER SUGAR
7 OZ BUTTON MUSHROOMS, SLICED
8 SMALL SOFT FLOUR TORTILLAS
5 OZ CHEDDAR CHEESE, GRATED
SMALL HANDFUL OF PARSLEY, CHOPPED
SALT AND BLACK PEPPER
GREEN SALAD, TO SERVE (OPTIONAL)

SERVES 4 WARRIORS
PREP TIME: 10 MINUTES
COOKING TIME: ABOUT 30 MINUTES

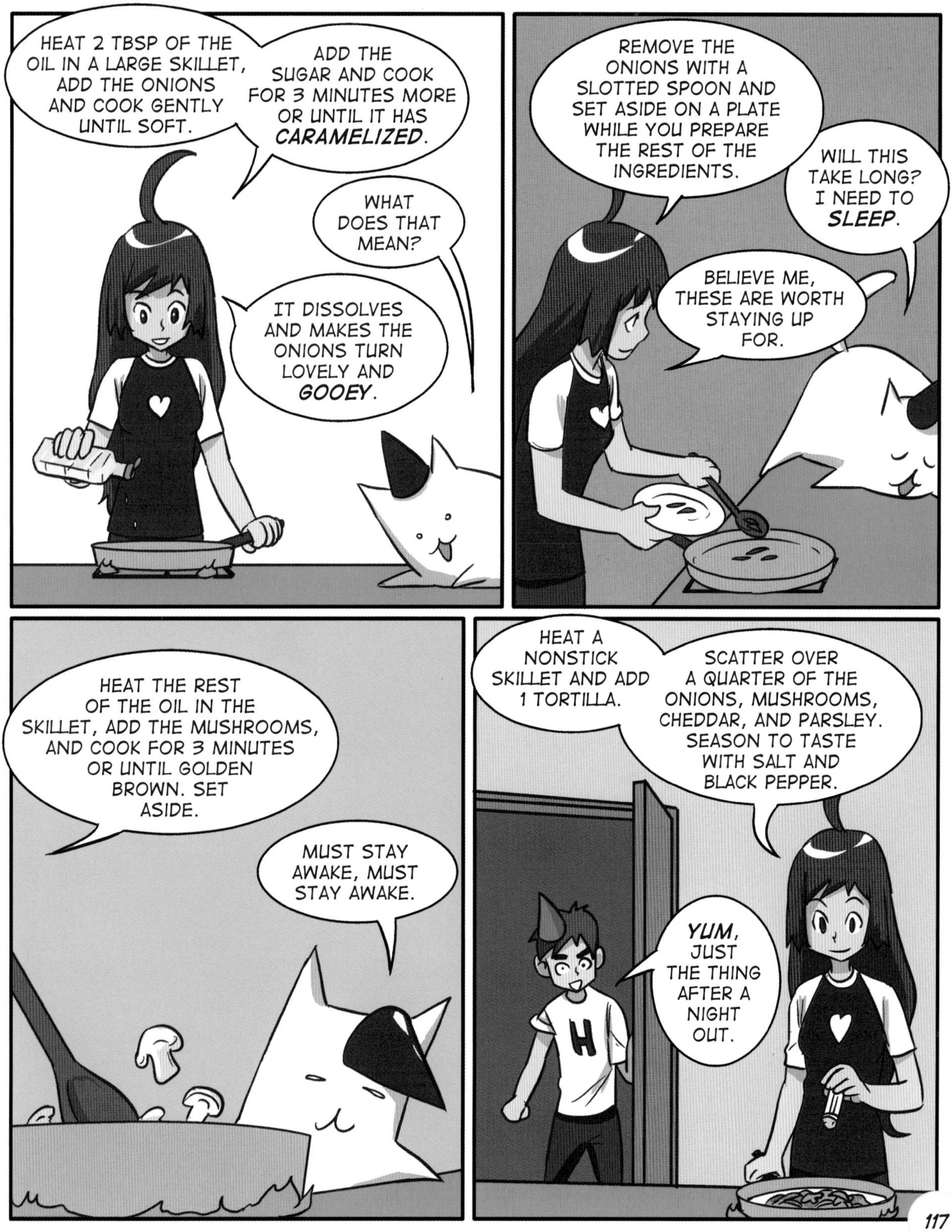

HEAT 2 TBSP OF THE OIL IN A LARGE SKILLET, ADD THE ONIONS AND COOK GENTLY UNTIL SOFT.
ADD THE SUGAR AND COOK FOR 3 MINUTES MORE OR UNTIL IT HAS **CARAMELIZED**.
WHAT DOES THAT MEAN?
IT DISSOLVES AND MAKES THE ONIONS TURN LOVELY AND **GOOEY**.
REMOVE THE ONIONS WITH A SLOTTED SPOON AND SET ASIDE ON A PLATE WHILE YOU PREPARE THE REST OF THE INGREDIENTS.
WILL THIS TAKE LONG? I NEED TO **SLEEP**.
BELIEVE ME, THESE ARE WORTH STAYING UP FOR.
HEAT THE REST OF THE OIL IN THE SKILLET, ADD THE MUSHROOMS, AND COOK FOR 3 MINUTES OR UNTIL GOLDEN BROWN. SET ASIDE.
MUST STAY AWAKE, MUST STAY AWAKE.
HEAT A NONSTICK SKILLET AND ADD 1 TORTILLA.
SCATTER OVER A QUARTER OF THE ONIONS, MUSHROOMS, CHEDDAR, AND PARSLEY. SEASON TO TASTE WITH SALT AND BLACK PEPPER.
YUM, JUST THE THING AFTER A NIGHT OUT.

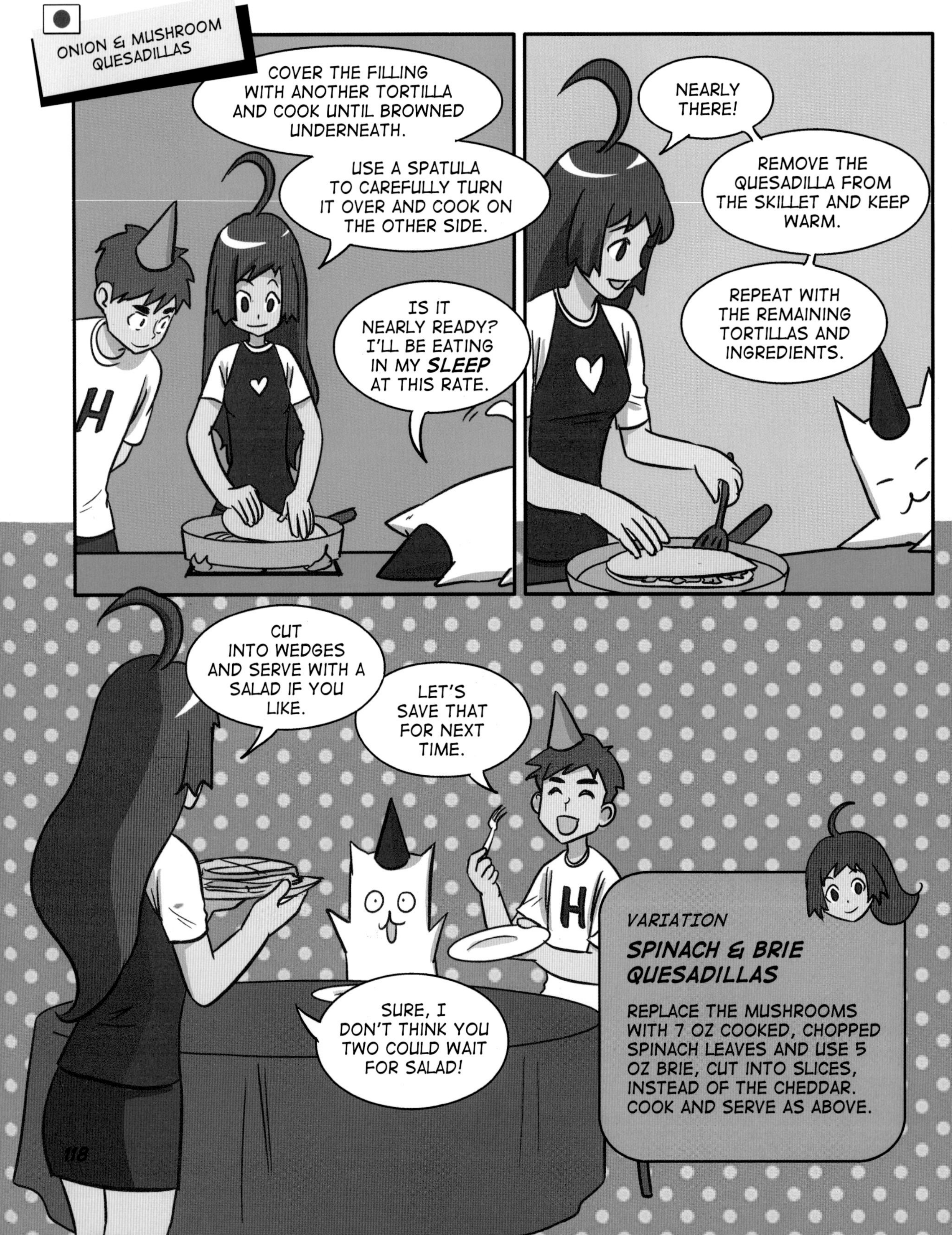
ONION & MUSHROOM QUESADILLAS
COVER THE FILLING WITH ANOTHER TORTILLA AND COOK UNTIL BROWNED UNDERNEATH.
USE A SPATULA TO CAREFULLY TURN IT OVER AND COOK ON THE OTHER SIDE.
IS IT NEARLY READY? I'LL BE EATING IN MY *SLEEP* AT THIS RATE.
NEARLY THERE!
REMOVE THE QUESADILLA FROM THE SKILLET AND KEEP WARM.
REPEAT WITH THE REMAINING TORTILLAS AND INGREDIENTS.
CUT INTO WEDGES AND SERVE WITH A SALAD IF YOU LIKE.
LET'S SAVE THAT FOR NEXT TIME.
SURE, I DON'T THINK YOU TWO COULD WAIT FOR SALAD!
H
H
VARIATION
SPINACH & BRIE QUESADILLAS
REPLACE THE MUSHROOMS WITH 7 OZ COOKED, CHOPPED SPINACH LEAVES AND USE 5 OZ BRIE, CUT INTO SLICES, INSTEAD OF THE CHEDDAR. COOK AND SERVE AS ABOVE.

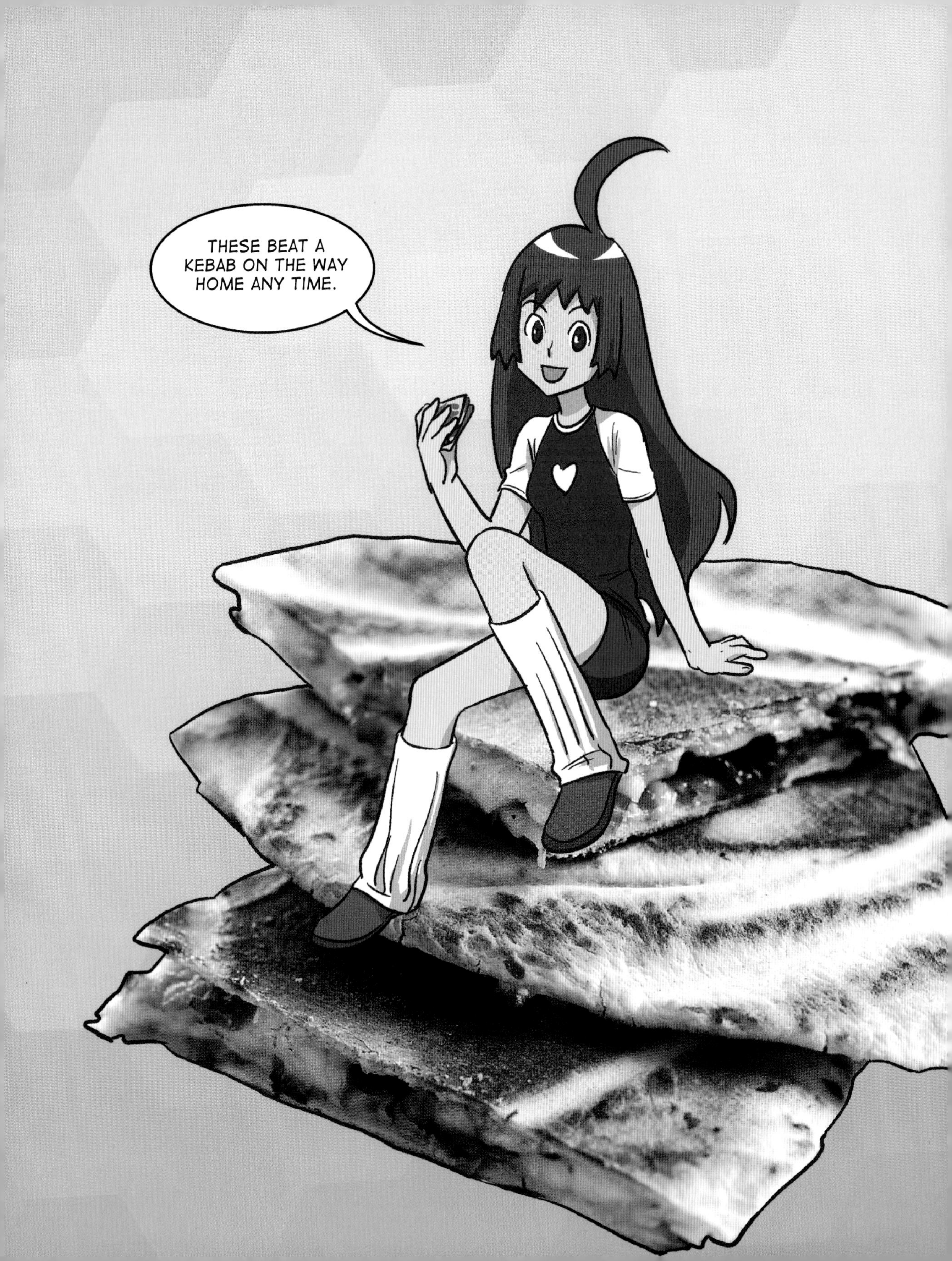
THESE BEAT A KEBAB ON THE WAY HOME ANY TIME.

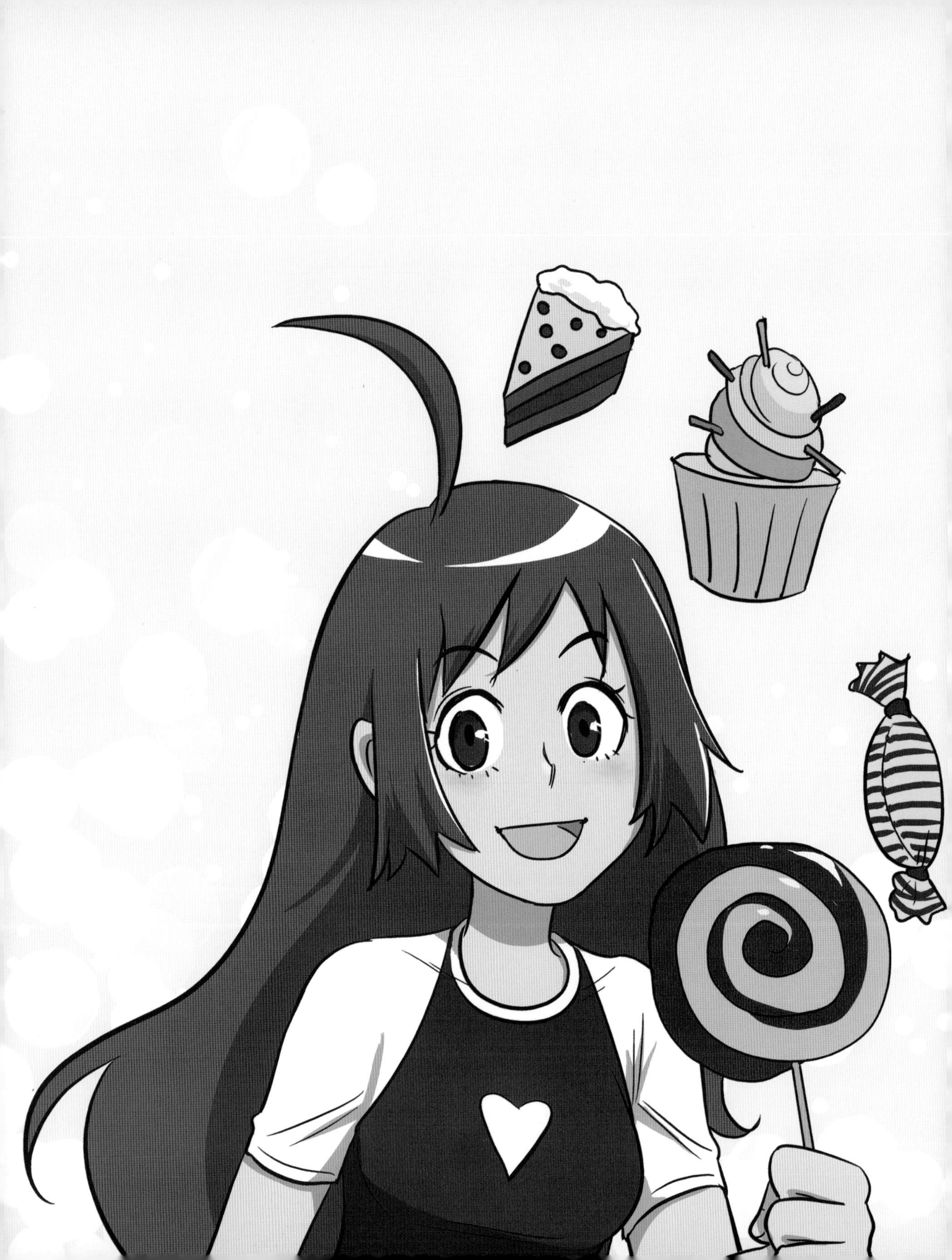

SWEET STUFF

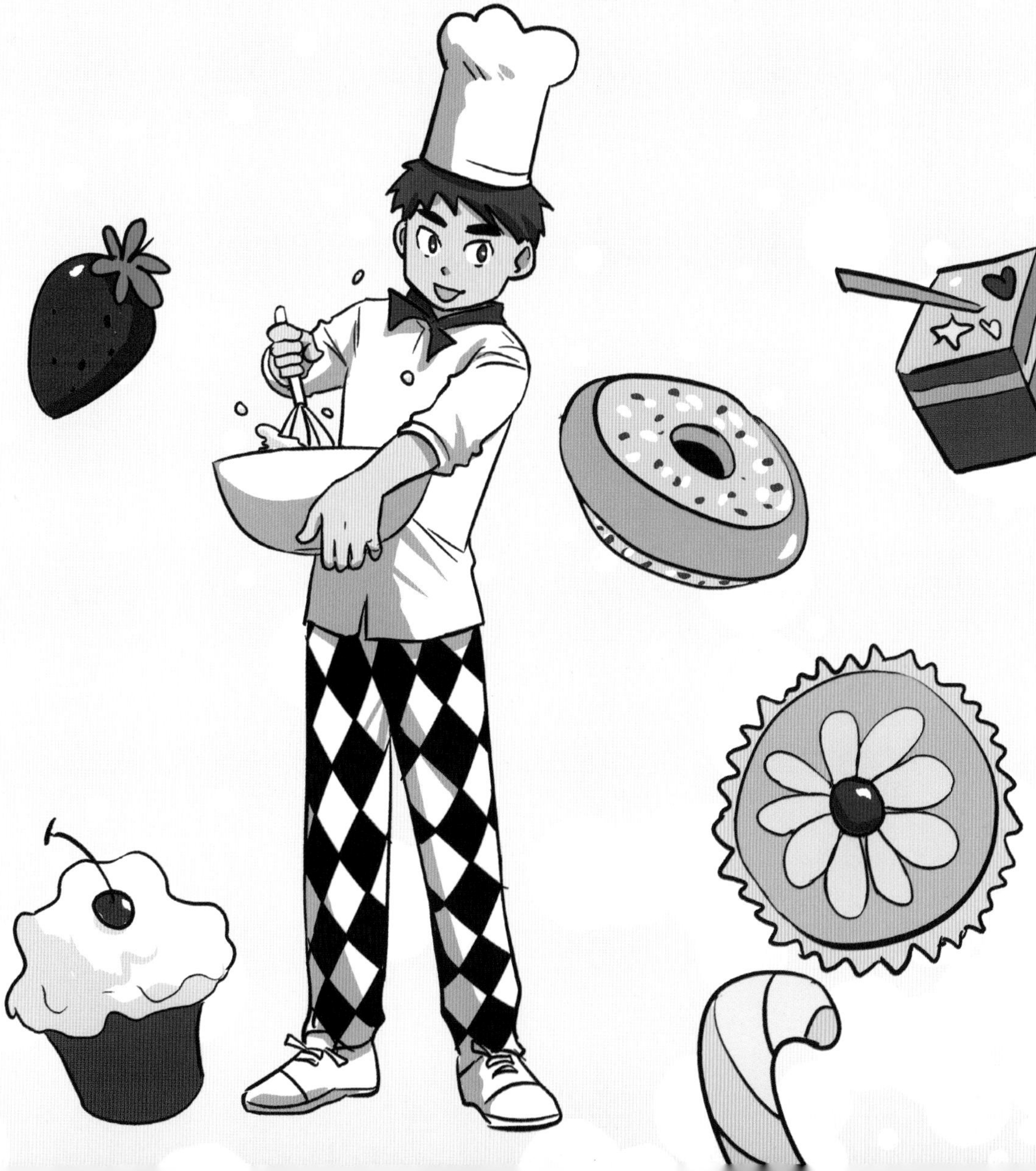

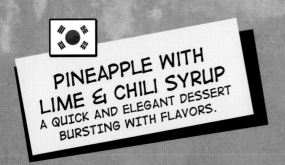

PINEAPPLE WITH LIME & CHILI SYRUP

A QUICK AND ELEGANT DESSERT BURSTING WITH FLAVORS.

1 BABY PINEAPPLE
3½ CASTER SUGAR
3½ FL OZ WATER
3 SMALL RED CHILIES, DESEEDED, AND CHOPPED
GRATED RIND AND JUICE OF 1 LIME
ICE CREAM, TO SERVE

SERVES 4 WARRIORS
PREP TIME: 10 MINUTES, PLUS COOLING
COOKING TIME: 10 MINUTES

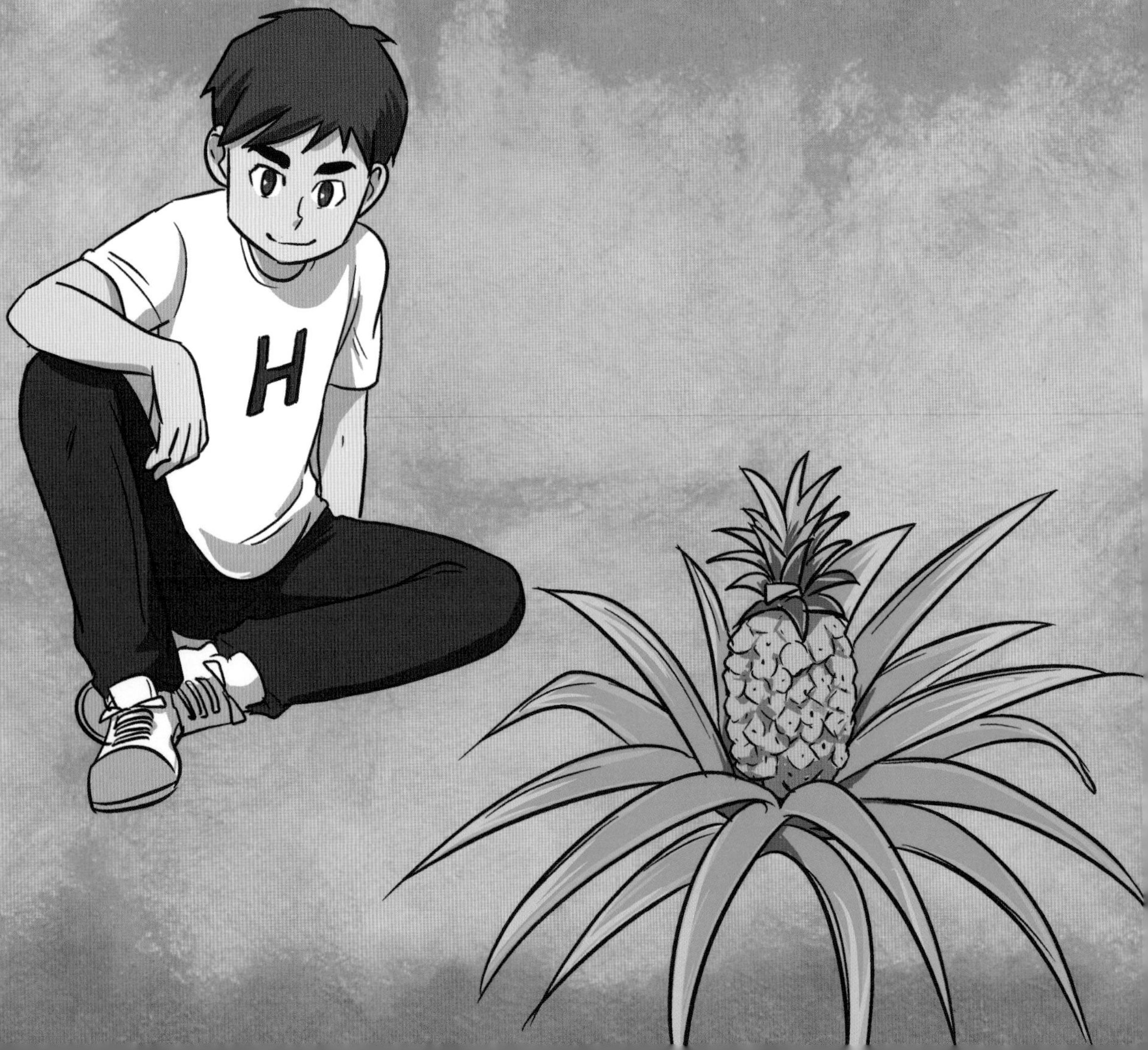
H

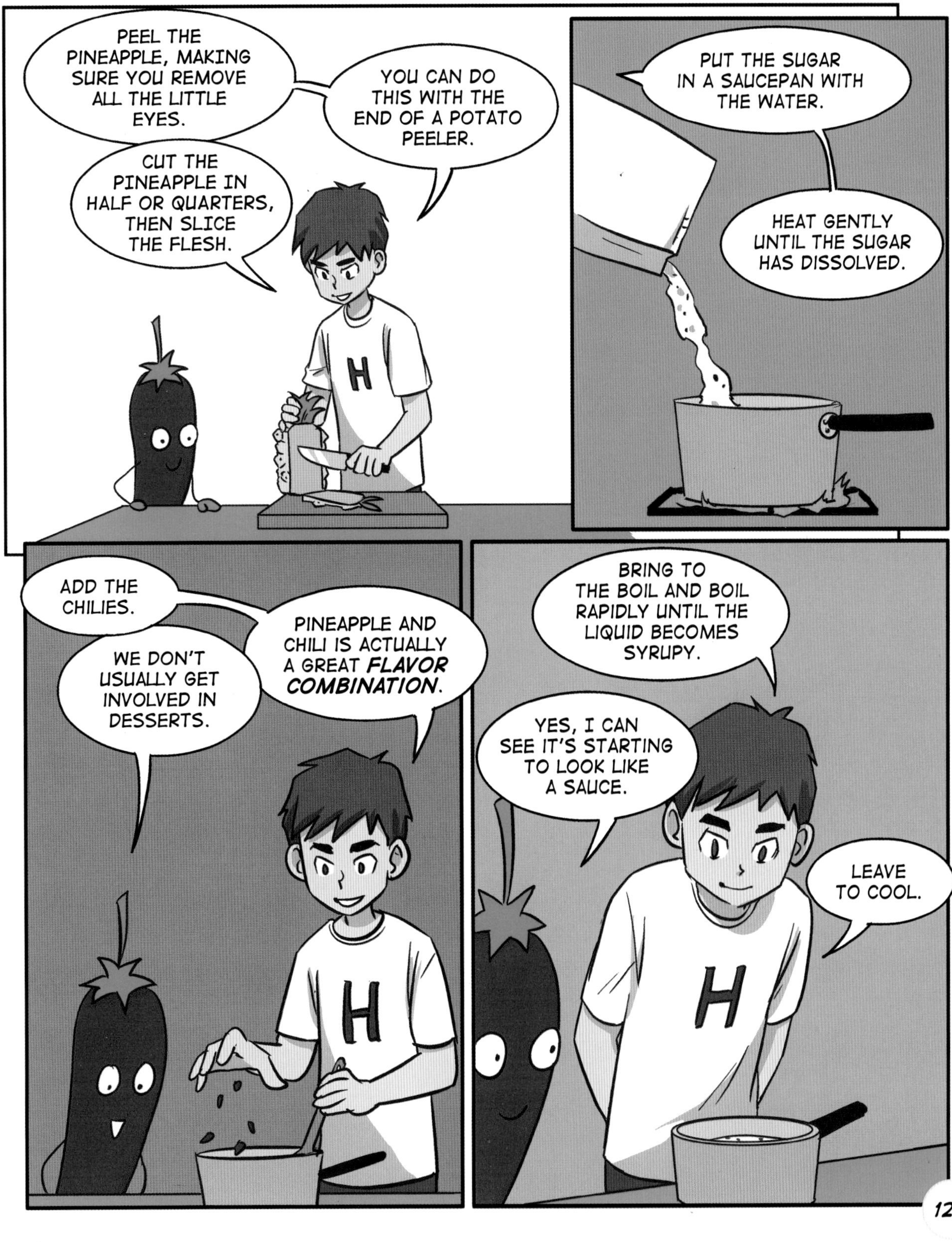

PEEL THE PINEAPPLE, MAKING SURE YOU REMOVE ALL THE LITTLE EYES.
YOU CAN DO THIS WITH THE END OF A POTATO PEELER.
CUT THE PINEAPPLE IN HALF OR QUARTERS, THEN SLICE THE FLESH.
PUT THE SUGAR IN A SAUCEPAN WITH THE WATER.
HEAT GENTLY UNTIL THE SUGAR HAS DISSOLVED.
ADD THE CHILIES.
PINEAPPLE AND CHILI IS ACTUALLY A GREAT ***FLAVOR COMBINATION***.
WE DON'T USUALLY GET INVOLVED IN DESSERTS.
BRING TO THE BOIL AND BOIL RAPIDLY UNTIL THE LIQUID BECOMES SYRUPY.
YES, I CAN SEE IT'S STARTING TO LOOK LIKE A SAUCE.
LEAVE TO COOL.

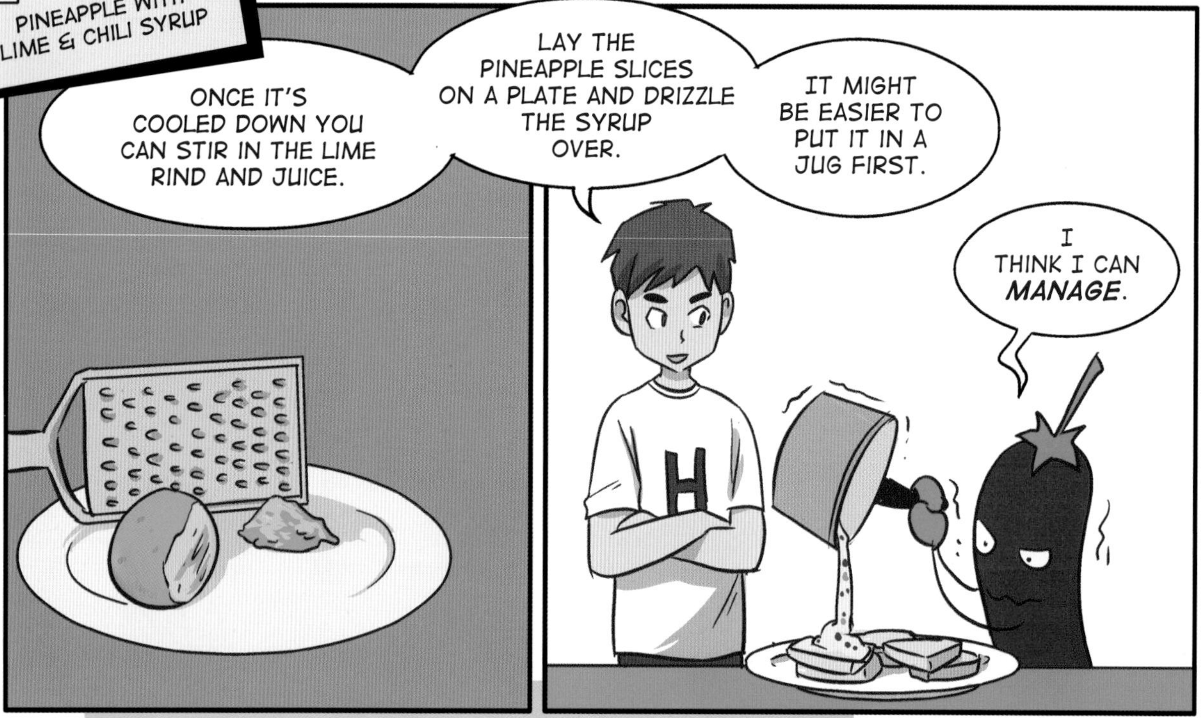
ONCE IT'S COOLED DOWN YOU CAN STIR IN THE LIME RIND AND JUICE.
LAY THE PINEAPPLE SLICES ON A PLATE AND DRIZZLE THE SYRUP OVER.
IT MIGHT BE EASIER TO PUT IT IN A JUG FIRST.
I THINK I CAN *MANAGE*.

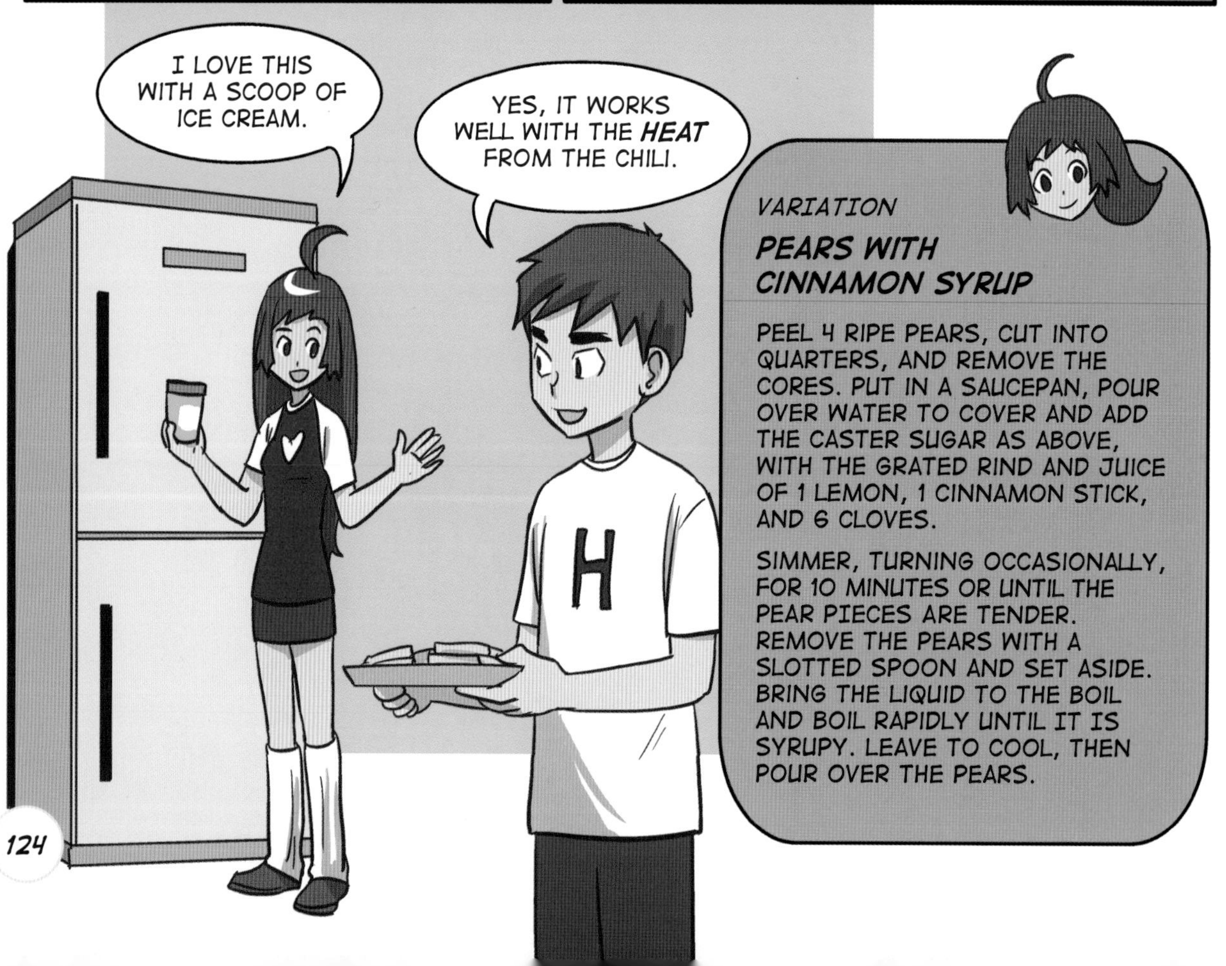
I LOVE THIS WITH A SCOOP OF ICE CREAM.
YES, IT WORKS WELL WITH THE *HEAT* FROM THE CHILI.

VARIATION

PEARS WITH CINNAMON SYRUP

PEEL 4 RIPE PEARS, CUT INTO QUARTERS, AND REMOVE THE CORES. PUT IN A SAUCEPAN, POUR OVER WATER TO COVER AND ADD THE CASTER SUGAR AS ABOVE, WITH THE GRATED RIND AND JUICE OF 1 LEMON, 1 CINNAMON STICK, AND 6 CLOVES.

SIMMER, TURNING OCCASIONALLY, FOR 10 MINUTES OR UNTIL THE PEAR PIECES ARE TENDER. REMOVE THE PEARS WITH A SLOTTED SPOON AND SET ASIDE. BRING THE LIQUID TO THE BOIL AND BOIL RAPIDLY UNTIL IT IS SYRUPY. LEAVE TO COOL, THEN POUR OVER THE PEARS.

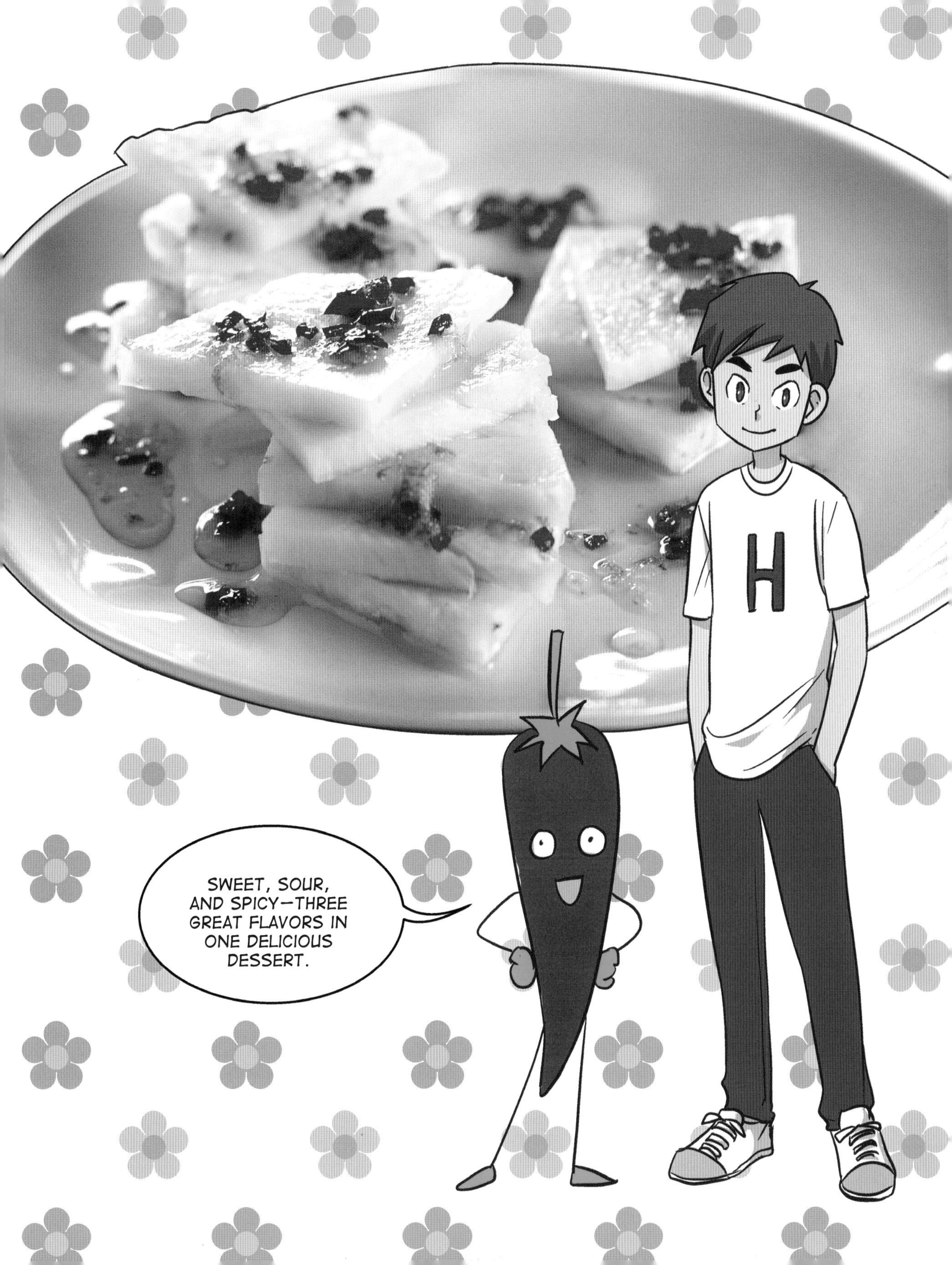
SWEET, SOUR, AND SPICY—THREE GREAT FLAVORS IN ONE DELICIOUS DESSERT.

BANOFFEE CHOCOLATE MUFFINS
CHOCOLATE AND BANANA IS A WINNING COMBINATION.

7½ OZ ALL-PURPOSE FLOUR, SIFTED
2 TSP BAKING POWDER
2 TBSP COCOA POWDER, SIFTED
3½ OZ CASTER SUGAR
3½ OZ DARK CHOCOLATE CHIPS
2 EGGS
2 SMALL RIPE BANANAS
2 FL OZ VEGETABLE OIL
4 OZ NATURAL YOGURT
READY-MADE TOFFEE SAUCE, TO SERVE

MAKES 12 MUFFINS
PREP TIME: 15 MINUTES
COOKING TIME: 18-22 MINUTES

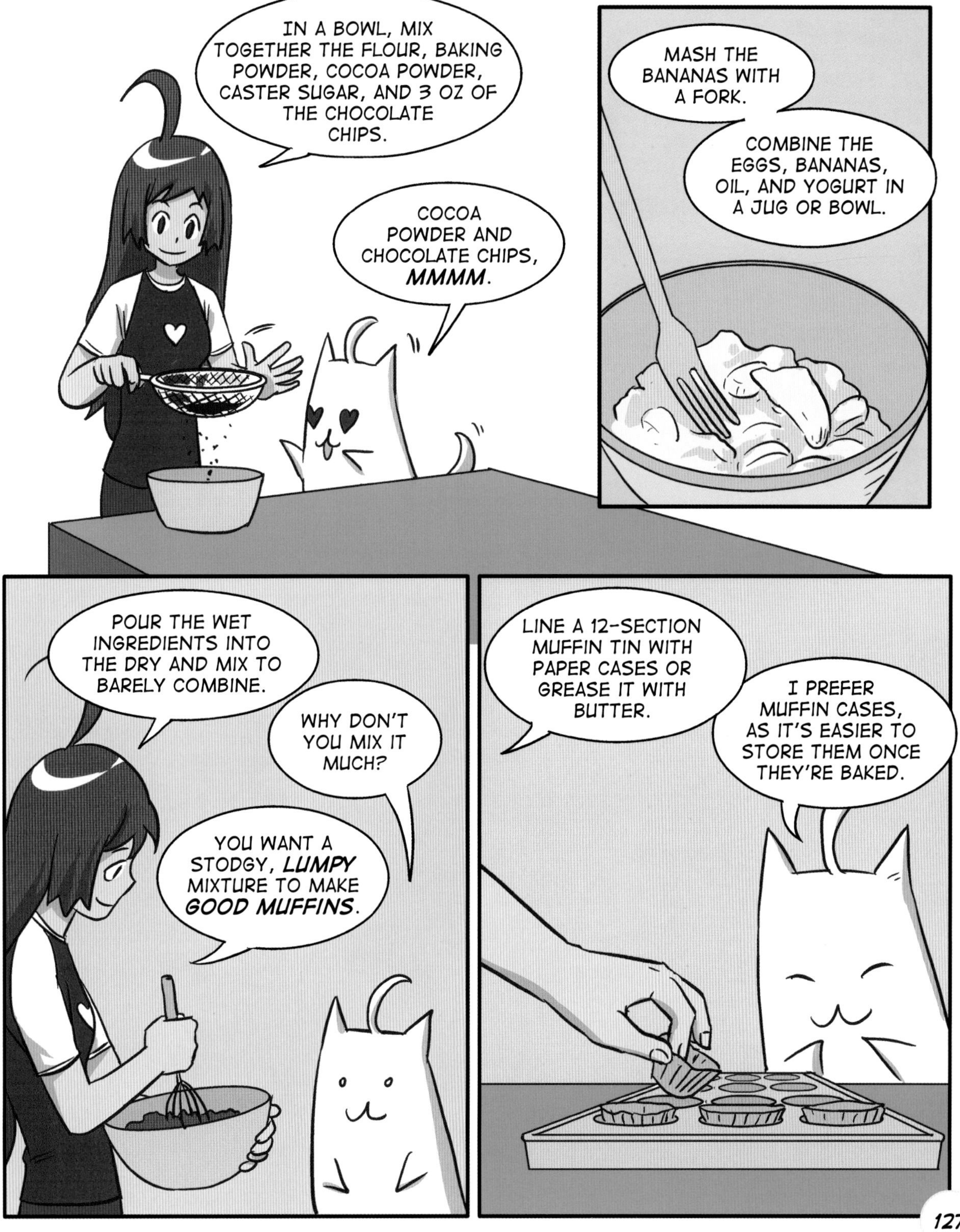
IN A BOWL, MIX TOGETHER THE FLOUR, BAKING POWDER, COCOA POWDER, CASTER SUGAR, AND 3 OZ OF THE CHOCOLATE CHIPS.
COCOA POWDER AND CHOCOLATE CHIPS, ***MMMM***.
MASH THE BANANAS WITH A FORK.
COMBINE THE EGGS, BANANAS, OIL, AND YOGURT IN A JUG OR BOWL.
POUR THE WET INGREDIENTS INTO THE DRY AND MIX TO BARELY COMBINE.
WHY DON'T YOU MIX IT MUCH?
YOU WANT A STODGY, ***LUMPY*** MIXTURE TO MAKE ***GOOD MUFFINS***.
LINE A 12-SECTION MUFFIN TIN WITH PAPER CASES OR GREASE IT WITH BUTTER.
I PREFER MUFFIN CASES, AS IT'S EASIER TO STORE THEM ONCE THEY'RE BAKED.

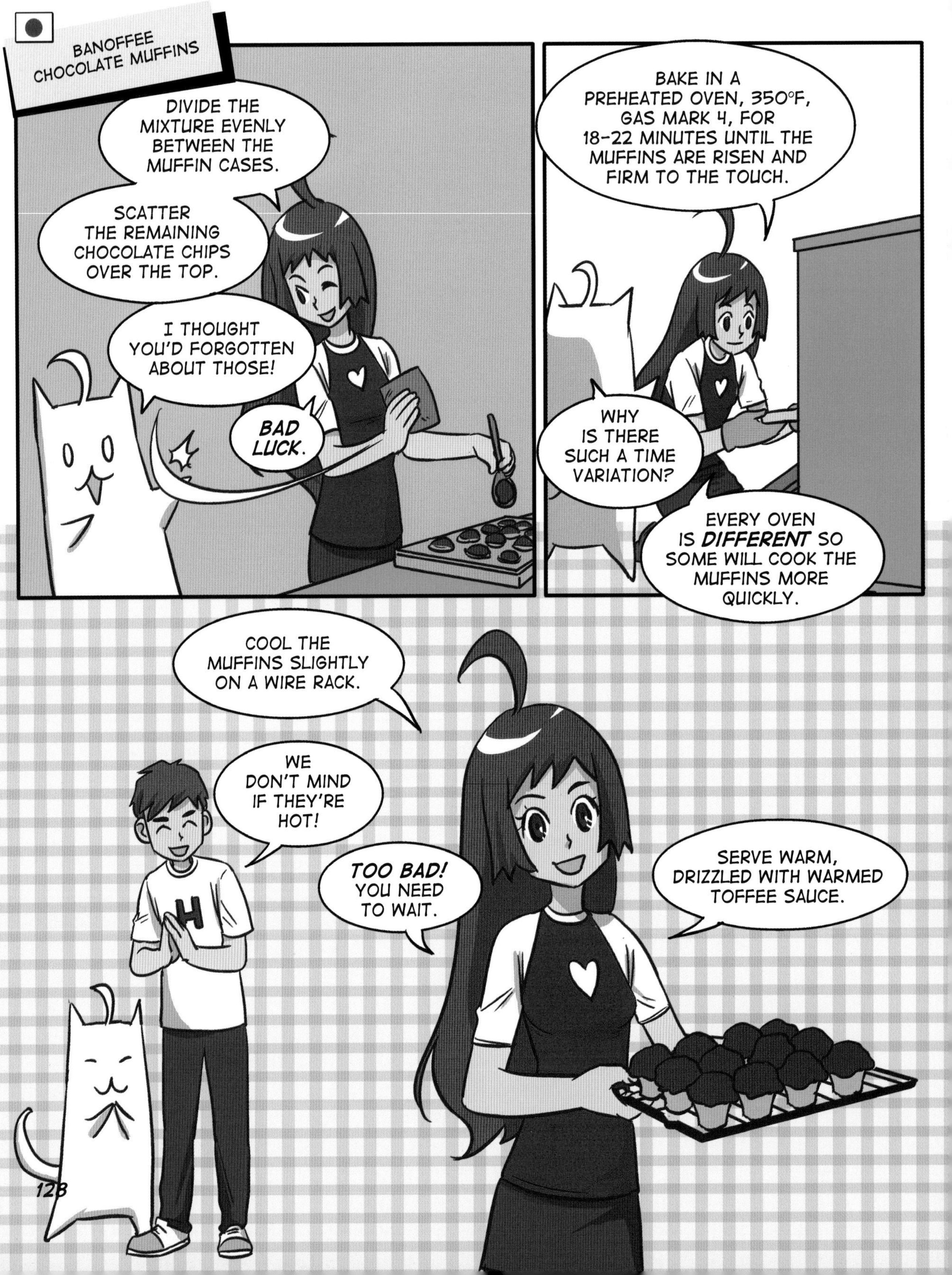
BANOFFEE CHOCOLATE MUFFINS
DIVIDE THE MIXTURE EVENLY BETWEEN THE MUFFIN CASES.
SCATTER THE REMAINING CHOCOLATE CHIPS OVER THE TOP.
I THOUGHT YOU'D FORGOTTEN ABOUT THOSE!
BAD LUCK.
BAKE IN A PREHEATED OVEN, 350°F, GAS MARK 4, FOR 18-22 MINUTES UNTIL THE MUFFINS ARE RISEN AND FIRM TO THE TOUCH.
WHY IS THERE SUCH A TIME VARIATION?
EVERY OVEN IS *DIFFERENT* SO SOME WILL COOK THE MUFFINS MORE QUICKLY.
COOL THE MUFFINS SLIGHTLY ON A WIRE RACK.
WE DON'T MIND IF THEY'RE HOT!
TOO BAD! YOU NEED TO WAIT.
SERVE WARM, DRIZZLED WITH WARMED TOFFEE SAUCE.

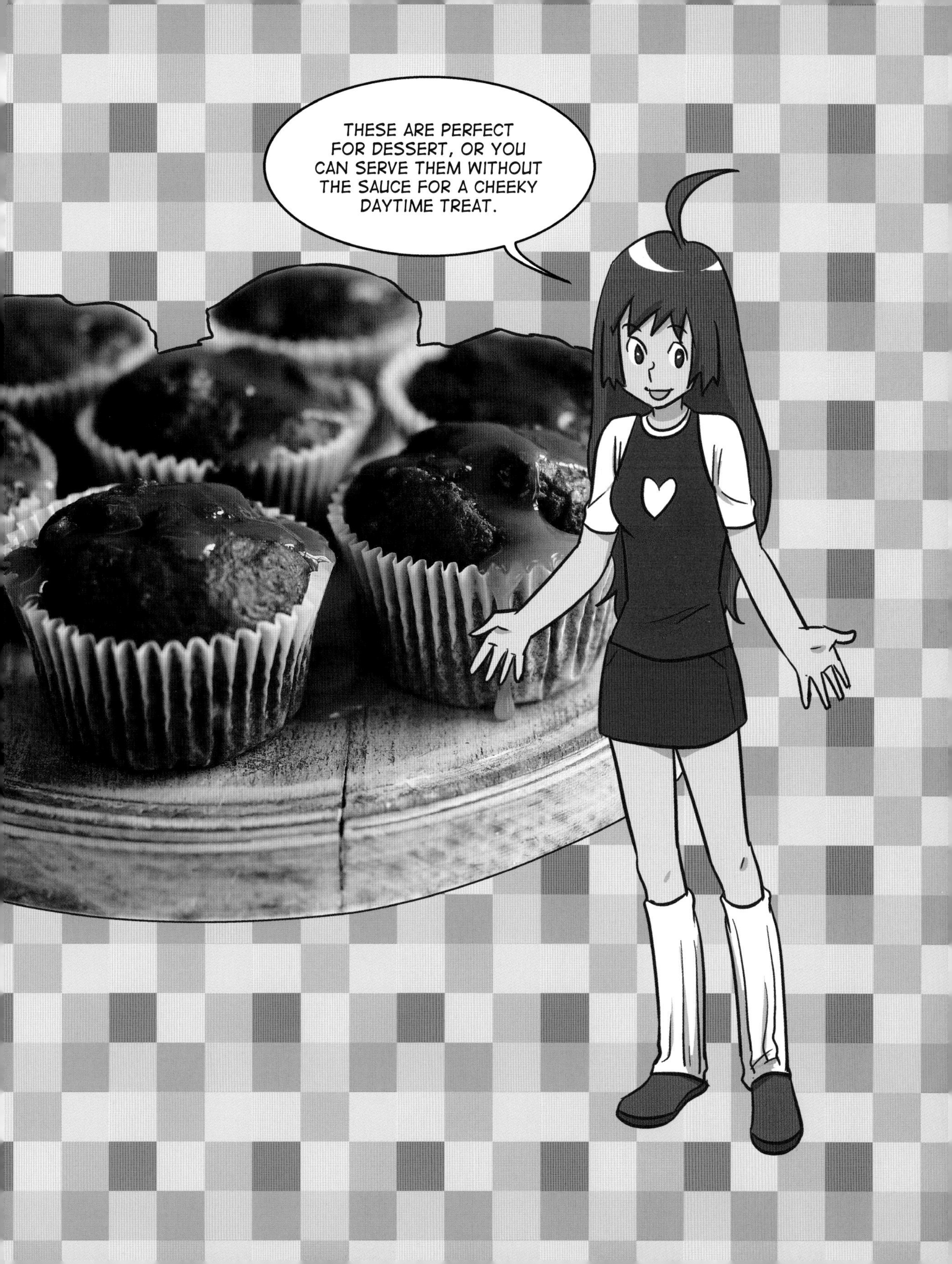
THESE ARE PERFECT FOR DESSERT, OR YOU CAN SERVE THEM WITHOUT THE SAUCE FOR A CHEEKY DAYTIME TREAT.

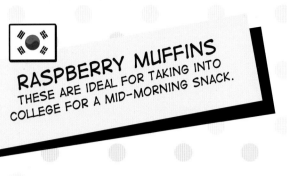

RASPBERRY MUFFINS

THESE ARE IDEAL FOR TAKING INTO COLLEGE FOR A MID-MORNING SNACK.

7 OZ PLAIN FLOUR, SIFTED
3 OZ CASTER SUGAR
2 TBSP GROUND ALMONDS
2 TSP BAKING POWDER
GRATED RIND OF 1 LEMON
3½ TBSP BUTTER, MELTED
¼ PINT BUTTERMILK
1 EGG, BEATEN
5 OZ FRESH OR FROZEN RASPBERRIES

MAKES 6 MUFFINS
PREP TIME: 15 MINUTES
COOKING TIME: 15-20 MINUTES

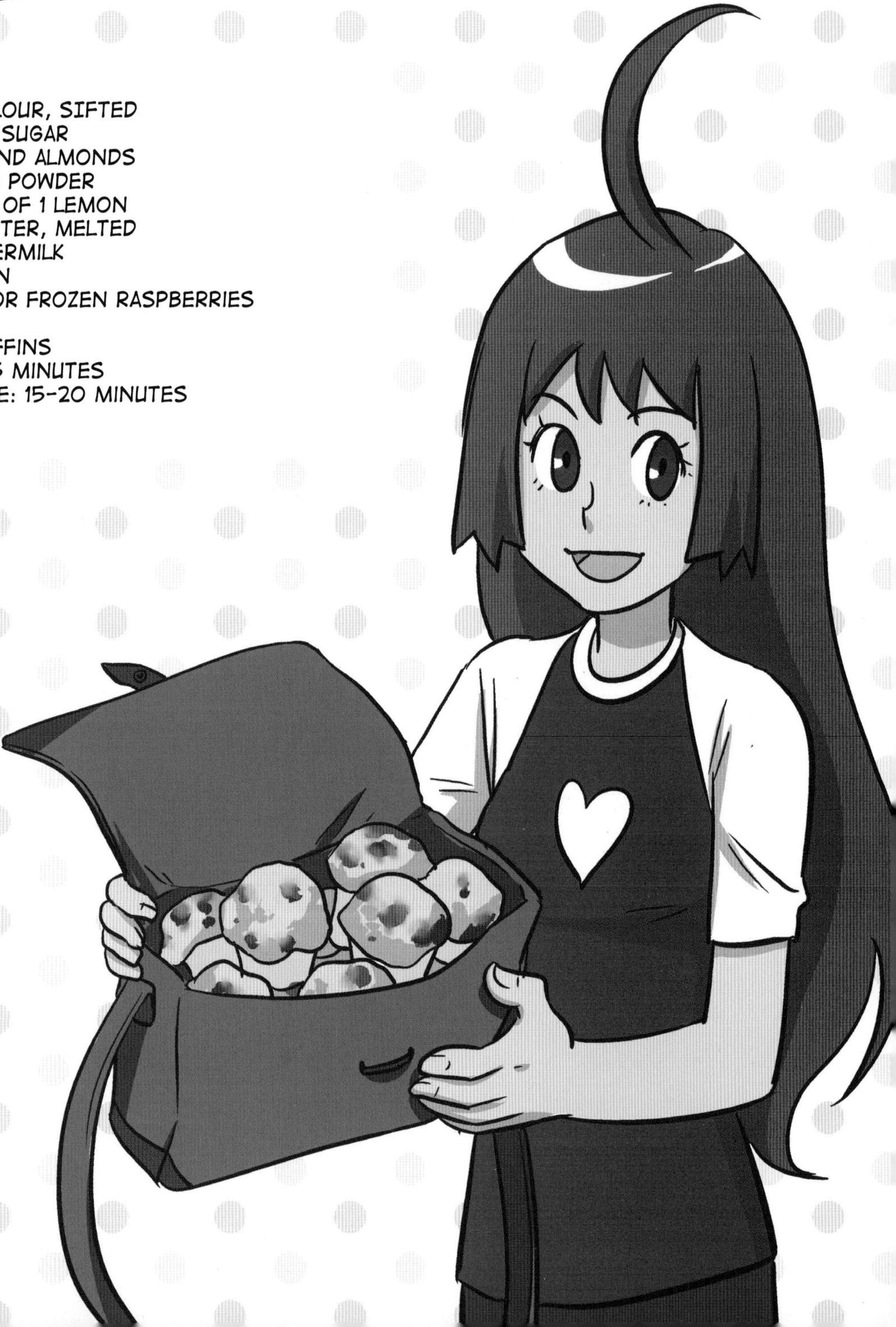

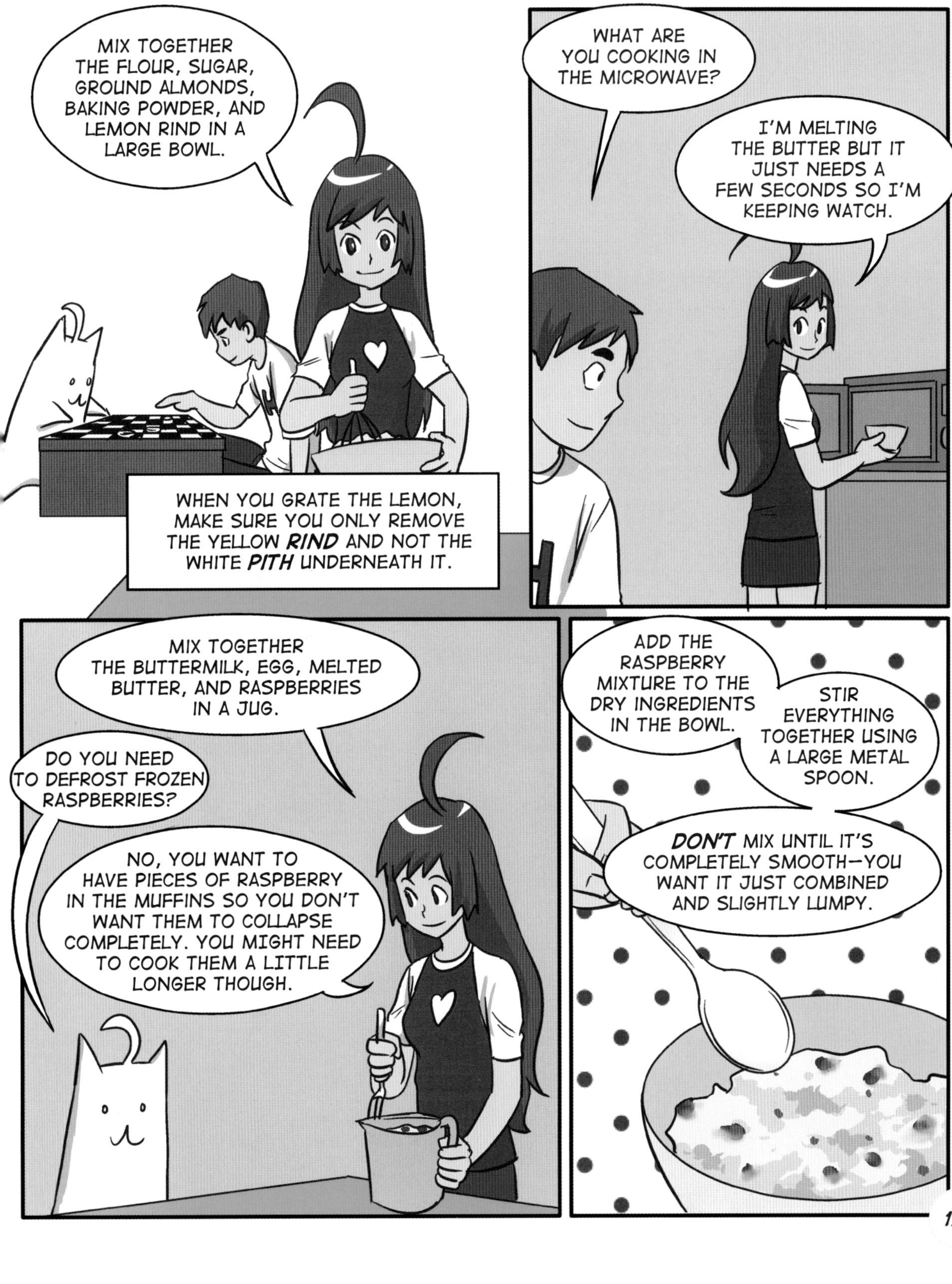
MIX TOGETHER THE FLOUR, SUGAR, GROUND ALMONDS, BAKING POWDER, AND LEMON RIND IN A LARGE BOWL.
WHEN YOU GRATE THE LEMON, MAKE SURE YOU ONLY REMOVE THE YELLOW **RIND** AND NOT THE WHITE **PITH** UNDERNEATH IT.
WHAT ARE YOU COOKING IN THE MICROWAVE?
I'M MELTING THE BUTTER BUT IT JUST NEEDS A FEW SECONDS SO I'M KEEPING WATCH.
MIX TOGETHER THE BUTTERMILK, EGG, MELTED BUTTER, AND RASPBERRIES IN A JUG.
DO YOU NEED TO DEFROST FROZEN RASPBERRIES?
NO, YOU WANT TO HAVE PIECES OF RASPBERRY IN THE MUFFINS SO YOU DON'T WANT THEM TO COLLAPSE COMPLETELY. YOU MIGHT NEED TO COOK THEM A LITTLE LONGER THOUGH.
ADD THE RASPBERRY MIXTURE TO THE DRY INGREDIENTS IN THE BOWL.
STIR EVERYTHING TOGETHER USING A LARGE METAL SPOON.
DON'T MIX UNTIL IT'S COMPLETELY SMOOTH—YOU WANT IT JUST COMBINED AND SLIGHTLY LUMPY.

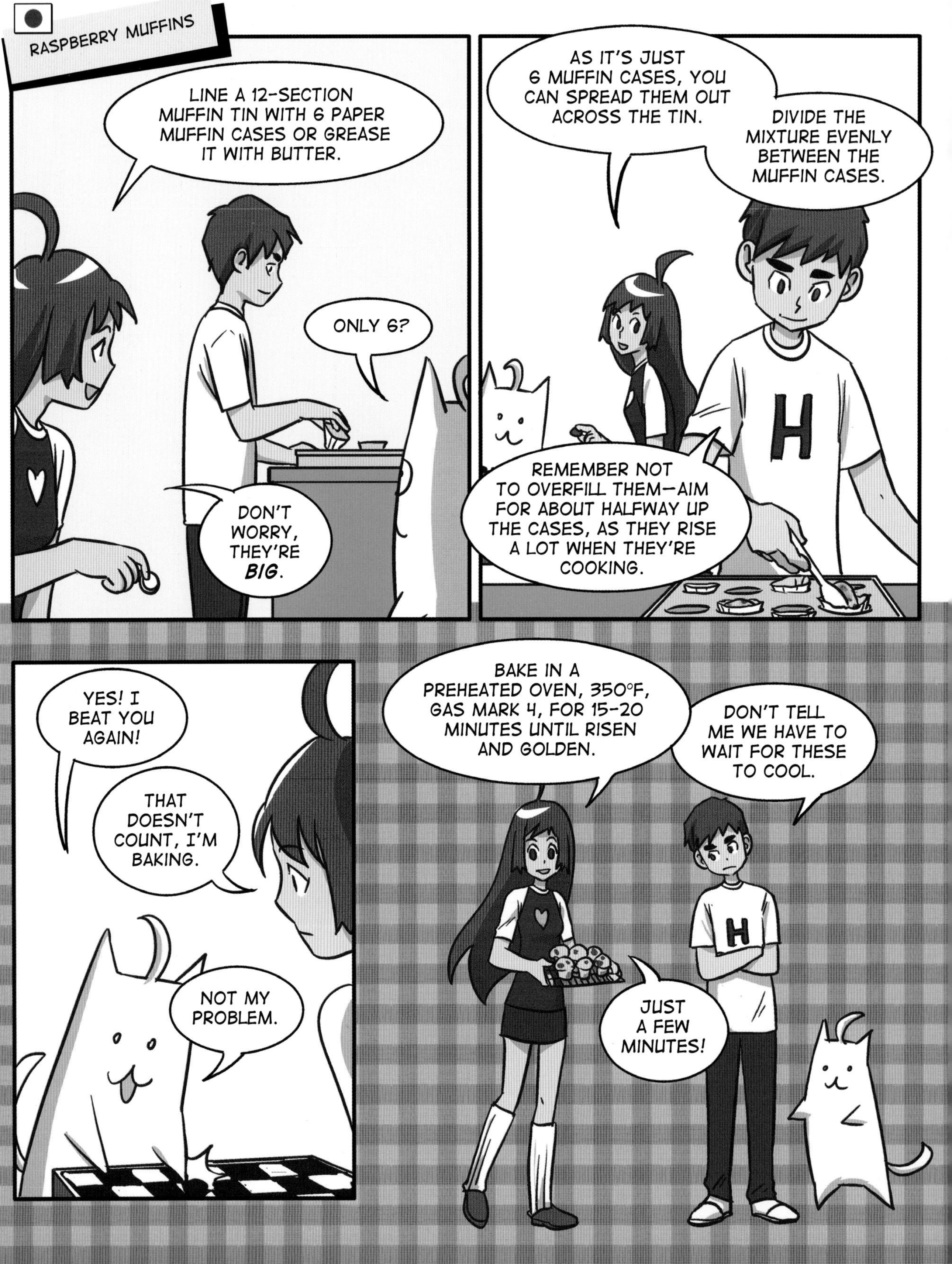
RASPBERRY MUFFINS
LINE A 12-SECTION MUFFIN TIN WITH 6 PAPER MUFFIN CASES OR GREASE IT WITH BUTTER.
ONLY 6?
DON'T WORRY, THEY'RE *BIG*.
AS IT'S JUST 6 MUFFIN CASES, YOU CAN SPREAD THEM OUT ACROSS THE TIN.
DIVIDE THE MIXTURE EVENLY BETWEEN THE MUFFIN CASES.
REMEMBER NOT TO OVERFILL THEM—AIM FOR ABOUT HALFWAY UP THE CASES, AS THEY RISE A LOT WHEN THEY'RE COOKING.
YES! I BEAT YOU AGAIN!
THAT DOESN'T COUNT, I'M BAKING.
NOT MY PROBLEM.
BAKE IN A PREHEATED OVEN, 350°F, GAS MARK 4, FOR 15-20 MINUTES UNTIL RISEN AND GOLDEN.
DON'T TELL ME WE HAVE TO WAIT FOR THESE TO COOL.
JUST A FEW MINUTES!

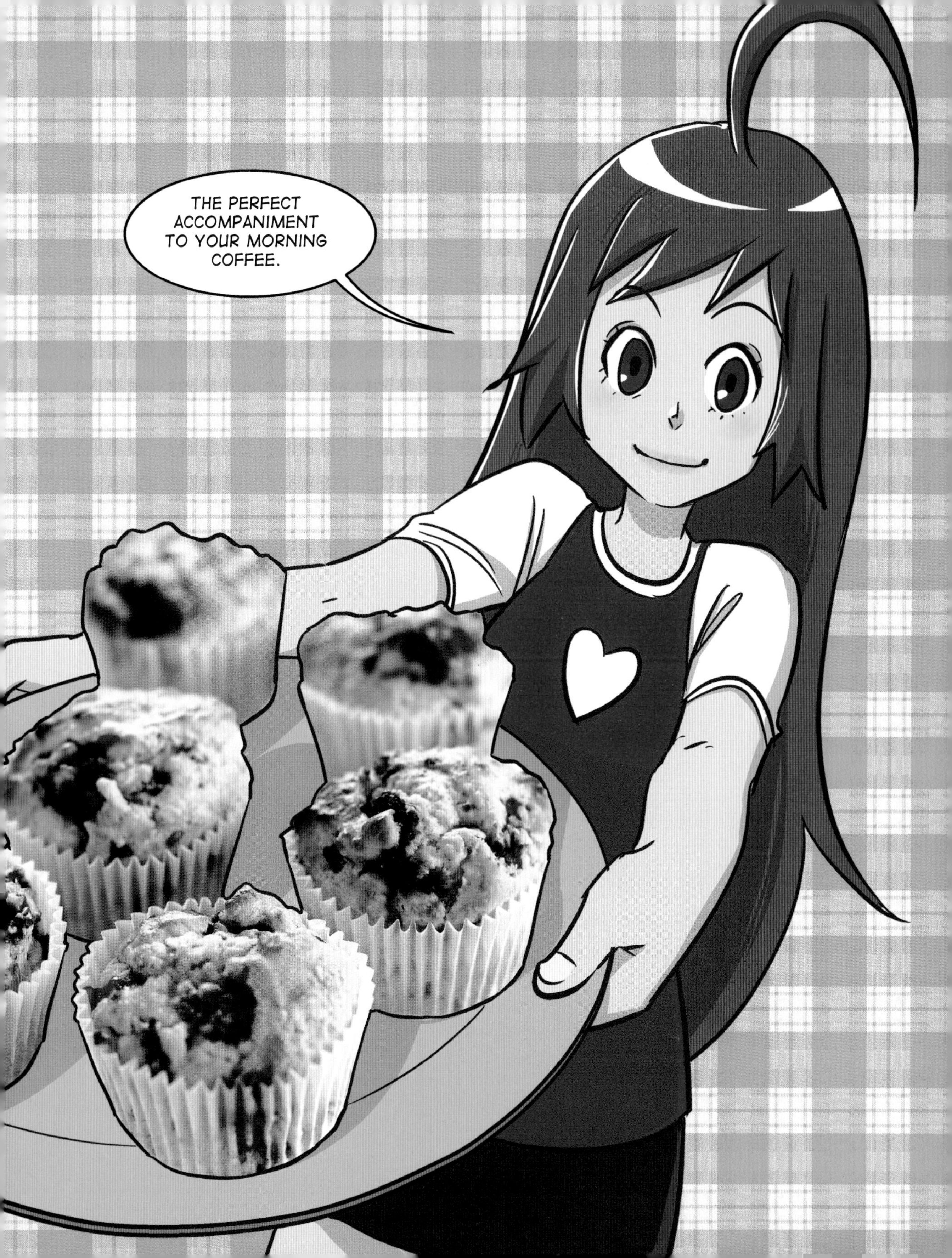
THE PERFECT ACCOMPANIMENT TO YOUR MORNING COFFEE.

CHOCOLATE CHIP COOKIES
THIS IS THE ONLY COOKIE RECIPE YOU'LL EVER NEED!

9 TBSP SOFT UNSALTED BUTTER, DICED
6 OZ SOFT LIGHT BROWN SUGAR
1 TSP VANILLA EXTRACT
1 EGG, LIGHTLY BEATEN
1 TBSP MILK
7 OZ PLAIN FLOUR
1 TSP BAKING POWDER
8 OZ DARK CHOCOLATE CHIPS

MAKES 16 COOKIES
PREP TIME: 10 MINUTES, PLUS COOLING
COOKING TIME: 15 MINUTES

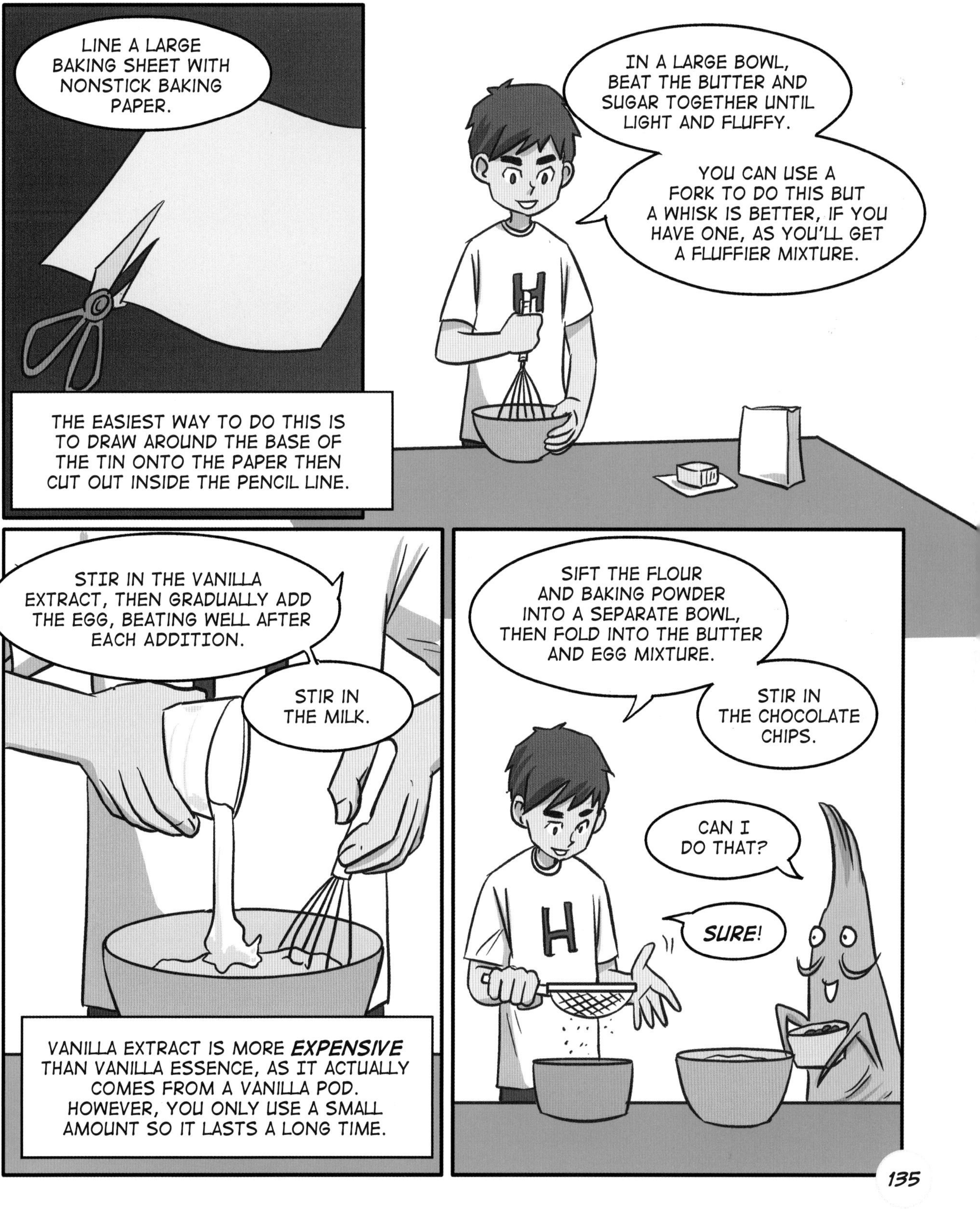
LINE A LARGE BAKING SHEET WITH NONSTICK BAKING PAPER.
THE EASIEST WAY TO DO THIS IS TO DRAW AROUND THE BASE OF THE TIN ONTO THE PAPER THEN CUT OUT INSIDE THE PENCIL LINE.
IN A LARGE BOWL, BEAT THE BUTTER AND SUGAR TOGETHER UNTIL LIGHT AND FLUFFY.
YOU CAN USE A FORK TO DO THIS BUT A WHISK IS BETTER, IF YOU HAVE ONE, AS YOU'LL GET A FLUFFIER MIXTURE.
STIR IN THE VANILLA EXTRACT, THEN GRADUALLY ADD THE EGG, BEATING WELL AFTER EACH ADDITION.
STIR IN THE MILK.
VANILLA EXTRACT IS MORE ***EXPENSIVE*** THAN VANILLA ESSENCE, AS IT ACTUALLY COMES FROM A VANILLA POD. HOWEVER, YOU ONLY USE A SMALL AMOUNT SO IT LASTS A LONG TIME.
SIFT THE FLOUR AND BAKING POWDER INTO A SEPARATE BOWL, THEN FOLD INTO THE BUTTER AND EGG MIXTURE.
STIR IN THE CHOCOLATE CHIPS.
CAN I DO THAT?
SURE!
H

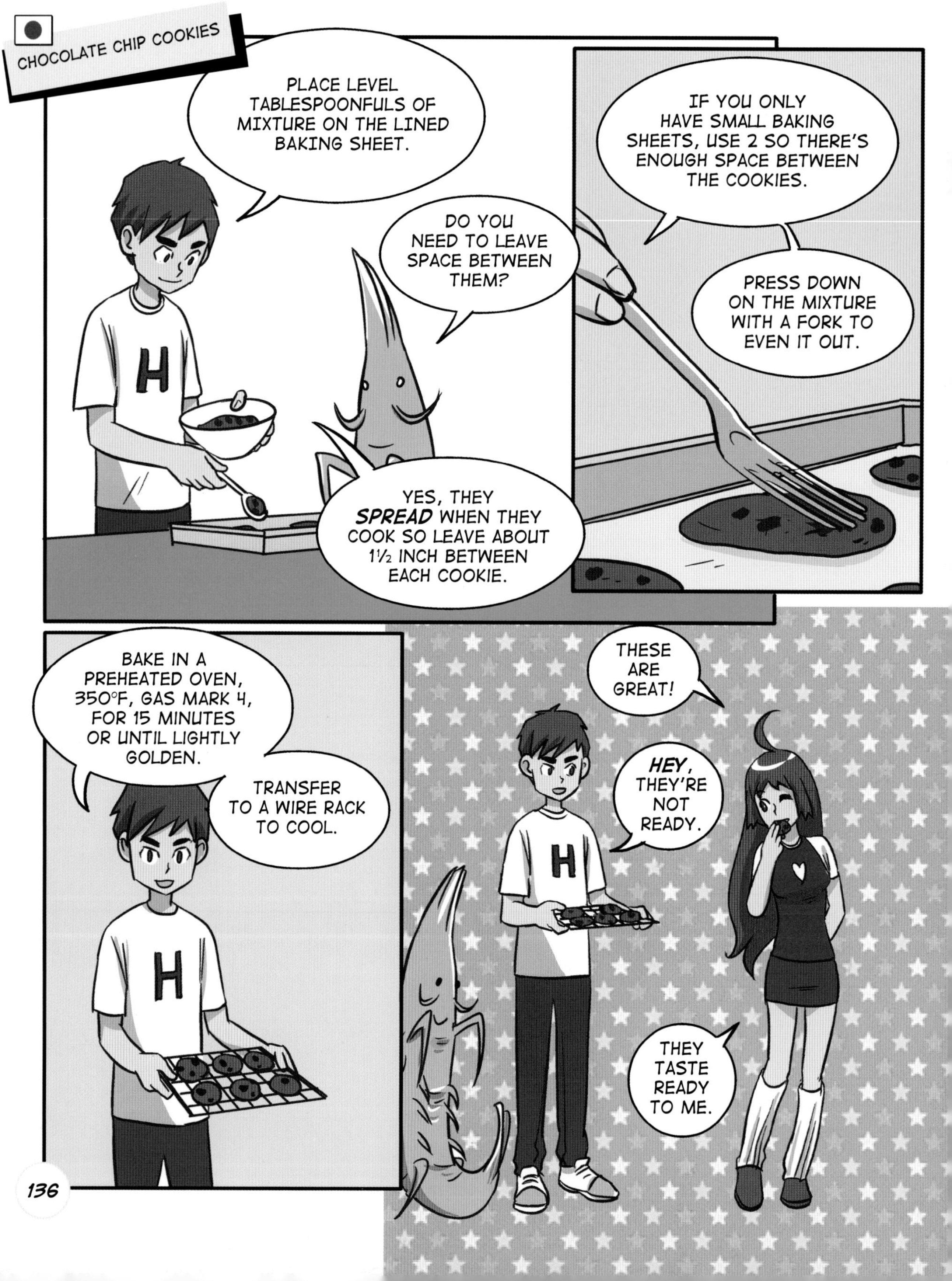
CHOCOLATE CHIP COOKIES
PLACE LEVEL TABLESPOONFULS OF MIXTURE ON THE LINED BAKING SHEET.
DO YOU NEED TO LEAVE SPACE BETWEEN THEM?
YES, THEY SPREAD WHEN THEY COOK SO LEAVE ABOUT 1½ INCH BETWEEN EACH COOKIE.
IF YOU ONLY HAVE SMALL BAKING SHEETS, USE 2 SO THERE'S ENOUGH SPACE BETWEEN THE COOKIES.
PRESS DOWN ON THE MIXTURE WITH A FORK TO EVEN IT OUT.
BAKE IN A PREHEATED OVEN, 350°F, GAS MARK 4, FOR 15 MINUTES OR UNTIL LIGHTLY GOLDEN.
TRANSFER TO A WIRE RACK TO COOL.
THESE ARE GREAT!
HEY, THEY'RE NOT READY.
THEY TASTE READY TO ME.

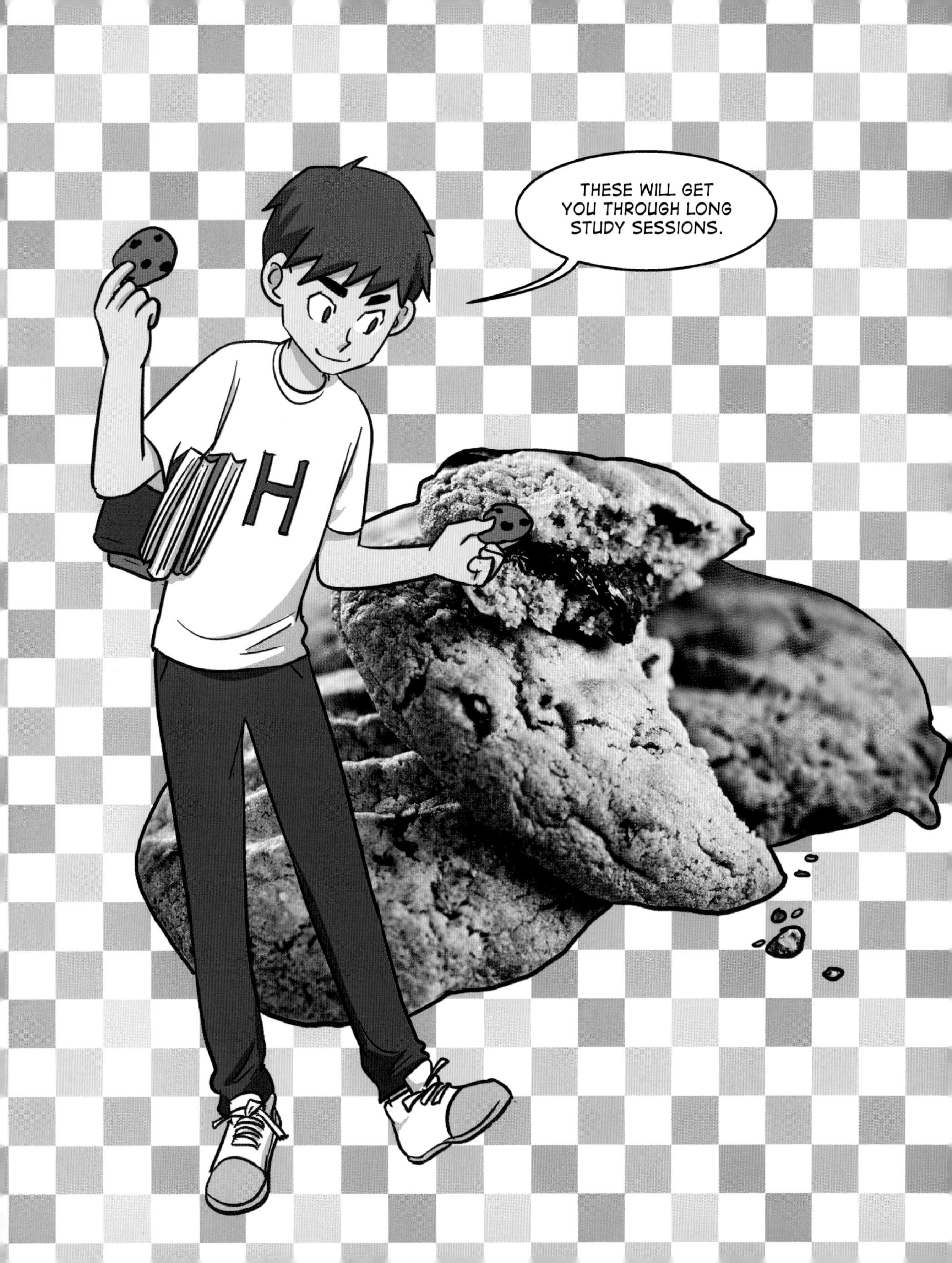
THESE WILL GET YOU THROUGH LONG STUDY SESSIONS.

VICTORIA SPONGE MUG CAKE
A CAKE COOKED IN A MUG—WHAT COULD BE SIMPLER?

3 TBSP VERY SOFT BUTTER
2 TBSP CASTER SUGAR, PLUS EXTRA
   FOR SPRINKLING
1 EGG YOLK, OR ½ BEATEN EGG
4 TBSP ALL-PURPOSE FLOUR
¼ TSP BAKING POWDER
¼ TSP VANILLA EXTRACT

1 TBSP STRAWBERRY JAM

SERVES 1 WARRIOR
PREP TIME: 3 MINUTES
COOKING TIME: 1½ MINUTES

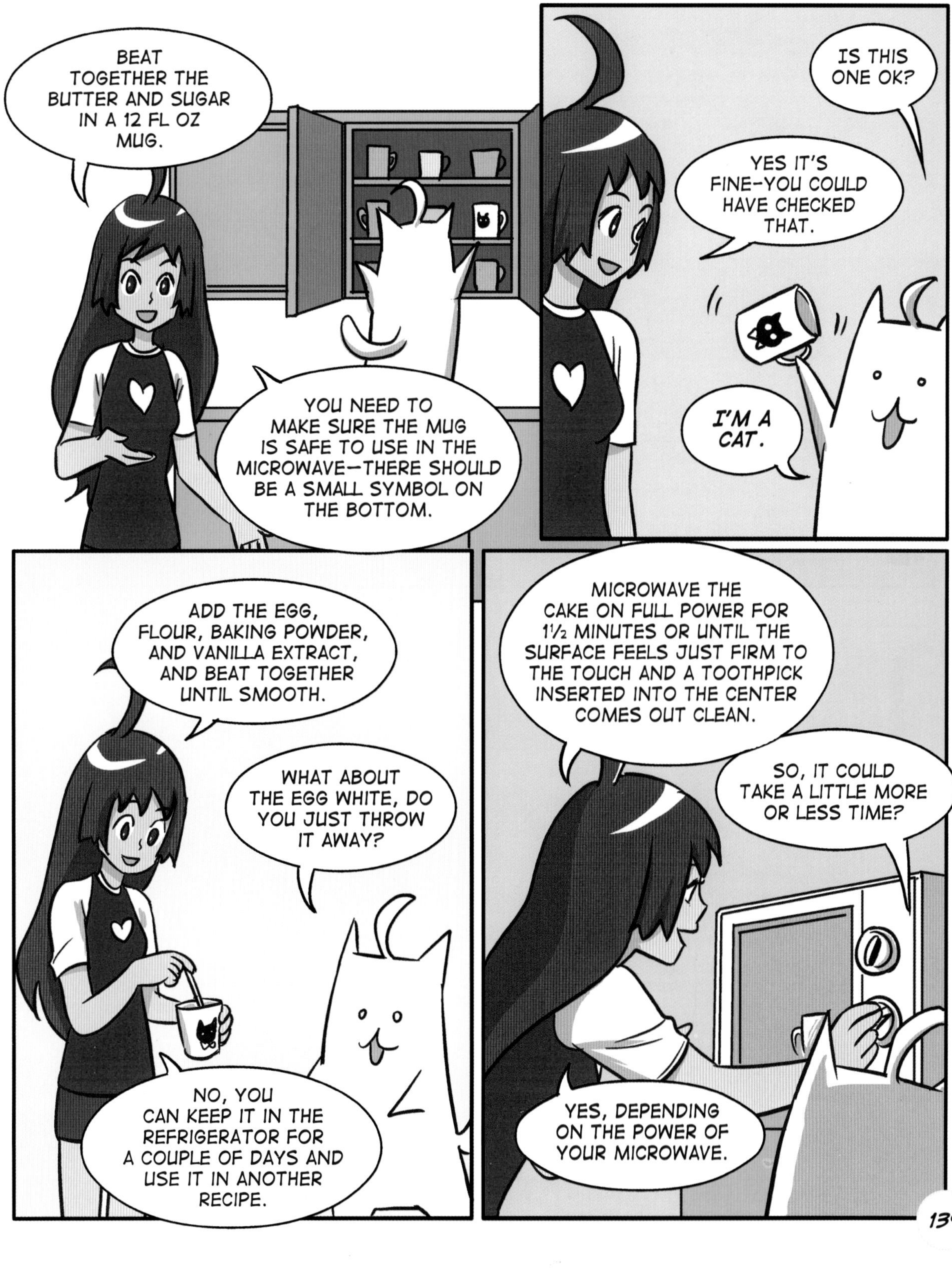

BEAT TOGETHER THE BUTTER AND SUGAR IN A 12 FL OZ MUG.
YOU NEED TO MAKE SURE THE MUG IS SAFE TO USE IN THE MICROWAVE—THERE SHOULD BE A SMALL SYMBOL ON THE BOTTOM.
IS THIS ONE OK?
YES IT'S FINE—YOU COULD HAVE CHECKED THAT.
I'M A CAT.
ADD THE EGG, FLOUR, BAKING POWDER, AND VANILLA EXTRACT, AND BEAT TOGETHER UNTIL SMOOTH.
WHAT ABOUT THE EGG WHITE, DO YOU JUST THROW IT AWAY?
NO, YOU CAN KEEP IT IN THE REFRIGERATOR FOR A COUPLE OF DAYS AND USE IT IN ANOTHER RECIPE.
MICROWAVE THE CAKE ON FULL POWER FOR 1½ MINUTES OR UNTIL THE SURFACE FEELS JUST FIRM TO THE TOUCH AND A TOOTHPICK INSERTED INTO THE CENTER COMES OUT CLEAN.
SO, IT COULD TAKE A LITTLE MORE OR LESS TIME?
YES, DEPENDING ON THE POWER OF YOUR MICROWAVE.

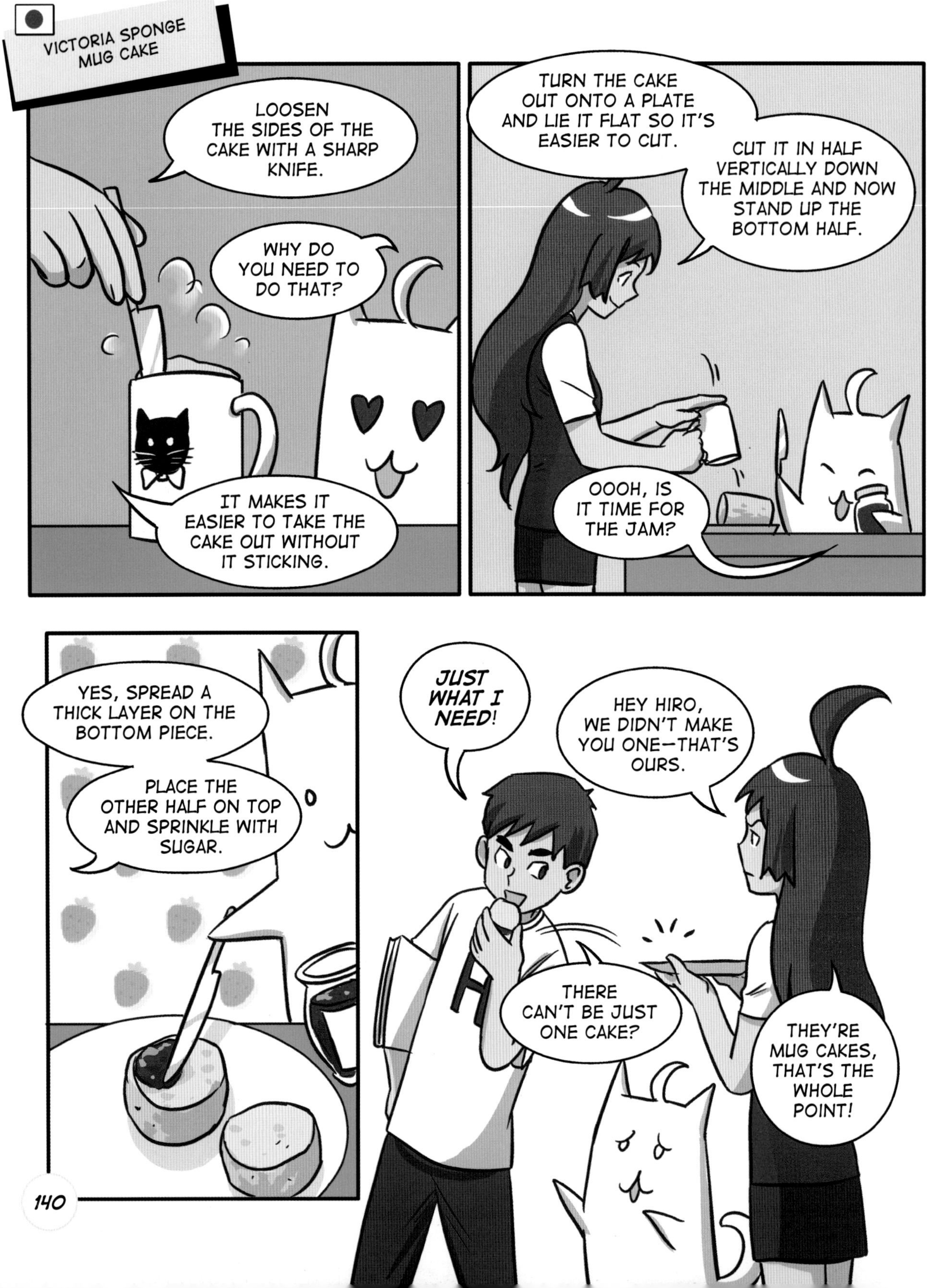
VICTORIA SPONGE MUG CAKE
LOOSEN THE SIDES OF THE CAKE WITH A SHARP KNIFE.
WHY DO YOU NEED TO DO THAT?
IT MAKES IT EASIER TO TAKE THE CAKE OUT WITHOUT IT STICKING.
TURN THE CAKE OUT ONTO A PLATE AND LIE IT FLAT SO IT'S EASIER TO CUT.
CUT IT IN HALF VERTICALLY DOWN THE MIDDLE AND NOW STAND UP THE BOTTOM HALF.
OOOH, IS IT TIME FOR THE JAM?
YES, SPREAD A THICK LAYER ON THE BOTTOM PIECE.
PLACE THE OTHER HALF ON TOP AND SPRINKLE WITH SUGAR.
JUST WHAT I NEED!
HEY HIRO, WE DIDN'T MAKE YOU ONE—THAT'S OURS.
THERE CAN'T BE JUST ONE CAKE?
THEY'RE MUG CAKES, THAT'S THE WHOLE POINT!

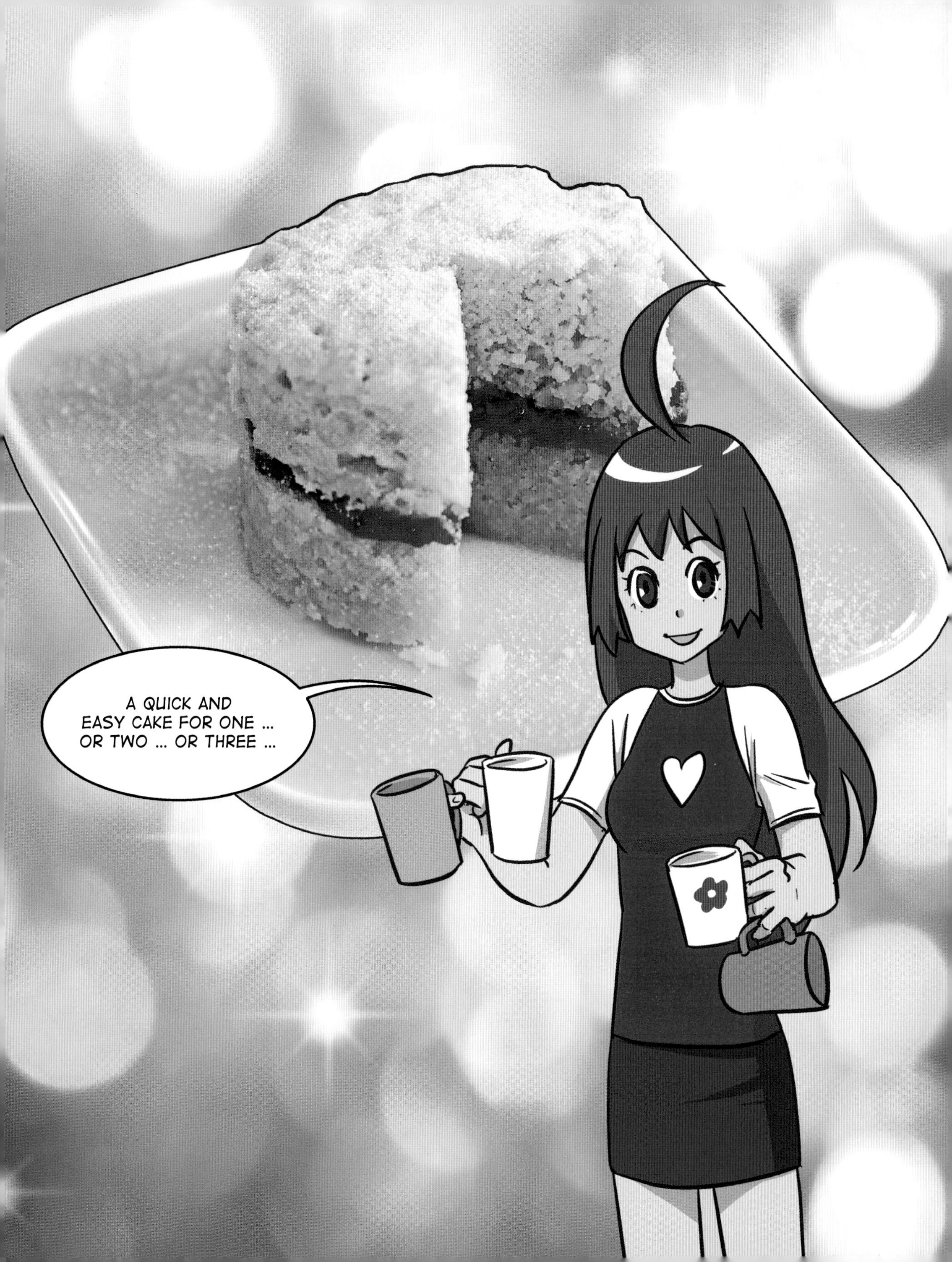
A QUICK AND EASY CAKE FOR ONE ... OR TWO ... OR THREE ...

A
almonds, ground 130–131
apricots 32
avocado 24

B
bacon 54, 55, 56
Baked Chicken with
    Fennel & Potatoes 12
baking powder 130–131, 134–135
bananas 126–127
Banoffee Chocolate Muffins
    126–129
basil 46, 48, 54, 56, 92, 94
bay leaf 34–35
Bean, Spinach, and Pasta Salad
    86
Bean Tostadas 24
beans
    baked 62
    black-eyed 80–83
    borlotti 88, 90
    cannellini 84–87
    kidney 24, 46, 88
beef
    minced 22, 30–31, 34
    stir-fry strips 26
Black-eyed Bean &
    Red Bell Pepper Stew 80–83
black olives 96, 98
broccoli 18–19
butter 38, 40, 50–51, 54, 56, 60,
    64, 74–76, 104–106, 109, 127,
    130–132, 138–139
    unsalted 34, 134
buttermilk 130–131

C
capers 67
carrot 34–35, 38–39, 80–84, 86,
    88, 89
cauliflower 104–107
Cauliflower Cheese 104–107
celery 30, 32, 34–35, 38–39,
    80–82, 84–85, 88–89
cheese

cheddar 22, 24, 26, 38,
    58–59, 66, 98, 104, 116–118
    feta 96, 98
    halloumi 94, 98
    mascarpone 58–59, 100–101
    mozzarella 108–110
    Red Leicester 104
    sauce 60, 66, 68
chicken
    breasts 10–13, 14–17
    stock 10, 34, 50
    thighs 18–21
chicory 10, 12
chinese greens 70, 72
chocolate 127–127, 134–135
Chunky Pasta Sauce 88–91
cinnamon 30, 32, 80–81, 124
Classic Bolognese 34–37
Classic Greek Salad 98
cloves 124
cocktail sausages 62
cocoa powder 126, 127
coconut milk 18, 19, 20
colander 60, 105, 106
Colourful Black-Eyed Bean
    & Vegetable Salad 82
coriander 14, 16, 20, 24, 30, 32,
    70, 72, 80, 82
Coriander & Apricot Couscous
    32
cornflour 66–67
couscous 30, 32–33
cream
    single 74
    soured 24, 28, 467, 48, 56,
    112, 114
    whipping 108
Creamy Garlic Mussels 74–77
cucumber 14, 16
Cucumber & Tomato Salsa
    14
cumin 80–81
cumin seeds 106
Curried Lamb Filo Pies 40
curry paste 18–19, 40

curry powder 30–31,
    112–113

D
dill 66–67

E
egg 20, 96–98, 108, 112–114,
    126–127, 130–131, 134–135,
    138–139 96, 97, 98, 108, 110,
    112, 113, 114, 126, 127, 138
egg plant 48, 92–93

F
fajita seasoning 22, 26
Fast Chicken Curry 18–21
fennel 12, 66–67
phyllo pastry 40
fish
    haddock 66
    sauce 70
    white 20, 66, 70
flatbreads 82
flour 54, 56, 116
    all-purpose 126, 138
    plain 104, 130, 134
food processor 67, 71

G
garlic 10–12, 34, 37, 46–48,
    50–51, 60, 62, 64, 70–72,
    74–76, 80–82, 84–85, 88–89,
    92–93
    bread 34, 37
ginger 70–71
Greek-style Omelet 96–99
Grilled Chicken Salsa 14–17
groundnut 70, 72

H
ham
    cooked 50
    cured 58
Hearty Bean & Vegetable Broth
    82
Hearty Minestrone 84–87

Hearty Potato & Cauliflower
    Soup 106
herbs, mixed 10–11, 80, 82

I
Ice Cream 122

K
ketchup 42–43

L
lamb, minced 38, 39, 48
Lamb & Egg Plant Chilli 48
leeks 10, 12, 66–67
lemon 20, 30, 32, 58, 60, 70–71,
    124, 130–131
lemon grass 70–71
lettuce 22, 24
lime 14, 16, 24, 82, 122, 124

M
Macaroni Cheese
    with Ham 58–61
malt vinegar 42
mango chutney 18
Meatball Tagine 30–33
milk 38, 40, 55, 58–59, 104–105,
    134–135
mint 10, 48, 82, 96–97
Mixed Bean Kedgeree 112–115
mushrooms 100–101
    button 56, 116–119
Mushroom, Tomato, & Courgette
    Lasagne 102
mussels 74–77
Mussels in Spicy Tomato Sauce
    76
mustard
    Dijon 58
    wholegrain 64

mustard mash 62, 64
mustard powder 104

O
olive oil 14, 18, 30, 32, 34, 38,
    46, 50, 58, 60, 62, 64, 76, 80,
    82, 84, 86, 88, 89, 92, 96, 98,
    100, 112, 116
olive oil & lemon dressing 58
One-pot Ratatouille 92–95
onions
    red 14, 24, 84, 86, 88, 97
    small 30
    spring 20, 54–55
Onion & Mushroom Quesadillas
    116–119
oregano 22, 46, 96–98
oyster sauce 72

P
pappadams 18
paprika 56, 76
parmesan 34, 36, 50, 52, 88, 90
parsley 10, 12, 50, 52, 54–55,
    58, 60, 62, 64, 66–67, 74, 76,
    96–97, 112, 114, 116–117
pasta
    al dente 36, 51, 59
    fettuccine 34
    macaroni 58–60
    penne 59, 88, 89
    short 86, 89
    soup 84
    tagliatelle 34
Pears with
    Cinnamon Syrup 124
peas 30, 32, 50–51, 66–67
peppers
    chili 14, 46, 50, 70, 76, 122
    jalepeño 26, 28
    red 22, 24, 26, 46, 48, 80,
    81–82, 92
    yellow 42–43, 92
peppercorns, green 66–67
pineapple 42–43, 122–125
Pineapple with Lime & Chili
    Syrup 122–125
Pork & Red Bell Pepper Chilli
    46–49
pork
    cubed 42

minced 34, 46
Potato & Bacon Patties 54–57
potatoes 10–12, 16, 38–39, 40,
    54–55, 64, 66, 68
Potato Gratin 108–111

R
raisins 30–31
raspberries 130–131
Raspberry Muffins 130–133
rice 20, 81–82, 112–113
    arborio 50–53
    basmati rice 44, 80
    boiled 14, 16, 42, 46, 48
    carnaroli 50
    long-grain 44, 112
risotto 50–53

S
salad 92, 100, 104, 108, 116
Salmon Fishcakes with Sour
    Cream & Mushroom Sauce
    56–59
Sausage & Bean Casserole
    62–65
sesame oil 72
shallots 80, 81, 82
    red 70–71
Shepherd's Pie 38–41
shrimp 15, 20, 52, 66–67
soy sauce 42–43
Spicy Fish skewers 70
Spicy Mexican Burgers 22–25
Spicy Pea & Ham Risotto 50–53
spinach 20, 58, 60, 84–86, 88,
    90, 100–102, 108–109, 118
Spinach & Brie Quesadillas 118
Spinach & Mushroom Lasagne
    102
Spinach with Olive Oil
    & Lemon Dressing 60
strawberry jam 138
sugar
    brown 42, 134
    caster 116–117, 122–125,
    126–129, 130–133, 138–140

INDEX

Surf & Turf 8–77
sweet potato 14, 16
Sweet & Sour Pork 42–45

T
Taleggio 100, 101
thyme 38–39, 62
toffee sauce 126, 128
Tomato & Onion Salad 100
tomatoes 14, 16, 32, 34, 35, 46,
    56, 88, 89, 92, 93, 96, 97, 98,
    102, 108, 110, 112, 114
    diced 18–20, 30, 34, 38, 54,
    62, 76
    passata 46
    paste 30–31, 38–40, 80–82,
    84
    sun-dried 80, 82
tortillas 24–28, 116, 118
Tray Bake Herb Chicken 10–13
turmeric 70–71

V
vanilla extract 134, 138
vegetable oil 20, 22, 26, 42, 106,
    126

vegetable stock 32, 80–82, 84,
    106, 112
vegetarian 78–119
Victoria Sponge Mug Cake
    138–141

W
wine
    red 86
    white 34, 74
wooden skewers 70

Y
yogurt 126, 127

Z
zucchini 30, 32, 92–93, 102

ACKNOWLEDGMENTS

For Eva and Quinn—my two
kitchen ninjas in training.